Local Economies in Turmoil

International Political Economy Series

General Editor: **Timothy M. Shaw**, Professor of Political Science and International Development Studies, and Director of the Centre for Foreign Policy Studies, Dalhousie University, Halifax, Nova Scotia

Titles include:

Steve Chan and A. Cooper Drury (*editors*)
SANCTIONS AS ECONOMIC STATECRAFT
Theory and Practice

Aldo Chircop, André Gerolymatos and John O. Iatrides
THE AEGEAN SEA AFTER THE COLD WAR
Security and Law of the Sea Issues

Diane Ethier
ECONOMIC ADJUSTMENT IN NEW DEMOCRACIES
Lessons from Southern Europe

Jeffrey Henderson (*editor*)
INDUSTRIAL TRANSFORMATION IN EASTERN EUROPE IN THE LIGHT OF THE EAST ASIAN EXPERIENCE

Jacques Hersh and Johannes Dragsbaek Schmidt (*editors*)
THE AFTERMATH OF 'REAL EXISTING SOCIALISM' IN EASTERN EUROPE
Volume 1: Between Western Europe and East Asia

Anne Lorentzen and Marianne Rostgaard (*editors*)
THE AFTERMATH OF 'REAL EXISTING SOCIALISM' IN EASTERN EUROPE
Volume 2: People and Technology in the Process of Transition

Gary McMahon (*editor*)
LESSONS IN ECONOMIC POLICY FOR EASTERN EUROPE FROM LATIN AMERICA

Árni Sverrison and Meine Pieter van Dijk (*editors*)
LOCAL ECONOMIES IN TURMOIL
The Effects of Deregulation and Globalization

International Political Economy Series
Series Standing Order ISBN 0–333–71708–2 hardcover
Series Standing Order ISBN 0–333–71110–6 paperback
(*outside North America only*)

You can receive future titles in this series as they are published by placing a standing order. Please contact your bookseller or, in case of difficulty, write to us at the address below with your name and address, the title of the series and one of the ISBNs quoted above.

Customer Services Department, Macmillan Distribution Ltd, Houndmills, Basingstoke, Hampshire RG21 6XS, England

Local Economies in Turmoil

The Effects of Deregulation and Globalization

Edited by

Árni Sverrisson

Assistant Professor
Department of Sociology
University of Stockholm
Sweden

and

Meine Pieter van Dijk

Professor
Erasmus University, and
Institute for Housing and Urban Studies
Rotterdam
The Netherlands

First published in Great Britain 2000 by
MACMILLAN PRESS LTD
Houndmills, Basingstoke, Hampshire RG21 6XS and London
Companies and representatives throughout the world
A catalogue record for this book is available from the British Library.

ISBN 0–333–79242–4

First published in the United States of America 2000 by
ST. MARTIN'S PRESS, INC.,
Scholarly and Reference Division,
175 Fifth Avenue, New York, N.Y. 10010
ISBN 0–312–23147–4
Library of Congress Cataloging-in-Publication Data
Local economies in turmoil: the effects of deregulation and globalization / edited
by Árni Sverrisson and Meine Pieter van Dijk.
p.   cm.
"Presentations and papers prepared for a joint meeting of the Working Group on
Industrialization Strategies and the Working Group on Changes in Eastern Europe and
North–South Relations, both within the European Association of Development Research and
Training Institutes (EADI) in Milan, September 19 and 20, 1997"–
–Acknowledgements.
Includes bibliographical references and index.
ISBN 0–312–23147–4 (cloth)
1. Small business—Case studies. 2. Structural adjustment (Economic policy)—Case studies.
3. Deregulation—Case studies. 4. Competition, International—Case studies. 5. Economic con-
ditions—1990—Case studies. I. Sverrisson, Árni. II. Dijk, Meine Pieter van. III. European
Association of Development Research and Training Institutes. Working Group on
Industrialization Strategies. IV. European Association of Development Research and Training
Institutes. Working Group on Changes in Eastern Europe and North–South Relations.
HD2341 .L6   2000
330.9—dc21   99–087607

This book is printed on paper suitable for recycling and made from fully managed and sustained
forest sources.

10   9   8   7   6   5   4   3   2   1
09   08   07   06   05   04   03   02   01   00

Printed and bound in Great Britain by Antony Rowe Ltd, Chippenham, Wiltshire

Contents

List of Tables   vii

List of Figures   viii

Acknowledgements   ix

Notes on the Contributors   x

List of Abbreviations   xiii

1   Introduction: Local Economies in Turmoil   1
    Árni Sverrisson and Meine Pieter van Dijk

Part I   Enterprises and Enterprise Strategies

2   Adjusting to an Opening Economy: Three Industrial
    Clusters in Brazil   19
    Jörg Meyer-Stamer

3   Social Embeddedness: Families and Firms in Tanzania   43
    Per Trulsson

4   Financing Small and Medium-sized Enterprises in
    Eastern Europe   60
    Debora Revoltella

Part II   Industrial Clusters and Networks

5   Structural Adjustment and Cluster Advantages:
    A Case from Peru   77
    Evert-Jan Visser

6   Innovation in Roof Tile and Copper Craft Clusters
    in Indonesia   95
    Henry Sandee and Piet Rietveld

7   Light Engineering Networks and Structural Adjustment
    in Zimbabwe   113
    Charles M. Halimana and Árni Sverrisson

v

Part III The Economic and Political Environment

8 A Macro-perspective on Small Enterprise Growth
in Southern Africa   131
Poul Ove Pedersen

9 Good Governance and Small Enterprises in Zimbabwe   150
Meine Pieter van Dijk

10 Economic Cultures and Industrial Development
in the South   167
Árni Sverrisson

11 Conclusion: Research Issues after Structural Adjustment 181
Meine Pieter van Dijk and Árni Sverrisson

References   193

Index   205

List of Tables

2.1 Comparing changes in industrial clusters in SC 39
4.1 Definitions of small and medium-sized enterprises 61
4.2 Share of small and medium-sized enterprises in the total labour force 61
4.3 Change in the use of sources of finance, 1993–94, by firm size 64
4.4 Firm size and financing through debt in 1994: stock analysis 64
6.1 Traditional tile producers and marketing chains in Karanggeneng 98
6.2 Traditional copper craft producers in Tumang, 1985 100
6.3 Logit regression analysis for adoption in Karanggeneng, 1993 104
6.4 Regression with innovation adoption as dependent variable in Tumang, 1985 106
6.5 Innovators selling to institutional consumers and final consumers 108
6.6 Comparison of traditional and press tile producers, census data, 1993 109
7.1 Age distribution of machines in light engineering firms in 1990 114
7.2 Volume of production indices, 1970–94 116
7.3 Imports (value) of selected categories of machinery, 1981–93 117
8.1 Sectoral distribution of small rural and urban enterprises 139
8.2 The small enterprise sectors in Kenya, Zimbabwe and Botswana 145

List of Figures

2.1 SC: structure of industry   21
2.2 Annual change in exports: SC and Brazil   22
2.3 Major textile firms in SC: returns on capital   28
2.4 Major ceramic tile firms in SC: return on capital   29
2.5 Production and exports of ceramic tiles in Brazil   30
4.1 Small and medium-sized enterprises by sector in 1994   61
4.2 Financing enterprises in the Czech Republic in 1994:
     a flow analysis   63
4.3 Bank interest rates on credits to best and worst clients
     in Hungary   67
8.1 Predictions of theories of small enterprise (SE) development   138

Acknowledgements

The contributions presented in this book originated as presentations and papers prepared for a joint meeting of the Working Group on Industrialization Strategies and the Working Group on Changes in Eastern Europe and North–South Relations, both within the European Association of Development Research and Training Institutes (EADI), in Milan, 19 and 20 September 1997. Our first and warmest thanks therefore go to Professor Sergio Allessandrini and Roberta Rabellotti at Universitá Commerciale Luigi Bocconi in Milan, who hosted the meeting and did everything to make it a pleasant, useful and educating experience for the participants. We also want to thank other participants in the meeting, whose presentations are not included here, who significantly contributed to the improvement of the book by their comments and suggestions. At the University of Stockholm, Susanne Urban assisted in various ways during the process of putting the book together, competently as always. Last but not least, the encouragement, suggestions and patience of Keith Povey, Tim Shaw and Aruna Vasudevan at Macmillan helped us through the final laps, when we needed it most. Thanks all!

Stockholm and Rotterdam

ÁRNI SVERRISSON
MEINE PIETER VAN DIJK

Notes on the Contributors

Meine Pieter van Dijk is Professor at the Economic Faculty of the Erasmus University in Rotterdam and at the Institute for Housing and Urban Studies in Rotterdam. He is author of *Burkina-Faso: le secteur informel de Ouagadougou*. He edited *Enterprise Clusters and Networks in Developing Countries* (with R. Rabellotti) and *Multilateralism versus Regionalism: Trade Issues After the Uruguay Round* (with Sandro Sideri). He has in addition published a large number of books, articles and reports on development issues. His current research interests include enterprise clusters in developing countries, the problems of women entrepreneurs and the development of urban infrastructure.

Charles M. Halimana is Senior Research Fellow at the Zimbabwe Institute for Development Studies, University of Zimbabwe in Harare. He is author of *The Role of Small Industrial Enterprises in Zimbabwe's Industrialization Future: Focus on Engineering Firms*, and has published a number of reports and articles on different development issues in Zimbabwe. His current research interests include the connections between social and economic development, ethnic constraints on development and the development and diffusion of engineering competence.

Jörg Meyer-Stamer is Senior Research Fellow at the Institute for Development and Peace, University of Duisburg. He also works as a consultant on local and regional economic development strategies for Fundação Empreender in Brazil, and for technical assistance agencies. He is author of *Technology, Competitiveness and Radical Policy Change: The Case of Brazil* and co-author of *Systemic Competitiveness: New Governance Patterns for Industrial Development*, as well as various reports and articles on the political economy of industrial competitiveness, industrial and technology policy, and other topics.

Poul Ove Pedersen is Director of Research at the Centre for Development Research in Copenhagen. He is author of *Small African Towns: Between Rural Networks and Urban Hierarchies*. He edited *Small Enterprises: Flexibility and Networking in an African Context* (with Dorothy McCormick) and *Flexible Specialisation: The Dynamics of Small Scale Industries in the South* (with Árni Sverrisson and Meine Pieter van Dijk). He has published numerous other books and articles on urban and regional development and small enterprises, especially in Africa. His current research focuses on the impact of globalization on economic development in Africa, with special emphasis on the role and structure of producer services.

Debora Revoltella is Research Associate at the Department of Economics, Bocconi University. She is the author of 'Financing firms in East European countries: an asymmetric information and agency costs approach', in *Corporate Governance in Central and Eastern Europe*. Her current work includes enterprise financing in transition economies, banking sector development and foreign direct investments in the banking sector in Eastern Europe.

Piet Rietveld is Professor of Transport Economics at the Faculty of Economics, Free University of Amsterdam and a fellow of the Tinbergen Institute. He is author of *Is Transport Infrastructure Effective? Transport Infrastructure and Accessibility: Impacts on the Space Economy* (with Frank Bruinsma) and edited *Networks in Transport and Communications: A Policy Approach* (with Cristina Capineri). He has published a large number of articles and papers on transport, technological innovation and development issues. Among his research interests are the impacts of transport infrastructure on land use and spatial development, the regional dimensions of development problems in developing countries and technological innovation.

Henry Sandee is a Senior Research Fellow at the Department of Development Economics, Free University of Amsterdam. He is the author of *Innovation Adaption in Rural Industry: Technological Change in Roof Tile Clusters in Central Java, Indonesia*. He has published a number of articles on small-scale industry development in Indonesia and elsewhere. His current research concerns innovation adoption in small-scale industries in Southeast Asia and the impact of the financial crisis on small industry development in Indonesia.

Árni Sverrisson is Assistant Professor at the Department of Sociology, University of Stockholm. He is author of *Evolutionary Technical Change and Flexible Mechanization: Entrepreneurship and Industrialization in Kenya and Zimbabwe*, and edited *Social Movements in Development: The Challenge of Globalization and Democratization* (with Staffan Lindberg). In addition, he has published a large number of reports and articles on technological change in small enterprise networks, sustainable technology, digital image technologies and social network theory, which remain his main research interests.

Per Trulsson is a sociologist and works at the regional office of the International Labour Organization in Harare. He is author of *Strategies of Entrepreneurship: Understanding Industrial Entrepreneurship and Structural Change in Northwest Tanzania*. His general research orientation concerns processes of structural change, and his current work includes studies of men and women who break gender barriers through their enterprising activities and other issues of enterprise development in Zimbabwe.

Evert-Jan Visser is Senior Research Fellow at the Netherlands Economic Institute, Department of Regional and Urban Development. He is author of *Local Sources of Competitiveness: Spatial Clustering and Organisational Dynamics in Small-Scale Clothing in Lima, Peru*. He has also published articles on sustainable forms of small enterprise financing in developing countries. His current work is concerned with policies enhancing the dynamism of small-firm clusters in developing countries, the relation between territory and trust, and scenario-based regional strategy formulation.

List of Abbreviations

ACI	Associations of Commerce and Industry
APEGA	Gamarra Association of Small Enterprises
BNDES	National Development Bank
CEO	Chief Executive Officer
CTC	Centre for Ceramics Technology
DEED	Department of Employment and Employment Development
DPT	Deregulation Project Team
ERP	Economic Recovery Programme
ESAP	Economic Structural Adjustment Programme
ETP	Employment and Training Programme
FACISC	Federation of ACIs
FIESC	Federation of Industries of Santa Catarina
GAPOOL	Gamarra T-shirt makers' Consortium
GDP	Gross Domestic Product
GNP	Gross National Product
GTZ	German Development Agency
ILO	International Labour Organization
ILOSDINFO	International Labour Organization Social Development Fund Information
IMF	International Monetary Fund
LOGAC	Loans and Grants Allocation Committee
MEDP	Micro-enterprise Development Programme
MFI	Micro-finance Institution
NBC	National Bank of Commerce
NGO	Non-governmental Organization
PAAP	Poverty Alleviation Action Plan
PHARE	Poland and Hungary: Aid for the Restructuring of Economies
R&D	Research and Development
SC	Santa Catarina
SCG	Sociedad de Consorcios de Exportacion de Gamarra
SDA	Social Dimensions of Adjustment
SDF	Social Development Fund
SE	Small Enterprise
SEDCO	Small Enterprise Development Corporation

xiii

SIDO	Small Industries Development Organization
SME	Small and Medium-sized Enterprise
SSN	Social Safety Net
SWP	Social Welfare Programme
UDI	Unilateral Declaration of Independence
ZIMPREST	Zimbabwe Programme for Social and Economic Transformation
ZISCO	Zimbabwe Steel Corporation

1
Introduction: Local Economies in Turmoil

Árni Sverrisson and Meine Pieter van Dijk

Two processes have changed the political and economic map of the world in the 1990s and created new challenges and opportunities for enterprises in the periphery of the global economy. These are the dissolving of 'planned economies' in Eastern Europe (Frank, 1996; Henderson, 1998) and the forceful promotion of structural adjustment programmes in the South.

Both these processes are essentially political. However, politics usually has an economic side, and in these cases, economic theories have come forward both to legitimize policy and to fuel criticism, as the case may be (cf. Lindberg and Sverrisson, 1997). Legitimatization has mainly drawn on the prescriptions of neo-classical economics. Deregulation of domestic economic life, less state intervention in economic activities, and fewer obstacles to international trade: these are the main tenets of neo-liberal policy.

Critics have focused mainly on the negative social consequences of these policies for the poor and powerless: economic planning, state capitalism and protectionism have had few advocates in the 1990s. Considerable efforts have also been devoted to social programmes and aid, particularly in the South, but also in Eastern Europe, in order to defuse what otherwise might become a threat to the ultimate goal: stable and orderly but also 'free' markets (cf. World Bank, 1990). However, these efforts are limited to selective interventions.

Earlier experiments in free market economics, from the nineteenth century on, have usually led to the revival of regulatory efforts in order to secure social and political stability and the continued legitimacy of the state. Failing this they have generated social revolutions or else 'free' markets have been maintained under the cover of armed dictatorship (cf. Schumpeter, 1942; Polanyi, 1957). Such solutions are still favoured by many.

However, the picture is more complex than this. The world is not only populated by poor people struggling along and global corporations closely integrated among themselves, and their respective advocates. The political logic of globally organized mass production, which transcends territorial borders, undermines states and replaces government planning with corporate planning, is perhaps dominant in the discourse conducted in public media. In practice, however, most people do not base their livelihood on working for global mass producers. Either they work in the now contracting state apparatuses, which for this reason can draw on a vested interest in their defence against free market politics, or they work in small and medium-sized units, local in scope and ranging from one-person enterprises and upwards (Pedersen, 1997). This is the case particularly in the Third World as it is likely to be in any economy predominantly based on agriculture and small-scale trading, but is also emerging as a significant phenomenon in Eastern Europe.

However, the many and heterogeneous forms of small-scale local production are not easy to grasp under the sweeping categorizations so characteristic of global and national politics. The workers and enterprise owners who populate this sphere of economic life are also much more difficult to distinguish from each other and organize separately, than the magnates of mass production and the workers they employ (cf. Scranton, 1997). Politically, the interests of small-scale producers and traders therefore tend to be subsumed under those of other groups with which they overlap to a smaller or greater extent: peasants, farmers, workers, professionals or burghers, as the case may be.

This situation is mirrored in academia. There is comparatively little work focusing on the internal and specific dynamics of local production systems and small-scale producers. During the current transformation of the world economy in particular, the problems and opportunities created in local economies therefore tend to be discussed on the basis of assumptions and stereotypes, if at all. This book is intended to help in opening up this area of research. Like all beginnings, it is in some ways hesitant and indeterminate. However, the problems discussed, the adaptation of local economic systems to the restructuring of the global economy, affect the lives of millions of people in profound ways, which is why both authors and editors have found the exercise worthwhile.

Local Economies and Structural Adjustment

The red thread woven through all the contributions included in this book is how local economies respond to deregulation and structural adjustment, under which heading we also subsume the changes taking place in Eastern Europe (Aage, 1997). The concrete issues and approaches which have guided the empirical work presented in this book address aspects of this more general problem. Conventionally, the effects of adjustment can be considered at three levels; micro, meso and macro. We have followed a similar classification and divided the contributions into three parts, each with its own distinctive theme, which focus, in turn, on enterprise level analysis, network/cluster analysis, and macro-level analysis. However, the middle level is, in this case, not inserted in order to account for everything that does not fit in the two others. If anything, it is the middle or meso-level concepts which provide a framework for the volume, and the chapters which address the micro- and macro-issues do so with a point of departure in the meso-level, more or less explicitly.

The first theme is the adjustment strategies of individual proprietors and managers and how they are formed by the past and present environment in which they operate, locally and globally. There is no single strategy which can be said to be characteristic of small- and medium-sized enterprises (SMEs). Each proprietor is rather faced with a concrete situation into which he or she carries the vestiges of the past, experience and hands-on knowledge which has been accumulated, economic capital in the form of machines and buildings and social capital in the form of business contacts, reputations among customers, and the like (Knorringa, 1995; Sverrisson, 1997). The form of adjustment can therefore be expected to depend on the interpretation and judgement each proprietor makes of the changes happening around each enterprise, its concrete forms and how he or she can manage to stay afloat or expand in the circumstances. This theme is the focus of the first part.

The second theme is interconnections between enterprises and their effects on adjustment. Previous research on SMEs has shown that small enterprises often develop in networks or clusters (Sverrisson, 1993; Pedersen *et al.*, 1994; van Dijk and Rabellotti, 1997). This theme is developed in a number of chapters in the second part. Are enterprises in clusters more likely to survive the effects of deregulation and adjustment? Are they in a better position to take advantage of opportunities such as export openings? Or is clustering in some cases an obstacle, which ties enterprises to traditional ways and hinders adjustment?

The third theme, which is discussed in part three, is political and economic environments. Under this heading the authors analyse the macro-economic, political, legal and cultural contexts of small enterprise growth.

Unavoidably, the themes overlap: they provide foci, not borderlines. This follows logically from the concern of the authors to understand the problems faced and choices made by entrepreneurs in their situated and complex totality, rather than purvey abstract prescriptions for how they should behave in an ideal world. However, although the agenda of the authors is empirical and scientific rather than political and normative, this does not preclude reflections on the policy implications of the findings presented here, and these are summarized in the last part of this introduction.

Enterprises and Enterprise Strategies

In Chapter 2, *'Adjusting to an Opening Economy: Three Industrial Clusters in Brazil'*, Jörg Meyer-Stamer reports findings from his studies of three clusters. One is made up of textile firms, another includes metal engineering and electromechanical appliances, and a third makes ceramic tiles. He introduces what remains a major concern throughout the book, namely the situated action of management within local political and economic contexts which refract the impact of structural adjustment in peculiar ways. In addition, he explores the usefulness of the concept of path-dependent action in a clustered context. The enterprises he studied have opted for a strategy of vertical integration in order to cope with an extremely volatile and turbulent business environment, which has become more so in the wake of structural adjustment and due to the vagaries of local politics. Hence, rather than networking horizontally, managers tend to stick to their basic strategy of self-reliance which served them well earlier. However, local business associations have become the vehicle of information interchange, stimulated common efforts to support vocational training in the area and supported collaborative improvements in design and quality. Although production links are still rare, other forms of networking suggest a new path for industrial development in Santa Catarina (SC), and that clusters imply positive effects even for firms which embody a vertically integrated production system.

Per Trulsson continues this theme in Chapter 3, *'Social Embeddedness: Families and Firms in Tanzania'*, in which he presents his findings from extensive fieldwork in north-west Tanzania. The companies he visited are also middle-sized and large rather than small. As Meyer-Stamer he explains vertical integration as a reaction to the uncertainty which has resulted from structural adjustment, particularly the changing role of the state, which was very strong earlier in Tanzania.

However, the conceptual framework he brings to this task is different from the one deployed by Meyer-Stamer. Trulsson rather develops aspects of Mark Granovetter's theory of the social embeddedness of economic activities, and links them to Göran Hydén's concept of an economy of affection, in which kinship obligations and other similar expectations on (relatively) wealthy people circumscribe the options which they can pursue. However, Trulsson finds that such ties are losing their importance and that affectionate trust is more and more limited to the immediate family. Rather than taking on relatives to work in their companies, the entrepreneurs studied would help them to set up their own, often very small, ventures and in other ways keep them at arm's length.

In explaining this, Trulsson combines a micro- and macro-analysis. He suggests *inter alia* that the sheer pressure created by structural adjustment calls for prudent personnel policies, but also mentions the past of the entrepreneurs in the state apparatus and parastatal companies as a contributing factor. However, he is careful to emphasize that the current transition of entrepreneurial behaviour remains embedded in a largely traditional social context, which creates opportunities to develop trust, but also inopportune demands that must be coped with.

An additional case of the situated character of business decision-making in a volatile environment is presented in Chapter 4, *'Financing Small- and Medium-sized Enterprises in Eastern Europe'*. In this chapter, Debora Revoltella presents her research on banking practices in the Czech Republic and elsewhere, how they affect the prospects of small- and medium-sized enterprises and by extension, the opportunities for entrepreneurship. On the basis of aggregated balance sheet data from a large number of firms, she shows that small- and medium-sized Czech enterprises rely mainly on internal funding and leasing. Noting that a good credit system needs a sound institutional basis, Revoltella goes on to analyse the Czech legislation which affects banking practices and financing options. She also compares it with Polish and Hungarian legislation in this area. She concludes that in spite of the differences between the countries, underdevelopment of financial markets and a fragmented and sometimes obsolete legislation is the root of the problem. Terms of lending, legal rules defining applicable sanctions and bankruptcy legislation are as yet inadequate.

Generally, bankers are also unfamiliar with the way small- and medium-sized enterprises operate. As a result, lending to small- and medium-sized enterprises tends to be seen as risky compared to other alternatives. Therefore, credit programmes are needed, which support small enterprises actively. Applicable legislation needs to be streamlined as well, in order to overcome both the adverse selection mechanisms evident now and the prevailing conception that lending to smaller enterprises is hazardous.

Industrial Clusters and Networks

In Chapter 5, '*Structural Adjustment and Cluster Advantages: A Case from Peru*', Evert-Jan Visser analyses critically the pros and cons of the argument that clustering provides dynamic advantages to the firms which participate, as well as to the cluster as a whole. On the basis of data gathered in two visits four years apart, he concludes that this has not been the case in the cluster he studied. The joint marketing efforts of firms in the cluster have not led to the dynamic development of the cluster or of single firms in it. Further, no successful initiatives have emerged through which marketing co-operation could be deepened and developed towards networked production and flexible specialization.

On the basis of this analysis Visser reflects on the current state of cluster theorizing and concludes that factors other than geographical proximity must be brought in to explain the development of micro-enterprise clusters. Analysis of the networks established among proprietors in a cluster and the potential of such networks for supporting technical and organizational improvements is a particularly needed and important step forward in this context.

In Chapter 6, '*Innovation in Roof Tile and Copper Craft Clusters in Indonesia*', Henry Sandee and Piet Rietveld present two different kinds of cluster dynamic, both of which, however, lead to technological and organizational change. On the basis of data collected by the authors in Indonesia they discuss the differential effects of producer networks and trading networks on technological change and vice versa. In both cases a transformation of formerly egalitarian producer networks to more hierarchical forms has been accompanied by technological change: in one case, this takes the form of subcontracting, in the other case, successful innovators start employing traditional producers as casual workers.

The workings of trading networks depend on the position of the intermediaries as well. Some of them connect producers to equally poor consumers in other rural locations, and the producers are consequently locked in a position of providing traditional and cheap products, which hinders innovation. Other intermediaries connect producers to better-off urban consumers, and linking with them facilitates innovation. In both cases, the trade-off between quality and price as competitive assets appears clearly. Lastly, some producers sell directly to consumers. They can then invest the trading profit, which in this case accrues directly to the producer, in machinery and better hand tools. This is particularly relevant in the case of tiles in which individual consumers make fairly large investments at long intervals. In the case of copper crafts, direct sales tend to be equal to small sales of cheap goods to other locals. Hence, both the network types, to which producers are connected, and the position of producers within these networks, are found to be important explanatory factors.

This theme is continued in Chapter 7, '*Light Engineering Networks and Structural Adjustment in Zimbabwe*', by Charles M. Halimana and Árni Sverrisson. First they analyse the manufacturing of elementary machinery and spares in Zimbabwe up to and immediately after the structural adjustment programmes of the 1990s. They then suggest that two countervailing factors have in particular influenced the changes taking place. On the one hand, the lifting of import restrictions has led to increased importation of machinery and vehicles, which in turn creates demand for supplementary products. An example is the extra fenders needed because of wildlife on the roads and not provided by vehicle manufactures. In addition, importing components to assemble products, and the importation of materials for making components then exported for assembly elsewhere has become possible to a larger extent. On the other hand, as spares for all types of machinery, as well as new machines, can be imported more easily, the local production of spares which thrived earlier behind protective barriers is facing crisis.

Light engineering companies respond to this situation in different ways. Some increase their product range, whereas others focus on a few standardized products or particular niches. Some have entered into a closer relationships with earlier customers and suppliers, whereas others have reorganized their networks. Some have developed contacts with global production networks, importing and exporting, whereas others develop hedging strategies predicated on maximal self-sufficiency combined with product diversification.

The explanation of this diversity is found in the previous histories of the companies concerned, and their response to crisis. Some have re-organized their operations more or less completely, sometimes via the legal instrument of bankruptcy, whereas others have adapted more evolutionary strategies, building on the financial, human and social capital they already possess. In the latter case, scope may be increased because earlier niches have become less lucrative, or decreased, because one or more niches, such as for example security equipment, have become more lucrative, due to structural adjustment.

Economic and Political Environment

Poul Ove Pedersen addresses the question: 'How can we explain growth' in Chapter 8, '*A Macro-perspective on Small Enterprise Growth in Southern Africa*'. First, he presents four different but possible explanations of growth in the small- and medium-sized enterprise sector. The first of these is based on the growth in labour supply which, if not absorbed by established companies, swells the ranks of the informal sector. The second explanation is based on growing demand for cheap products, which creates opportunities for self-employment in the informal sector. Both types of explanation have a common root in population growth as the independent variable, but they identify different intermediary mechanisms.

The third type of explanation is based on increased commercialization of agriculture. As the number of commercial transactions increases and the prevalence of household production decreases, opportunities are created for small enterprises, either in rural areas, which leads to an increase in non-agricultural activities, or in urban areas, due to the migration fuelled by increased efficiency of agriculture, land shortage, etc. The fourth type of explanation sees the increase in small informal enterprise as a part of an industrialization process which both creates openings for manufacturing enterprises but also increases the opportunities for trade in their products.

If the first two types of explanation suggest a straightforward connection between central variables and take the structures in which they operate as given, the latter two types of explanation, in contrast, focus on the effects of historical change.

One way to decide which explanation works is to consider how well different predictions generated by each explanation fit available data, which are presented by Pedersen. However, no explanation predicts observed variations in the size and composition of the small enterprise sector particularly well, neither over time nor across countries. Pedersen concludes, on the basis of a detailed discussion of the data, that a composite theory is needed. It should include the effects of secular change as well as the effects of variation in population growth. An adequate theory should also be able to distinguish the short-term effects of structural adjustment programmes (the shocks) from their long-term effects on secular trends.

In Chapter 9, '*Good Governance and Small Enterprises in Zimbabwe*', Meine Pieter van Dijk analyses the effects of liberalization on SMEs in Zimbabwe. He argues that against the present economic background the chances for the development of small enterprises are dismal. Many formally established manufacturers perceive small- and medium-sized enterprises as illegitimate competitors which should be eliminated. At the same time, a number of initiatives from the government and donors aimed at helping small- and medium-sized enterprises have encountered problems, ranging from inadequate repayment rates to completely missing the intended target group.

Van Dijk suggests that a large part of the problem is to be found in the business environment created before independence. A transition in Zimbabwe calls for the establishment of a neutral framework for different kinds of enterprises, what has been called 'good governance,' rather than sector specific efforts. Van Dijk analyses what this would imply for Zimbabwe, focusing on a number of regulations still in force which directly work against the interests of small entrepreneurs. However, the structural disadvantages of small enterprises are such that continued efforts to ameliorate the by now well-known problems of small entrepreneurs are needed. However, these tasks do not need to be carried out by central government agencies, and should be entrusted to local governments and non-governmental organizations (NGOs) both of which can more easily tailor support measures to the manifest needs of their clients.

In Chapter 10, '*Economic Cultures and Industrial Development in the South*,' Árni Sverrisson analyses the bifurcation between the global production culture and a variety of local production cultures, on the basis of material gathered in different African countries over a number of years. Sverrisson observes that the coexistence of these two varieties of production system seems to be a universal characteristic of industrialization processes. He then proceeds to discuss what this means for the South today.

Sverrisson draws on two different network approaches, social network analysis and analysis of socio/technical networks, and identifies a number of features which characterize the more dynamic local economic cultures in the South. The first of these is gradual mechanization based on the sharing of benefits in networks and clusters. When, for example, a wood lathe is acquired by one small enterprise, it can also supply all others with turned components of furniture. The second is division of labour and task specialization within clusters, often but not always connected to mechanization. The third is the mobilization of outside contacts to acquire technical information, and their fast diffusion within clusters. This is combined with innovative local interpretation of technologies leading to flexible production practices. Fourth, the presence of individuals who through the possession of core technologies or by organizational means (or both) act as brokers of information and opportunities is also essential. Lastly, the prevalence of craft production and polyvalent or all-round skills of workers is found in a large number of growing local economies.

However, most local economies tend to be inward-oriented, and connections with the global economic culture are few and far between. The development of such connections is necessary for the sustained development of local economies, yet they rarely develop to the point where they can reach out to larger markets. Local demand is limited, and can be satisfied with elementary products, and the learning implied by dealing with demanding and discerning customers, which is a prerequisite for export activities, is absent in most cases. These obstacles are intensified by structural adjustment: cheap imports, particularly of textiles, flood African markets, for example. The original reason for inadequate learning, widespread poverty, has become more severe. Further, the main repositories of advanced technological capability, that is import substituting, government owned or parastatal companies, are folded down and very little has appeared instead.

Future Research Issues

The conclusions from these studies can be grouped under two main headings, research conclusions and policy conclusions. The research conclusions are discussed in detail in Chapter 11, and we will only indicate the main points briefly here. The rest of this introduction is then focused on policy conclusions.

In Chapter 11 the research conclusions are grouped around five themes. The first is focused on the effects of structural adjustment on local economies in general and the effects on enterprise clusters in particular. This leads on to a discussion of research issues pertaining to the relationship between local economies and the global system. The second theme is centered on the cluster concept, which more than any other has shaped alternative approaches to industrialization, and we discuss ways and means of transcending what we see as an impasse: a large number of clusters has been documented, but their trajectories differ widely and no single explanation of their development or its absence seems to be adequate. Our suggestions in this regard is to bring in both network analysis and typologies of clusters and cluster trajectories, and generally more systematic consideration of cluster histories, as exemplified by Visser and Meyer-Stamer in this volume. The third theme is 'the new dualism,' that is the existence of informal clusters of small enterprises around the established clusters of more dynamic and larger ones. This phenomenon, which has been noted by several authors (e.g. Sverrisson, 1993; Nadvi and Schmitz, 1994) has not been systematically explored, and we suggest how that could be done. The fourth theme is innovation in small enterprises in the South, which has attracted some attention over the years. However, it is not clear whether innovation in the strict sense or creative imitative practices are the most suitable strategies and we indicate how this issue could be resolved. Lastly we summarize the preceding discussion and outline what we see as the next step in developing alternative approaches to industrialization – going beyond flexible specialization to multidimensional and context oriented analysis, in which certain universal mechanisms can be identified, with the outcome revolving on their combination rather than on any single factor.

Small Enterprise Policies and Structural Adjustment

What does all this imply for small enterprise policies? A first and perhaps obvious conclusion is that policies and other interventions aimed at individual firms are not likely to be very effective, if their local environments are not affected simultaneously. Such policies tend to reproduce enclaves of vertically integrated industrial development rather than the diffusion of new production methods, technological and organizational, and improvements for the entire community. Conversely, interventions which aim at enhancing local, regional and national conditions will not lead to the desired result, if firms are unable to adapt and reorganize their operations accordingly.

Humphrey and Schmitz (1996) have suggested, on the basis of research along similar lines as the contributions presented here, that policies to support small- and medium-sized enterprises need to be customer-oriented, collective and cumulative, resulting in what they call a triple C approach. In what follows we explore the implications of this approach on the basis of the different contributions in this book.

Customer-orientation implies that the needs of customers are studied in detail, which amounts to focusing on niches and often temporary variations in, e.g. styles and designs preferred, rather than working on the assumption of anonymous markets where price is the only tool of competition. This accords well with what is known about how most locally oriented companies actually operate, and the task of policy and government intervention then becomes to create the channels which facilitate the flow of information which is relevant to such strategies, as suggested by Sverrisson, Visser and van Dijk in their contributions. At the same time, it is neccessary for customers to be able to get at least some overview of what is being offered. This is one of the main strengths of clusters of enterprises in similar activities: customers can, by visiting a cluster, both express their preferences to a large number of enterprises, and conversely, acquire information about what is available from many, competing, firms. Similarly, suppliers can and do establish themselves in such clusters for parallel reasons.

However, if clustering ensures smooth operation of the connections between local customers and local companies, and between them and their suppliers, it cannot, in itself, facilitate links with customers elsewhere. For this purpose, brokers of some kind are neccessary, as Halimana and Sverrisson as well as Sandee and Rietveld point out in their chapters in this volume. This problematic can be approached in three rather different ways.

The first alternative is commercial. Merchants promote products but more significantly, they also gather information about markets which is relayed to producers through the mechanism of ordering and the provision of designs, colour schemes, etc. A problem which inevitably arises here is that merchants tend to limit access to the information at their disposal to the firms to which they are connected, and they also claim, of course, a large share of the profit, which can lead to a situation in which it is rational for individual producers to avoid merchants if they can (cf. Sverrisson, 1993; Sandee, 1995).

The second method is government based and financed. An appropriate agency, local or national as the case may be, employs consultants which study markets abroad, in urban agglomerations, etc. in order to figure out how local firms can, by focusing on particular niches, make an inroad in these markets. This information is then made available to all producers (and merchants as well). A further step is to establish marketing agencies which connect local producers with customers elsewhere, via government intervention, and eventually with government ownership. However, as in the case of merchants, the cut of the marketing agency is likely to be large, and in addition, such agencies have often turned out to be less than adequately effective in practice. In the case of customers with exacting demands according to fairly well defined standards, e.g. in food processing and exports of food products, government intervention can be necessary, however, but then in the form of information about such standards, inspection of facilities and organizing appropriate educational and training efforts rather than direct marketing, which moreover can often been done better by, or at least in co-operation with, actors located in the importing country.

The third form is based on branch associations or co-operative marketing agencies owned by the producers themselves. When effective, such units can gather information about prospective customers, relay orders, represent producers at fairs and other such occasions, and organize training. The hard nut to crack is how to facilitate the establishment of such associations, and decide when this is feasible. Although the success stories here are legion, unpremeditated imposition of such forms from above, as for example has happened with co-operatives in several African countries, is counterproductive. Policies in this area are therefore limited to support to associations and co-operatives which form spontaneously. The idea can be promoted but not the thing itself (cf. Visser, van Dijk, Meyer-Stamer, this volume).

This leads us naturally to the collective aspects of enterprise improvement policies. In order to intervene on behalf of some collective, it must be organized, and as it is not feasible for the government (or externally funded development projects, for that matter) to create an organization on behalf of a group of producers, or force them to organize in order to acquire assistance, be it in the form of credit, marketing or technical consultancy, this severely limits the policy options in this area. In essence, government agencies are reduced to working with existing collectives and organizations. However, it is by now well documented that clustering and networking frequently arise spontaneously among producers in the South. There is therefore no shortage of possible candidates for this type of support, and in the view of the current capacities of the relevant agencies and organizations, the supply of potential beneficiaries will not run out in the near future.

However, most such interactive activities are not formalized in associations or organizations. This flows from the sad state of democratic participation in most countries rather than from any intrinsic economic logic. It is difficult to form an association in a country where arranging a public meeting without permission from the authorities is a prosecutable offence. In the long run, therefore, development strategies, which include the active participation of producers in managing their own mutual affairs call for political and not only economic reforms. Attempts to circumvent this obstacle by creating specific organizations among the receivers of some kind of assistance cannot really solve this problem: first, because they exclude those who do not benefit directly, and include only a part of a given cluster or network, and secondly, because the membership is in such cases usually oriented toward individual benefits (ultimately to the detriment of local competitors) rather than collective improvement.

As for the cumulative character and long-term consistency of support, this is a well documented requirement for success. However, deep seated uncertainties created by turbulent economic and political conditions make this difficult, as is documented in several contributions in this volume. Such conditions tend to focus the efforts of producers on the short-term adaptions neccessary for survival rather than long-term measures needed for growth (cf. MacGaffey, 1987; Tripp, 1997 and Trulsson, this volume). The limited time span of most development projects strengthens this tendency to get what you can while it is available, and let the future take care of itself.

This does not mean that uncertainties cannot be overcome, or at least reduced, either through vertical integration, if in a networked rather than in-house form, or looser co-operation arising spontaneously or taking commercial initiatives, government initiatives or active associations as the point of departure. In this process, government action can help, essentially in two ways. First, the government can pursue systematic procurement policies which support such improvement efforts there are, particularly among small- and medium-sized enterprises, and in sectors which are for historical or other reasons particularly disadvantaged, as well as otherwise create a level ground for competition. In any country, after all, the government is the largest, if not the most lucrative and quick-paying customer. Second, governments can and should pursue policies which reduce uncertainty, by increasing the information available, avoid economic shocks (such as delaying devaluations of currencies and other financial measures until they assume catastrophic dimensions), and ensure adequate infrastructure conditions.

However, in the long run, growth depends on technological change. Amidst crisis management and demands for democratization, formulating and consistently maintaining coherent technology policies has proved difficult. Developing appropriate educational programmes for engineers and craftsmen is a high priority in any industrializing country, but in spite of the almost trivial character of this observation, such programmes are inadequate, to say the least, in most countries in South. On-the-job training can fill some of the gaps in the short term. However, the problem-solving skills needed to sustain technological change, as distinct from day-to-day production, are rarely acquired through practice alone. In order to learn from experience, reflection is necessary, and the tools of reflection are theory, be it physics, materials science, agronomy or accounting. Therefore, underdevelopment will remain as long as these tools are only available to privileged minorities.

In such cases, structural adjustment and deregulation will merely expose the weak, local economic systems to the full force of global competition, with severe consequences. In other cases, hopefully, where technological and organizational capabilities are better developed, structural adjustment creates increased opportunities for at least the most advanced segments of local economies.

Part I

Enterprises and Enterprise Strategies

2
Adjusting to an Opening Economy: Three Industrial Clusters in Brazil

Jörg Meyer-Stamer

Research on industrial clusters and industrial districts in developing countries is moving from the first stage, namely finding and describing industrial districts, to the second stage, i.e. analysing the internal dynamics of these districts. This chapter adds a further dimension by comparing three clusters which have been facing the same macro-economic, regulatory and political conditions and yet show different performances. It is based on field research that was conducted in three industrial clusters in the southern Brazilian state of Santa Catarina (SC).[1]

In the past, particularly during the 1980s and early 1990s, growth rates and exports of industry in SC were significantly above average. Management and workers were better qualified and often possessed specific technological know-how and implemented long-term strategies. Firms did not need to struggle in all areas at the same time in order to survive, because until 1990 Brazilian markets were closed to most products that could be manufactured locally. Apart from that, chronically high inflation discouraged the formulation of long-term strategies and created an environment that penalized inter-firm transactions. Moreover, during the process of latecomer-industrialization suppliers and supporting activities emerged only slowly, and often as quasi-monopolies. Under these conditions it was rational for firms to internalize as many activities as possible. This reduced uncertainty and transaction costs, and excessive vertical integration and lack of externalities were not penalized in protected local markets. Thus emerged an extremely non-co-operative business culture which does not change easily even after the overall incentive struture has changed dramatically due to the transition from import-substituting industrialization to an open economy.

However, the comparison between different clusters reveals that under certain conditions the behaviour of firms can change profoundly, towards co-operation and collective efficiency. These conditions include the exhaustion of incremental strategies, the presence of change agents and the existence of business associations and role models which show alternative paths. The most important changes are attempts to stimulate co-operation between firms (intensified supplier relationships, techno-logical learning, collective action to lobby for a better business condi-tions) and attempts to shape the supporting environment (creating or amplifying the scope of training and technology institutions). Most changes occur inside the business community. The political–adminis-trative system at municipal and state level is more inert.

The Focus of the Field Research

Clustering is one of the salient features of industrial development in SC (the absence of state-owned and large multinational firms being the other two). There are five major industrial clusters (Figure 2.1):

- *The textile cluster.* Main products are casual wear and home textiles. The main location is the Itajaí Valley in the north-eastern part of the state; the largest city there, Blumenau, was founded by German immigrants in 1850. The development of the textile industry, which started in 1880, was initially a chance event due to the arrival of immigrants who were experienced in this trade and sensed a business opportunity (Hering, 1987).
- *The metal engineering and electromechanical cluster.* Major products are household appliances, electrical motors, compressors, transport equipment, and car parts. It is located in the coastal region in the north-eastern part of the state, around the largest city of the state, Joinville, which was also founded by German immigrants in 1851. The development of the cluster was initiated by individual entrepren-eurs in the 1930s (Ternes, 1986).
- *The food processing industry* in the western part of the state specializes in broilers and the processing of chicken, turkey, and pork. It is based on a few large processing firms and a huge number of small farmers who raise the animals. This industry was started in the 1950s, mainly by Italian immigrants.
- *The ceramic tile cluster* around the cities of Criciúma and Tubarão in the southern part of the state. This also started on the basis of individual entrepreneurship of Italian immigrants in the 1950s.

Figure 2.1 SC: structure of industry (according to VAT contribution, 1994)

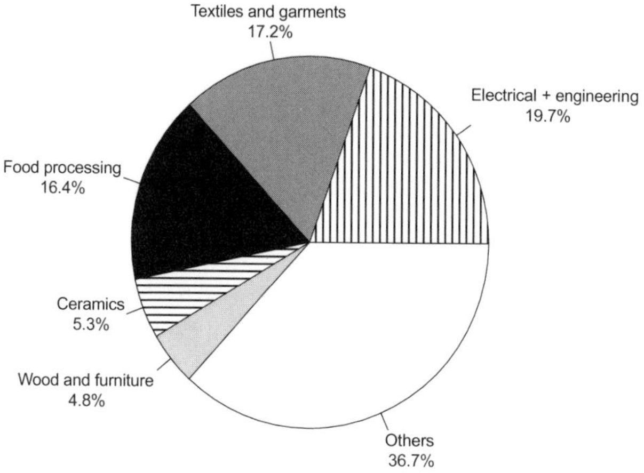

Textiles and garments
17.2%

Electrical + engineering
19.7%

Food processing
16.4%

Ceramics
5.3%

Wood and furniture
4.8%

Others
36.7%

Source: FIESC.

- *The furniture cluster* in the north-eastern interior region around the city of São Bento do Sul. It started on the basis of individual entrepreneurship of mostly German immigrants in the 1920s.

In my research I have investigated three of these clusters: textiles and clothing, metal engineering and electromechanical, and ceramic tiles. This choice was determined by staff shortages and the expectation that these three clusters would be instructive in terms of how firms under pressure strive to improve their competitiveness. Local observers report that the food processing industry is extremely competitive, and that the furniture industry is stagnant.

The metal engineering/electromechanical and the ceramic tile industry are both dominated by medium-sized and large firms. We identified only few micro- and small industrial firms which are suppliers and subcontractors of other firms. The textiles and clothing industry consists of two types of firms. On the one hand, there are verticlly integrated, medium and large, casual wear and home textiles firms which are entirely operating in the formal sector. On the other hand, there are micro- and small casual wear firms which are at least partially operating in the informal sector.[2] In the casual wear industry, both segments coexist in a complicated relationship. For the formal sector firms, the informals are important competitors. The informals also copy the designs of formal sector firms. Moreover, the cluster environment facilitates the business of the informals as qualified workers and inputs are easily available.

Past Successes, Present Challenges

Over the last decades the growth of Gross Domestic Product (GDP) per capita in SC has been consistently higher than in Brazil as a whole,[3] and during the 1980s export performance has been better than the Brazilian average (Figure 2.2), and this has to a large degree been due to highly dynamic industrial development. Contrary to the experience in other parts of Brazil where industrial development has been stimulated, particularly since the 1950s, by massive State support, direct State intervention, and direct foreign investment,[4] in SC it was mainly the result of local entrepreneurship. This is not to say that the State did not play a role in SC's industrial development; the State government launched a

Figure 2.2   Annual change in exports: SC and Brazil

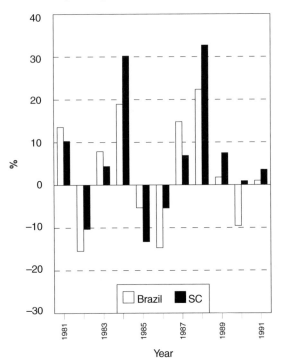

Source: Foreign Trade Department, Central Bank.

programme in the 1970s that contributed significantly to the dynamism in some sectors, particularly food processing and ceramic tiles; and many firms grew rapidly because they had access to (often subsidized) investment funding from the single most important State agency in industrial development, the National Development Bank (Frischtak and Atiyas, 1990). Yet it is important to understand that entrepreneur-ship and entrepreneurial dynamism have played a larger role, and access to State agencies and the capacity to mobilize political support and protection a smaller role, than in other industries in other parts of Brazil. Accordingly, the emphasis on individual achievement is an important element in the local business culture, and is a point industrialists emphasize whenever the opportunity arises.

Looking into management practices of firms in SC, it soon becomes obvious why they have shown an above-average performance in the past, i.e. in the phase of import-substituting industrialization which was the model followed by Brazil until 1990. On the whole, the beha-viour of Brazilian firms in this era was characterized by limited efforts to increase efficiency, quality, and innovative capability (Moreira, 1993; Meyer-Stamer, 1997a). Even leading firms were way behind interna-tional best practice (Sequeira, 1990). Yet many firms in SC did not follow this pattern. Firm owners maintained contacts with the countries they or their forefathers had emigrated from, and often developed a clear idea of how a serious firm' should look like. Supported by a certain sense of superiority, particularly among the German immigrants, entrepreneurs sought to build firms that more or less matched European counterparts. This meant in practice that firms invested in up-to-date equipment, or in the training of their employees, or paid above-averages wages and benefits to develop a stable workforce, or built up Research and Devel-opment (R&D) departments, or upgraded their management systems continuously.[5] Well-known examples of outstanding strategic vision are the foundry Tupy in Joinville and the ceramic tile firm Eliane in Cri-ciúma, both of which initiated vocational training. Further, quite a few firms from SC regularly show up among the best Brazilian firms. Cloth-ing firms in SC have a much higher average productivity than in the rest of Brazil, and account for 32.8 per cent of the production but about 90 per cent of Brazilian casual wear exports (Romero *et al.*, 1995: 121).

We found that, on the whole, firms achieved an above-average per-formance mainly due to their intra-firm effort and with little interaction with other firms, be they suppliers, subcontractors, customers, or rivals, or with supporting institutions. For instance, medium and large textile firms tend to be completely integrated vertically except that they usually do not own cotton plantations. Many metal engineering and electromechanical firms have their own foundry; and one of the electromechanical firms actually has its own forest plantations which supply wood for the boxes it uses for shipment, and the resin, which is an important input for its own industrial colour plant. Several firms in all branches had their own internal training programmes in basic education and vocational training. This is particularly striking because the public vocational training system which has schools in all major cities of SC is financed completely by compulsory contributions by industrial firms.

Sometimes, if rarely, firms overcame their anti-co-operative disposition. For instance, many textile firms have been under pressure since the 1980s to set up wastewater treatment stations. In this area the benefits of collective action due to economies of scale are obvious. In one of the municipalities, Brusque, 11 firms set up a common wastewater treatment plant. Elsewhere, major firms built their own plants (which have a price tag of between US$4 and 8 million). Literacy programmes for workers are another example. In one municipality, Jaraguá do Sul, firms started a joint training programme with the Association of Commerce and Industry and the local government (firms send pupils and contribute funds, and the state provides teachers). But again, in all the other municipalities, firms have at best achieved individual agreements with the local government or pursue such efforts by themselves.

At the outset, we expected to encounter 'superclusters' like the one identified by Schmitz (1995a) in Sinos Valley in the neighbouring state of Rio Grande do Sul. However, while there was clustering, there were no, or only incipient, industrial district-like structures, according to Schmitz' definition (Schmitz, 1995a: 10) which includes six distinct features: geographical and sectoral concentration of firms, predominance of small- and medium-sized firms, vertical disintegration (at the firm level), co-operative competition, a socio-cultural identity which facilitates trust, and active self-help organization. Although firms of the same branch are concentrated in various places they are as self-sufficient as possible.[6] In fact, many interviewees emphasized the disadvantages of clustering, like the easy availability of alternative employment opportunities for workers (which raises employee turnover) or how easy it is to start a new business (which increases local competition), and neglected the positive clustering effects which are present, such as ready availability of special inputs or services like repair and maintenance. To the casual observer (in particular those observers who are aware of the industrial district phenomenon elsewhere) all this would be quite surprising, and in fact quite irrational as the firms forego the advantages that strong co-operative links can provide, like more rapid learning processes and increased competitiveness through concentration on core competence. However, this can be seen as the result of rational behaviour in the context of the past development path, and at the same time as a structure that continues to live on and makes it difficult for firms to adapt to new conditions.

The Rationality of Isolation in the Old Development Path

A high degree of vertical integration and the lack of interactin among firms used to be quite rational in the past, and this for five reasons.[7] First, there was the simple fact that in many areas there just were no suppliers, or suppliers were unreliable, or showed predatory behaviour. For instance, a constant complaint among metal engineering firms used to be that State-owned steel mills used to deliver their product in the quantity, the quality, and at the moment they found convenient rather than according to the orders of their customers. This has changed since the privatization of these firms in the early 1990s. It is also important to understand how price formation and placement of orders worked in the high-inflation past. Suppliers used to adjust their prices every three months or more often. So there was a strong incentive for the customer to place an order on day 89, that is on the day before the price adjustment. A typical reaction of suppliers to this was to try to economize on quality or quantity, or to delay delivery, claiming a machine breakdown, a power cut, or some other contingency. All in all, relations between suppliers and customers used to be quite hostile.

Secondly, high inflation and the frequent attempts of the government to deal with it created extremely turbulent and unpredictable business conditions.[8] Economic stabilization plans caused turmoil all across industry as firms tried to understand the new rules of the game. Even minor interventions such as changes in price adjustment rules, foreign exchange regulations, or changes in interest rates and credit regulations caused problems. There was a strong incentive for firms to try to insulate themselves as much as possible from this environment, and vertical integration was one means of doing this.

Thirdly, the regulatory regime used to be, and actually continues to be, complex, contradictory, and lack transparency. It is in fact almost impossible for an entrepreneur to be a law-abiding citizen, respecting all tax, safety, and other regulations that exist (Stone *et al.*, 1992). Therefore, firms have various matters to hide at any given time. This creates a situation where firm owners and managers are suspicious of any contact that goes beyond arm's-length business transactions. Firm owners repeatedly told me that this was one reason why they would neither let outsiders enter their premises, nor enter into any kind of information exchange with other business people.

Fourthly, many firm-owners pointed out that their firms had been extremely profitable in a protected market, so what to do with these massive profits?[9] Locally, status was derived from economic success rather than conspicuous consumption. Firm owners did not lead a frugal life, but the amount of money they could sensibly spend was limited. One option was to acquire real estate, but few apparently opted for this on a large scale. Another option was financial investment, reputedly common. We could not investigate this as firms were extremely unwilling to discuss their financial situation, and published data show this for only a handful of firms. The preferred option was, however, to use the money to integrate vertically. So if a firm suffered, say, from unreliable suppliers of fabric, it would not necessarily calculate whether it should invest in this activity but rather decide that it would be a good and sensible thing to take last year's profit and build a weaving mill.

Fifthly, there was no penalty on limited efficiency in the past. Competition was limited in most product markets, and where it existed the main competitive weapon was heavy advertising rather than good quality or low prices. In fact, low-price strategies in final products markets were not feasible in the high-inflation environment that existed until 1994 because customers just would not notice; shops adjusted their prices at different points in time, so that there were vast price differences for a given product between shops anyway, and customers were already quite annoyed with that. Consequently firms could pursue idiosyncratic strategies rather than converging to some kind of best practice. This did not only apply to vertical integration but also to inter-firm co-operation and interaction with supporting institutions. Inter-firm co-operation always involves some transaction cost, and business people may find that this cost is quite high, not least because it involves emotional stress in a fairly small community where everyone knows each other, and many are related and have a long history of intra-family feuds. Consequently, it can be difficult to interact in a 'businesslike' manner. Moreover, co-operation, in particular in terms of deliveries and subcontracting, will necessarily involve conflicts from time to time. Endless haggling between firms on price and delivery conditions was not unusual. The same problems apply to interaction with supporting institutions, which is exacerbated by the usual problems of interaction between private firms and public institutions with a different logic of action, for instance regarding time-horizons.

Changes in Economic Conditions and Firm Behaviour

The Brazilian government abandoned the import-substitution strategy in 1990 and gradually opened for imports (Meyer-Stamer, 1997b). Within the new framework firms which are not competitive are penalized. One option to increase their competitiveness could be to use the advantages that clustering can offer, i.e. to increase the use of external suppliers of inputs and specialities. Being good is to a certain degree a function of the ability of a firm to concentrate on its core competence (Prahalad and Hamel, 1991). This view is supported by findings from industrial economics that the density of externalities is a key factor in explaining innovative capacity and competitiveness (OECD, 1992). Moreover, the discussion on clustering and industrial districts emphasizes that specialization and close interaction among firms can substantially increase their overall competitiveness, particularly when they are proximate, due to reduction of uncertainty (increasing trust) and of transaction-costs.[10] Therefore, the high degree of vertical integration and the lack of interaction among firms in clusters in SC would appear quite irrational under the new conditions.

Further, it can be argued that the five reasons for non-co-operation mentioned above are not valid any longer. First, some firms have shown that it is perfectly possible to run manufacturing operations with a low level of vertical integration. For instance, there was an Italian manufacturer of equipment for the paper industry who chose Joinville in the mid-1970s as a location for his Brazilian affiliate exactly because of the presence of the metal-engineering cluster, and has ever since operated with a very low level of vertical integration. This medium-sized firm is highly competitive as it dominates the Brazilian market and has an export ratio of about 50 per cent. We observed a number of firms who are actively shaping their supply structure, for instance by persuading employees in areas like machining or maintenance to set up their own small firm and supply their former employer. Moreover, with the end of inflation, inter-firm transactions are much less risky. Complaints about predatory behaviour of suppliers were rare and certainly much less frequent than in another study we conducted in 1991 (Meyer-Stamer *et al.*, 1991).

Secondly, overall economic turbulence has been reduced with the stabilization of the economy, even though one cannot fail to notice that the Brazilian central government still has a tendency to interfere in the economy in a very detailed manner and stabilization is far from complete (Dornbusch, 1997). But today competition is, in many industrial branches, a much more important issue than turbulence, and competition forces firms to limit their activities to those areas where their core competencies lie.

Thirdly, the regulatory environment has improved much less than firms and the government would like to see. There can, however, be little doubt that the central government is seriously working on this (Ministério da Fazenda, 1997).

Fourthly, the profitability of firms has decreased since 1990 (see Figures 2.3 and 2.4), and many find it increasingly complicated to keep their equipment up to date due to lack of funds, something that compromises their competitiveness as a substantial part of the machinery (especially in spinning and weaving) dates from the 1970s and is much less productive than up-to-date equipment. Credit-financed investment is not an attractive option either as real interest rates are consistently in the two-digit-range.

Fifthly, today there clearly is a penalty on limited efficiency. Respondents in some of the highly vertically integrated firms argued that their firms suffer from their integration, and that they had a size-related competitive disadvantage due to high overhead costs and reduced flexibility.

Figure 2.3   Major textile firms in SC: return on capital

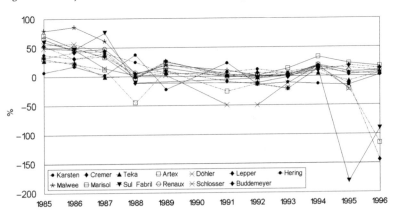

Note: The *Balanço Anual* did not provide data on all the firms for all the years. The year 1990 is excluded because it was extremely turbulent even by Brazilian standards (*Plana Collor I* stabilization programme) and caused extreme deviations in performance data in many firms.
Source: *Gazeta Mercantil*, various issues.

Figure 2.4   Major ceramic tile firms in SC: return on capital

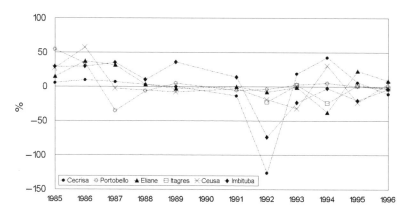

Source: *Gazeta Mercantil,* various issues.

Micro-level Adjustment: the Case of the Ceramic Tile Industry

The ceramic tile firms were the first to come under serious pressure, initially because the country was on the verge of hyper-inflation in 1989/1990, and the economy stagnated due to macro-economic stabilization efforts. This led to the collapse of the construction market, and the sales of the firms decreased accordingly (see Figure 2.5). At the same time, real interest rates went up and penalized firms which had previously pursued debt-financed expansion and modernization strategies.

Today, these firms claim to be close to leading Italian and Spanish competitors in terms of production technology, and they have introduced new management techniques more widely than firms in other branches. They have developed a strong effort in training at all levels; in one large firm, all employees will have completed primary education by 1997, which is quite unusual among industrial firms in Brazil, and in one medium firm 98 per cent of the employees have completed secondary education, and 39 per cent have completed or are attending courses in higher education. Firms are co-operating informally with each other, business associations play a very active role, and the industry has been active in shaping its supporting environment.

It seems that in the ceramic tile cluster there is at least some information in the air. There is substantial informal information exchange

Figure 2.5   Production and exports of ceramic tiles in Brazil

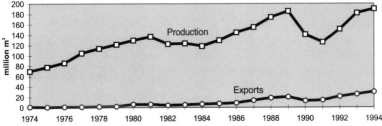

Source: *Informe Setorial*, No. 7, 15 Sept. 1995.

going on between professionals from tile producers; unlike in other branches, it is perfectly normal for them to visit competitors' factories. Behind this is, first, the notion that local firms should stick together to maintain their position *vis-à-vis* domestic competitors, especially from a cluster in the state of São Paulo. Secondly, engineers claim that production technology is on the whole standardized so there is little risk of disclosing crucial secrets. Competitive advantages lie rather in specific design and in logistics, i.e. the ability to deliver a wide variety of products fast without having huge stocks. Suppliers of inputs and vendors of equipment are other agents who stimulate exchange among firms. For instance, if a vendor (typically an Italian firm) has installed equipment in one of the firms, it will be used as a showcase for other firms.

Business associations are more active in the ceramic tile industry than elsewhere and firms from SC do actually maintain close contacts with their associations. First, there is the local *sindicato* of the tile industry, which has been playing a pivotal role in stimulating exchange among firms. Secondly, there is Anfacer, the National Association of Tile Manufacturers. Anfacer plays an important role in stimulating technological exchange among firms, *inter alia* by organizing an annual congress of the industry and by maintaining a separate institute, founded in 1993, the Brazilian Ceramic Centre, which is active in training, research, and consumer information. Unlike in other branches, firms from SC play a very active role in Anfacer.

Local firms and the *sindicato* are also important in shaping the supporting environment. One of the two largest firms set up their own technical school long ago and opened it for students from competing firms in 1991. Together with the state's Federation of Industries (FIESC), in co-operation with the Federal University of SC, and with some financial support from the state, the firms founded CTC, the Centre for

Ceramics Technology, modelled after a similar institution in Spain. Moreover, firms have pressed the local university to offer a special course for technicians in ceramics technology, and lobbied the state intensively to authorize this course, so that it began after one year of preparations, much faster than usual. In order to explain this diverging experience, two factors appear to be important. First, fierce rivalry and non-co-operation has led some firms to the brink of bankruptcy. The two largest firms were involved in a race to become the largest tile producer in the 1980s, investing in new factories and taking over smaller firms, to a large extent based on development bank credits. When sales decreased dramatically after 1989/90, both were extremely vulnerable. Medium-sized firms report that the two large firms have not at all been open to co-operation in the past. Moreover, medium-sized firms may have sought some distance from the two largest as they feared to be taken over as well. All this has changed after the crisis of the late 1980s/early 1990s – out of necessity (i.e. the need to consolidate), due to the interventions of creditors (which forced the family out of the management of one of the large firms), and due to moderation by two persons, the president of the *sindicato* and the president of the local Chamber of Commerce and Industry, who brought the large firms together to settle their dispute.

Secondly, this industry found a role model in Italy's industrial tile districts in the 1980s. Local firms started to develop close links with firms in Italy, in particular with equipment suppliers and manufacturers of inputs, but also with their Italian competitors. Italian representatives and technicians frequently visit the region, and they behave in the way they are used to, i.e. based on the notion that firms, even competitors, co-operate. Moreover, managers and employees of local firms frequently visit Italy and thus have started to develop a notion of what things are like in industrial districts there.

Changes in the Textiles/Clothing Industry

Initially, the gradual lifting of import restrictions had little impact on clothing manufactures. Things changed after the government launched a stabilization programme in July 1994, which successfully fought inflation. One of the results was a boom in consumption, partly fuelled by increased confidence, partly by the reintroduction of consumer credits. The local industry did not have the capabilities to meet increased demand. All of a sudden, Brazil looked like a very interesting market for foreign suppliers:

As a result, the number of clothing items produced in Brazil increased by almost 10% in 1995 to reach an all-time record of 4.1 bn pieces. This compares with 3.8 bn items in 1994 and 3.0 bn in 1992 and in 1993. At the same time, Brazil's clothing imports rose even more dramatically, increasing from 18,500 tons in 1994 to an estimated 77,000 tons in 1995. This compares with a modest 7,700 tons in 1993.

Knight, 1996: 41ff

At the end of 1994 and in 1995 the government decided that the economy was overheated and curbs on consumer credit and higher interest rates followed. However, commercial links with foreign, mainly East Asian suppliers were established by now and did not crumble over-night. The result was increased price competition in local markets.

A few textiles and clothing firms, particularly casualwear producers, have initiated a profound change, starting to leave the established development path. These are large firms which are located at the centre of the textiles cluster, i.e. in the municipality of Blumenau. Reacting to increased competitive pressure, they sought ways to reduce costs, and they found subcontracting. Some firms combined down-sizing with programs to encourage employees to set up subcontracting firms. The barriers to entry for subcontracting firms in sewing, and to a lesser extent in embroidery, are low, because factory space, machines, and qualified workers are easily available. Apart from this, severance pay which normally amounts to one month's wage per year of employment with the firm often serves as the starting capital for a micro-enterprise. In other words, the barriers to de-verticalization and stronger network-ing are not necessarily high in terms of measurable costs. However, increased subcontracting presupposes a change in the mentality of managers in large firms.

It is important to note that the externalization strategy is limited to large firms in Blumenau. Medium firms in Blumenau and medium and large firms in other municipalities, including neighbouring ones retain the self-sufficiency strategy or even try to increase vertical integration. Asked to comment on the strategy of the large firms in Blumenau, they will point out that they have been doing fine so far and do not see any immediate reason to change their ways. Rather than asking themselves fundamental questions about the way they do business, managers assume that cutting costs is enough, which they try to achieve by investing in new, more productive equipment and by cuts in personnel.

Most managers do not see that foreign competitors are more agile, flexible, and customer-oriented. To match them on these factors would imply a radical change in the way local firms do business – a move from passive to active adjustment. They would have to introduce new patterns of internal organization (flat hierarchies, employee empowerment, customer-driven organization) and external relations (de-verticalization, concentration on core competencies, introducing just-in-time delivery and co-operation with suppliers in engineering). This is one of the preconditions to move up-market which is unavoidable as local production costs are just too high to compete with low-price imports from East Asia.[11] Other conditions include a bigger effort in fashion design and changes in sales channels.

It was only in late 1996, after two years of crisis, that adjustment in the textile cluster went beyond the activities described above. This was mainly due to the commitment of the president of the largest and oldest firm in Blumenau, a longstanding leader in technology, both equipment and management techniques. The president organized a visit of local owners and managers of textile firms to Italian industrial districts in order to learn about best practice, particularly in terms of inter-firm relationships and a highly developed supporting environment that creates 'specialized factors' (Porter, 1990). This visit gave rise to an ongoing dialogue among a number of medium and large firms on measures to create collective efficiency, especially by improving information flows among firms (e.g. on credit standing of customers and prices of key supplies), by stimulating the emergence of new training courses at the vocational schools, by creating a quality brand for products from the region, and by studying the feasibility of setting-up a technology centre. To a certain extent, these activities got formalized in that this person was elected president of the Chamber of Commerce and Industry in Blumenau.

The interaction between the business sector and the political sphere has, so far, followed the traditional pattern: The textiles industry bargained for, and in the end received, fiscal incentives at the state level (Weiss, 1997).

This reflects the current practice in Brazil: Location strategies at the state and local level rarely amount to more than fiscal incentives, particularly for new investors, and provision of real estate. Creative policies that try, for instance, to shape the meso-level, i.e. create and amplify institutions that support the firms, are so far rare exceptions (Meyer-Stamer, 1997c). Firms and business associations have only very recently started to articulate their demand in this respect *vis-à-vis* state and local governments.

The Metal Engineering and Electromechanical Industry

In the metal engineering and electromechanical industry competition has increased to a different degree for different firms. One can distinguish three types of firms. First, there are firms operating in a global market. A firm like WEG (which is among the five leading manufacturers of electrical motors world-wide) has a well-defined strategy to increase its presence in key markets, and Embraco (which is the world's No. 2 in the manufacturing of compressors for refrigerators) has actually turned itself into a veritable multinational firm, setting up factories in China and Italy.

Secondly, there are firms which have to upgrade due to pressure from their customers. This includes car parts suppliers and suppliers of firms of the first group. Upgrading in these cases typically follows the pattern described by Fleury (1995: 82ff) i.e. firms implement total quality concepts or a just-in-time-strategy which in the end amount to much the same, namely a profound restructuring of intra-firm practices.

Thirdly, there are firms which have low export ratios and frequently enjoy a natural protection' in the domestic market and have a solid position in their niche. Major explanatory factors are high barriers to entry due to specific technological know-how, the structure of the distribution channels, and specific design preferences of Brazilian customers. Examples would be a manufacturer of plumbing equipment that is the only Brazilian firm that produces automatic valves for taps, or a manufacturer that masters the complex, skill- and labour-intensive process of assembling bodies for urban and overland busses.

Externalization of activities remains in all three groups restricted to simple services like cafeterias, security, cleaning, and transport, thus reflecting a Brazil-wide trend. The majority of the large- and medium-sized metal-engineering firms do not seriously consider reducing their vertical integration, e.g. by subcontracting certain tasks like machining and polishing to independent small workshops which are available.

Two main factors explain the different trajectory of this cluster. First, there is the fact that firms are affected in different ways by the profound structural change underway in Brazil's industry since 1990. The perception of a crisis, shared by most important actors, which was the main element in initiating changes in the other two clusters, is missing here. Secondly, and related to that, local actors do not perceive the local industrial structure as a specialized cluster. In their view, the region has a highly diversified industrial structure. In fact, it is more diverse than, say, in the Itajaí valley – apart from electromechanical and metal engineering there are two large textile firms both in Joinville and Jar-aguá do Sul, and two important plastics manufacturers in Joinville. This has important implications for collective consciousness – the sense of everybody sharing the same fate, which one can observe both in Criciúma and Itajaí Valley, is missing here.

The Changing Role of Business Associations: Embarking on a New Path

The role of business associations has started to change profoundly over the last years, with some of them trying seriously to provide various ser-vices to their members and to support the emergence of competitiveness.

For the firms, membership in industry associations (*sindicatos patronal*) is mandatory. They are organized by branch at the municipal level. The main role of the industry associations consists in collective bargaining. Yet some of them have recently started to broaden their profile. For instance, the textiles industry *sindicato* in Blumenau has explored pro-curing abroad, e.g. in Argentina. It also has adopted an active role as a political lobbyist for the industry. The ceramics industry *sindicato* in Criciúma has played an important role in lobbying for the construction of a pipeline to provide the local industry with natural gas.

The FIESC is the umbrella organization of the *sindicatos*. Owing to the initiative of a new president who entered office in 1992, FIESC has played an active role in preparing firms for globalization and increased competition. It organized journeys of groups of local business people to international exhibitions, e.g. the Hanover fair. It has invested in pub-licity campaigns for the state of SC abroad. It has set up a very well-equipped centre for foreign trade information. It plays an important role in informing local firms about the necessities implied by the introduc-tion of the ISO 14000 system of eco-auditing norms. It has organized the creation of a venture capital fund. All this, however, has only to a limited extent been accompanied by organizational development, in particular a professionalization of an entity which has always tended to be quite politicized, so that FIESC's future performance will depend on the initiative and effort of the future president.

Apart from the *sindicatos*, there also exist Associations of Commerce and Industry (ACI) with voluntary membership at the municipal level; there is also an umbrella organization (Federation of ACIs, FACISC) which is, however, only influential if its president is an important person with well-established links to politicians. Traditionally, they were something like clubs of local business people (Müller-Glodde

1993). Their basic tasks were to administrate the register of firms and to provide their members with legal advice. Many of them had no professional staff at all, and even the largest ones employed just a handful of people. In the northeastern part of the state the impetus for change came through a German technical co-operation project which established a partnership between around initially three ACIs (in 1991; by 1996 the number had grown to 17) and the Chamber of Craft and Trade of Munich. Essentially, it was the result of a broader German government initiative to get German private business more actively involved in development co-operation by stimulating and financing twinning arrangements with business associations in various developing countries. As the northeastern part of the state had been an area of German colonization local actors liked the idea of this partnership although they did not see the profoundness of the change it would induce. In fact, the visits to their German partner provoked a serious shock among representatives of the ACIs as they noted the impressive size, the large number of employees, and the broad spectrum of services provided by the Chamber in Munich. After these experiences, the presidents of ACIs were much more open-minded about the changes proposed by the project staff.

These changes, which took about five years to materialize, resulted essentially in three things. First, and most importantly, the role definition of the ACIs changed as they increasingly developed services geared to the demands of the members, tried to attract new members, especially among small and medium firms, and became more active in lobbying *vis-à-vis* local government. Secondly, there was an increase in the number of employees as ACIs started to employ consultants to serve their members. Thirdly, sectoral working groups were formed in the ACIs which united business owners and managers from one sector or were organized around a given problem, e.g. environmental protection. In many cases, the sectoral working groups established for the first time a forum for exchange of business-related issues between local firms, thus playing an important role in challenging path dependence'[12] and overcoming traditional behaviour.

The Role of Local and State Government

Location policies at the municipal level hardly exist in SC, except in the largest municipalities. This refers, first of all, to initiatives in Joinville and Blumenau to attract a car assembly factory.

Apart from that, the only local initiatives in location policy worth mentioning concern the software industry where Florianópolis, Blumenau, and Joinville set up business incubators. They were only to a small extent financed locally, but local government lobbied strongly at the state and federal level to raise funds. At the state level, things were not much different. The Kleinübing administration (1991–94) delegated industrial policy-making to the Federation of Industries which was, unfortunately, not prepared to deal with such a task as it lacked specialized professionals and adequate internal structures. But it succeeded in launching some individual projects, mostly technology centres. With the Paulo Afonso administration (1995–98) things got worse. With a different party background, relations with the Federation of Industries changed from close to hostile. In terms of industrial policy, some sectors succeeded in lobbying for inclusion in a tax incentive programme. But in the second half of the mandate period, the state government was hardly able to pay the wages of its employees, and it was involved in a major scandal and thus struggling for survival. Industrial policy took the back seat under these circumstances.

To understand the small scope of activities at the local level, several aspects of the polity have to be pointed out. First, it is important to remember that any kind of industrial policy has always been a central government activity, i.e. there is no tradition of decentralized location policy. Accordingly, local policy-makers often do not perceive that location policy should be part of their activities. It should rather be left to firms and business associations.

Secondly, political turbulence at the local level is not smaller than that the state or federal levels. It is quite rare that a ruling party or coalition remains in office for more than one term. And even during its term, there will be frequent changes in office. Thus, it is quite remarkable if a municipal secretary for economic development stays in office for more than, say, two years. Accordingly, the pattern of action is mostly ad hoc rather than pursuing a longer-term strategy (which usually does not exist anyway in the form of a written document).

Thirdly, Brazil's political system is to a large extent based on clientelism (Avelino Filho, 1994). As parties are weak each politician has to make sure that he make a certain number of people happy in order to become (re-)elected (Mainwearing, 1992; Avritzer, 1995). Elections are less the act of a sovereign people to determine its representatives to serve the common good than an implicit deal between citizens and politicians where votes are traded for material or other benefits. One of the effects of this political model is its limited ability to pursue strategies, i.e. to stick consistently to a certain line of action for a certain period of time. Long-term strategies are exceptions which are only possible if a party or coalition stays in power for more than one term and is not overly divided internally. Under the prevailing conditions, political action typically amounts to realizing a variety of projects – in the sense of undertakings which are clearly located and limited in time, like constructing a new road or a new school (what is called *obras* in Brazil). It is not by chance that substantial amounts of the State's income on all levels are earmarked; this is seen as the only way to assure that certain tasks are fulfilled over time.

It is important to note that with changes in the ACIs a change in political practice at the municipal level occurred in some places. This typically took two forms. First, ACIs started to define more clearly what they expected from their local government, for instance in terms of local infrastructure provision, public transport, local environmental issues, or education. Secondly, key ACI actors started to play a more active role in political life, i.e. by taking up jobs as secretaries for economic development or even as mayors. What was new about this was the fact that this did not so much indicate personal ambitions to make a political career. Instead, it represented the willingness to transfer the dedication and professional values of a key group of civil society into the public service.

Conclusions

A comparison of the main findings in the three clusters (Table 2.1) shows that those two clusters where we found radical change (ceramic tiles and textiles/clothing) have several features in common: they have experienced an external shock which in retrospective appears as the turning point in the cluster's trajectory; they are facing intense competitive pressure, and they are fairly homogeneous, i.e. all firms are facing roughly the same problems. In these two cases it is already obvious, or it is becoming obvious, that incremental change will not suffice to thrive in the changed environment. This is much less obvious in the third cluster, the metal engineering and electromechanical industry. A handful of leading firms like Consul, Embraco and WEG were never really adjusted to the old development model, i.e. they were more competitive than they had to be, and for them change is incremental indeed. The mediocre firms show a tendency to overestimate their competitive potential and it is possible that they will not have to face fierce competitive pressure for some time. Thus, anybody who tries to argue for radical change in this cluster is likely to preach to deaf ears.

A further parallel between the two first clusters regards the role of change agents, associations, and points of entry to inter-firm co-opera-

Table 2.1 Comparing changes in industrial clusters in SC

	Ceramic tiles Criciúma	Textiles/garments Blumenau	Engineering Joinville
Degree of cluster's specialization	high	high	medium
Competitive pressure	high	high, increasing	medium
Competitive advantage	logistics (quick response despite low stocks), design	price and quality; sales channel and competence of sales representatives	product technology
Turning point	macro-economic crisis 1989/91	overvaluation and imports 1994/95	none so far
Change agents	owner of large firm, president of ACI, institutional investors	owner of largest firm, institutional investors	
Role of business associations	very important	small, but increasingly important	medium, stagnating importance for medium and large firms
Points of entry to inter-firm cooperation	benchmarking, vocational training, technology institute	benchmarking, vocational training (technology institute?)	vocational training

tion. In both clusters certain individuals played a crucial role in uniting firms and organizing change. They got indirect support from institutional investors to the extent that these shoved out conservative family management in some highly indebted firms, and local observers argue that professional managers, and newcomers in the local community are more open to inter-firm cooperation than families with a decade-long history of local feuds. Business associations played an important role as the *locus* of exchange between firms. The internal structure of these associations, where the president may be in a position to reign autocratically, is both an asset and a curse: a strong, visionary president may introduce radical change within a short period of time, but if a successor is weak everything may fall apart again. Apart from co-operation via associations, firms started to co-operate via joint bench-marking exercises and by working more closely with vocational schools.

Another, rather ironic, parallel regards the nature of localized competition. Competition between local firms is strong both in the textiles/ clothing and the ceramic tile industry, whereas it is limited in the metal engineering/electromechanical industry. Yet ceramic tile firms co-operate much more intensely, and some textiles/clothing firms are starting to do so, than firms in the metal engineering/electromechanical cluster. This underlines an observation made by Lazonick in his critique of Michael Porter's work. Lazonick points out that 'Porter's own documentation and analysis of the determinants of global competitive advantage reveal...that an emphasis on competition to the exclusion of co-operation is unwarranted' (Lazonick, 1993: 3). The case of SC helps understand why fierce local competition and co-operation may coexist: because firms have no alternative. Local firms cater for precisely the same market, something that forces them to constantly upgrade and innovate, not only in terms of processes and products but also in terms of design and sales strategies. Due to proximity innovations can hardly kept secret for long so that there is an upward spiral that involves many local firms. At the same time, firms do not only compete locally but also with firms in other parts of the country and abroad. This can establish a logic of collective action along two lines. First, local firms may notice that it is costly to undertake activities like vocational training, measuring and testing, or wastewater treatment, on an individual basis; and they may understand that they can no longer afford costly individualism due to pressure from competitors elsewhere. Secondly, local firms may perceive that competitors elsewhere enjoy unfair advantages, like tax relief and subsidies in the case of national competitors or dumping and exemption from certain regulations in the case of imports. This may lead local firms to mount a joint political effort, like the one of the textiles/clothing industry to receive tax incentives. In both cases, it seems to be crucial that somebody assumes leadership.

The SC experience suggests that clustering simultaneously hinders and supports adjustment to changing conditions. More precisely, it hinders adjustment initially as it favours path-dependent behaviour. Path dependence means that firms try to pursue a well-established behavioural pattern, but in a more intensive way, rather than take the risk of trying something completely different early on. During the first phase of adjustment this behaviour is reinforced by clustering as firms cannot fail to observe each other, and even in an environment where little information is in the air some kind of local consensus will emerge regarding what is the most appropriate strategy in trying to adjust.

Clustering makes adjustment easier later on, as soon as key actors have understood the limitations of path dependent behaviour. In this phase, the key challenge is to move from passive to active advantages of clustering.[13] Passive advantages of clustering include the availability of specialized suppliers, business service firms, and skilled labour. These elements are present even in those regions where interaction between firms is very low. Active advantages include the strengthening of core competencies through purchasing more from external, often specialized suppliers plus a systematic effort to upgrade them, the learning-by-interacting benefits of close inter-firm co-operation and a dense flow of information, and the creation of specific supporting institutions.

Notes

1. Initial field research was conducted between February and April 1996 as part of the trainee course of the German Development Institute (Meyer-Stamer *et al.*, 1996). I am indebted to the trainees who participated in the field research, Bernhard Adam, Stefan Bantle, Alexandra Lauer, and Daniela Mohaupt. Moreover, I am indebted to the Instituto Euvaldo Lodi of the Federation of Industries of Santa Catarina, in particular Silene Seibel, and the Associations of Commerce and Industry in Blumenau, Brusque, Criciúma, Jaraguá do Sul, and Joinville, which did a tremendous job in helping us to organize and carry out the field-work. Finally, I am indebted to executives of firms, supporting institutions, and government agencies in sharing a lot of their valuable time with us. An invitation by the Federation of Industries to spend another three weeks in the region in August 1996 gave me the opportunity to conduct additional interviews, and to discuss the findings with various local stakeholders. For comments on earlier drafts I am indebted to Stefan Bantle, Herbert Brücker, Barbra Fritz, Irfan ul Haque, Rainer Müller-Glodde, Hubert Schmitz, Imme Scholz, Árni Sverrisson, and participants in a workshop at IDS in Brighton, April 1997.
2. This means that they are not registered and/or do not pay taxes and/or do not pay social security contributions for their employees and/or sell directly to final consumers, without charging sales tax, or to informal vendors.
3. Santa Catarina's share in Brazil's GDP grew from 2.68 per cent in 1970 to 3.18 per cent in 1980 and 3.33 per cent in 1990 (FIESC, 1995: 90).
4. See Moreira (1993). The case studies of de Soto (1993) and Shapiro (1994) illustrate the crucial role government guidance has played in the passenger car industry and in the pulp and paper industry, two of the most important and dynamic branches in Brazilian industry.
5. For instance, while visiting well-known, competitive Italian spinning and weaving firms in November 1996, the owners and chief executive officers (CEOs) of some leading textiles firms from SC were surprised to see that, unlike their own firms, many of those firms used neither bar-code systems (which are an important element in rationalizing intra-firm logistics) nor last-vintage cutting technology (which can reduce the waste ratio substantially and save time due to computerized control).

6. It has been pointed out in the discussion on flexible specialization that loneliness vs. integrated in networks' may be a more important issue today than large vs. small (Poon, 1990).

7. This section mainly draws on explanations businessmen from SC gave us when we inquired about inter-firm relationships.

8. In their institutionalist analysis of the Brazilian business environment, Stone *et al.* (1992: 18) found that in times of crisis around 40 per cent of orders used to be renegotiated between firms.

9. Profitability of industry has been high in Brazil all through the 1970s and 1980s (Meyer-Stamer, 1997a: 48), largely due to the low level of competitive pressure and the necessity to finance investments internally as long-term credit was only available from BNDES.

10. On clustering see Porter (1990), on industrial districts Nadvi and Schmitz (1994) and Schmitz (1995b). For the specific case of ceramic tiles see Russo (1985) and Porter (1990: 210ff). On the knitwear industry see, for instance, Lazerson (1990).

11. A seamstress in Blumenau will typically earn about US$380–450 per month. The effective cost to the firm is twice that amount due to social charges and other indirect labor costs (World Bank, 1996).

12. The term is borrowed from Arthur (1994).

13. This distinction has been suggested by Nadvi (1997).

3

Social Embeddedness: Families and Firms in Tanzania

Per Trulsson

This chapter describes and analyses how entrepreneurs in north-western Tanzania understand and deal with the complexities they face in acquiring the resources needed for their industrial processing activities. One of the most salient findings is that entrepreneurs primarily sought to integrate the acquisition of resources. Further, Tanzania is very much what Göran Hydén (1987) has termed 'an economy of affection', where ascription rather than achievement is the basis for 'trust' in most inter-personal relations, economic relations included. However, this study also suggests that this kind of inter-personal relationship might slowly be giving way to more impersonal and achievement based social relations of the kind prevailing in developed market economies.

The theoretical groundwork is laid in the first section, where the concept of social embeddedness is explained and related to the structural adjustment process. After a brief background section, the existence and content of 'trust' is discussed in relation to three categories, external organizations, own employees and members of the extended family. In conclusion, the results are summarized and evaluated.

Structural Adjustment and the Embeddedness of Entrepreneurship

Over two decades Tanzania pursued development along the lines of self-reliance and African Socialism.[1] By the mid-1980s this development path had become an impasse. Supported by the World Bank and other donors, Tanzania abandoned the socialist development path in 1985 and embarked on a neo-liberal path to development. An Economic Recovery Programme (ERP) was launched, initiating a process of structural adjustment. Incentives to act in a manner desired by policy-makers are provided by monetary incentives rather than legal punishment in this approach. Consequently, as pointed out by neo-institutionalists such as Oliver Williamson, a crucial aspect of institution-building and the development of a market economy is 'getting the prices right' (Nicholson, 1988). In theory, if the prices are right, the incentives for action will be correct. If entrepreneurs are understood as rational economic beings that respond to price incentives, 'right' prices will contribute to a more efficient economic system.

Why is it important to induce entrepreneurial activity? Following the Schumpeterian conception of 'entrepreneurship', it may be understood as a key aspect of societal change – entrepreneurs are 'agents of change'. They have a unique capacity to see and respond to new opportunities; they break new paths and show others where to go. They can break the dead-lock of an ailing economy and bring new life to it. This capacity makes them very different from other business people. The effect entrepreneurial action may have on societal change has been explained succinctly by Etzioni in terms of the 'societal function of entrepreneurship':

> The societal function of entrepreneurship is to provide *adaptive* reality-testing; that is, to *change* existing obsolescent societal patterns (of relations, organisation, modes of production) to render them more compatible with the changed environment.
>
> Etzioni, 1987: 177

Entrepreneurs are, therefore, expected to be agents of change within a relatively stable institutional framework. In their unorthodox behaviour, entrepreneurs often break with the kind of action that societal institutions suggest. As others see the success of the entrepreneurs and follow in their footsteps, such institutions become subject to transformation pressures.

This chapter is focused on the changes taking place in the informal aspects of economic life. The ways in which personal relations impact on the acquisition of resources are described and analysed. Given the importance of family relations in resource accumulation, particular attention will be paid to the close and often troublesome relationship between family and enterprise.

In the field of industrial development, there has been a renewed and surging interest for theories that concern flexible specialization and the development of industrial, or Marshallian, districts (Pedersen *et al.*, 1994; van Dijk and Rabellotti, 1997). A central proposition of these theories is that regional collaboration among small entities is essential for their ability to compete with foreign producers. Core ingredients of such relations are a large degree of trust and a shared understanding of mutual benefits that contributes to collective efficiency. The importance of social networks is therefore accorded great value (Knorringa, 1995). In the East African context, Göran Hydén has argued that the state in Tanzania is an entity of its own, that it is 'suspended in mid-air over society' (Hydén, 1983: 7). Hydén then describes the functioning of society in Tanzania and Kenya in terms of an 'economy of affection', i.e. 'an economy in which the affective ties based on common descent, common residence, etc. prevail' (Hydén 1980: 18). In this kind of economy 'investment in social relations is the dominant logic guiding... social and economic life' (Hydén 1995: 8).

It is in this context that Mark Granovetter's (1985) understanding of economic activity as being 'socially embedded' seems particularly appealing. Granovetter argues against Williamson's neo-institutional understanding of economic action, which Granovetter maintains is under-socialized. There is more to economic exchange than just rational economic behaviour and organization of economic exchange within impersonal institutional arrangements, i.e. hierarchies or markets, he contends. Granovetter also argues against over-socialized conceptions of human behaviour such as that of James Duesenberry, where notions of a generalized morality provide the basis for explaining human behaviour. Both conceptions are wrong, argues Granovetter, because they perceive human action as an atomized feat, free from the constraints placed upon actors by their immediate social context. Instead, he argues that human action must be understood as a socially embedded activity, where actors rely neither exclusively on a generalized morality nor institutional arrangements. His approach 'stresses instead the role of concrete personal relations and structures (or 'networks') of such relations in generating trust and discouraging malfeasance'. In this respect, he argues:

> Better than the statement that someone is known to be reliable is information from a trusted informant that he has dealt with that individual and found him so. Even better is information from one's own past dealings with that person.
>
> Granovetter, 1985: 490

Fundamental to Granovetter's perspective is therefore personal relations and personal judgment about the reliability of other actors, i.e. the perceived ability of an actor to be able to trust other actors to measure up to certain expected standards, e.g. not to cheat on him/her. Granovetter points out that his perspective, for example, has implications for when one may expect to see vertical integration of firms rather than pure market transactions between them:

> Other things being equal, for example, we should expect pressures toward vertical integration in a market where transacting firms lack a network of personal relations that connects them, or where such a network eventuates in conflict, disorder, opportunism, or malfeasance.
>
> ibid., 1985: 503

This leads us to examine the role of trust in explaining the prevalence of integration in organizing economic activities.[2]

The study reported here was undertaken in three regions of northwest Tanzania – Kagera, Mara and Mwanza regions. Twenty-six African Tanzanian industrial entrepreneurs were interviewed. All but one were men. Not surprisingly, considering Tanzania's socialist and centralized past, three-quarters of them had previously been state employees; many in high positions, from which they benefited by access to information and networking opportunities.

The entrepreneurs employed anything from 6 to almost 800 people, with the majority in the range of 6 to 30 employees, i.e. they were small-scale industrialists. Virtually all of them employed members of the extended family. The production activities covered a wide range of products, e.g. leather purses, fruit juices, corrugated card-board boxes, and electric stoves. Most entrepreneurs had also previously been engaged in less innovative production activities, and were often running several ventures at the same time, many of which were common in the area. Some of the wealthier entrepreneurs also engaged heavily in cotton and coffee handling, formerly co-operatively controlled. While engaging in cotton processing, the affiliated activities of making cooking oil and cotton cakes for animal feeds were often picked up.

Locally available products such as cotton seed, fish and timber, are the basis of production. Among the material inputs produced in other parts of Tanzania, paper for printing was most common, but also metals such as aluminium and steel. Very few material inputs were imported. The technological sophistication involved ranged from almost entirely manual production to quite sophisticated and computerized machinery. Most technologies were of an intermediate kind. The machinery was often second hand of western origin, or new from Asia. The majority of the entrepreneurs had at some point been assisted by the Small Industries Development Organization, SIDO, and/or the National Bank of Commerce, NBC, in acquiring machinery. This was particularly true for small-scale industrialists, but also for the first ventures of several entrepreneurs now operating on a larger scale. Most products were consumed locally. However, semi-finished products (coffee, cotton and fish) and leather articles were exported to neighbouring African countries.

Building Cash-mountains and Avoiding Bottlenecks

In Tanzania, policy changes are frequent. Although structural adjustment began in 1985, uncertainty still prevails among entrepreneurs about future directions of change. Such changes can create windfall profits for those who are well positioned, but changes may also close down anticipated windows of opportunity or even ruin market advantages already achieved. The formal institutional framework is still under reconstruction and can hardly be relied upon to provide a stable basis for economic activity. State policies are, however, only part of the general environment for economic activities.

One of the most frequently discussed constraints to entrepreneurial activities is access to credit. At NBC, and SIDO, for instance, the procedures to obtain loans were often very cumbersome. Entrepreneurs mentioned waiting for their loan approvals up to two years, never quite knowing the status of their applications. In addition, it was rather common to have to bribe an officer or two (or compensate the officer for his poor salary). In asking about the prevalence of such practices, I got answers like the following:

> Well, I reserve my comment on that [laughter]...but you cannot avoid it...It's not worth talking about....No, actually it is an open secret, so it's why I say it's not worth talking about it. The entire system is corrupt, so there is no place you can go without, you know.

This entrepreneur's remark that the prevalence of corruption in the system 'is an open secret,' illustrates the frequency of such agreements. Another entrepreneur attests to this and adds an estimate of the usual financial cost of corrupt deals: 'Interest now is around 40 per cent, if you borrow, what can you pay? You cannot pay, and for that they need *chai*, 10 per cent, it becomes 50 per cent. And it takes one year to get the money...' Still, he also says: 'if the country is like that you have to do like that.'

Another entrepreneur provides further testimony about the prevalence of corruption, and suggests that a corrupt lending agreement may include the idea that the loan should not be repaid at all. There are indications of both in the material. The entrepreneur says:

> For instance, if you lend me one million and indirectly you ask me to give you back 200,000. After processing my loan, then I will assume that we are friends. And don't think that you come back to me with strict terms again, changing from the understanding we have, the illegal understanding that we have.

The parties to a corrupt deal become 'partners in crime', and none of them wants to disclose the illegal procedures for making the deal. There is a kiswahili saying: 'kukopa arusi, kulipa matanga'. This basically means,'to lend is to wed, to pay is a funeral'. Lending is the beginning of a relationship. To ask someone to repay is tantamount to terminating that relationship. In an economy where relationships are important for survival, it might appear wise not to ask that loans be repaid. This is especially true if the lending agreement was corrupt from the very beginning.

However, seven out of the 26 entrepreneurs have never borrowed money from a formal financial organization. They are not against it in principle, but simply think it is too expensive. Like one of them says: 'How can you make a profit when the bank takes 35 per cent? You will only be working for the bank.' Instead, these entrepreneurs prefer to build up their 'cash-mountains', little by little, or 'pole-pole' as they say. Indeed, many of the entrepreneurs who have borrowed from financial organizations prefer this way of financing, and have only borrowed once or twice in order to 'take-off', i.e. to make a major investment. Hence, internalizing the acquisition of financial resources is a common strategy.

The uncertainties related to ascertaining an adequate supply of material inputs are no less. To illustrate some of the complexities, let us take the experiences of one of the fish processors, Thomas.[3] When Thomas began his operations there were relatively few competitors in the vicinity. He did not have any fishing boats of his own and he found sending refrigerated lorries to buy fish at local fish markets to be a troublesome venture. Instead he decided to create an organization for collection of fish very similar to that which the co-operatives use for bringing cotton seed from farmers to the ginneries. He made arrangements with a number of local fishermen that he assisted them to get e.g. fishing nets, boats and even out-boarders, if they in return promised to supply him with their catch at a predetermined price. The system operated for a while until Thomas found out that many fishermen cheated on him. They brought only a small portion of what they caught to him, while they retained most of fish to sell at the higher market price. Thomas terminated the system, kept a few of the fishermen that he had found reliable, and started to build up his own fleet of boats.

Another kind of problem in obtaining material inputs is related to the bottle-necks in production that others are experiencing. Bottle-necks were a standard feature of the Tanzanian socialist production system. Transports failed, foreign exchange resources were lacking and/ or management was poor, to mention only a few factors. Many of these problems persist today. When the rains are plentiful many rural roads become very rough, or even impassable, delaying collection of agricultural inputs. Conversely, absence of rain also creates problems with access to material inputs. Since the prime source of electricity generation in Tanzania is hydropower, ample rains are required or else power is cut. However, even if the rains are good, electricity supplies cannot be depended upon. For this reason virtually all the entrepreneurs who need electricity for their processing activities have bought their own diesel generators and are consequently producing their own electricity when so required. Nevertheless, power cuts are likely to create problems for suppliers. Consequently, bottlenecks in production may arise anyway.

However, timeliness has rarely been an important issue in Tanzania. Before trade liberalization, small-scale industrial production was more a matter of producing at all, than producing on time. However, for producers who want to meet foreign demand, for producers who want to become what the entrepreneurs themselves consider to be 'serious', timeliness is increasingly becoming an important issue. An example to illustrate this is Simon, who produces leather articles like purses and belts for export. Simon relied upon supplies from the local tannery, ailing from the beginning. Simon's closest associate, however, was a former employee of the tannery and knew the trade well. He also had close personal contacts at the tannery, but in spite of this, they were sometimes very late in delivering. This bothered Simon somewhat but he did not think of alternative solutions until one time when it was absolutely crucial to have the supply of leather ordered in order to produce for a particular occasion. As he was let down this time, he started to look into the possibility of a mini-tannery in-house, i.e. internalizing the supply of this inputs.

Internalization of supply or vertical integration may be understood as a way to reduce uncertainty, or increase control over the supply of inputs. Rather than relying on external sources to supply the requisite inputs, the entrepreneurs prefer to rely on themselves. This is partly a matter of distrusting others. However, it is *also* a matter of knowing about the obstacles and preferring to be on top of the situation, even at a cost (Rotter, 1966).

Employee Relations: the Enterprise as Family

Most of the enterprises in the study were small-scale, i.e. employing 5–49 employees. For most of the work, few skills, which could be taught on the job, were required. Finding a qualified workforce was therefore not much of a problem for the entrepreneurs. Their main concern was being able to trust the workers to do the job properly. There were several reasons for this, e.g. poor salaries, a low work morale inherited from the socialist period, and the character of employment agreements.

The entrepreneurs screened most job applicants themselves, even in relatively large companies, in order to reduce the risk of employing the wrong people. Entrepreneurs in charge of smaller companies often employed members of their extended family, partly because it was expected of them, and partly because the entrepreneurs thought they might be trusted or at least were easier to control than others. In the larger companies, the essential thing was to find employees for higher ranking positions that could be depended upon, not only to do their own job but also to make sure that the lower level employees did theirs. In this respect higher employees may be thought of as 'trusted employees', a term introduced by Peter Whalley to point out that to the employer the crucial aspect of higher-ranking employees in a company is not that they can do a job, but that they can be trusted to do it (Whalley, 1986: 58–65).

Ten entrepreneurs have high ranking employees. Charles explains: '[We ask] somebody who knows him since five years ago. If that man is known and this and this.' Using friends and other contacts is a common approach among entrepreneurs for obtaining educated higher staff. The entrepreneur inquires among people he knows, who know the prospective employee, about his or her personal characteristics. If the impression is positive, and preferably based upon long-term acquaint-ance, the entrepreneur is likely to employ the person, even if his or her qualifications do not perfectly match the work tasks. To the entrepren-eurs, the crucial aspect of employing a person is the issue of trust. As pointed out by Ahmed: 'You know, Tanzania is not like Europe where you get everything straight. You go sometimes to pay something with no paper. You don't get receipt. You don't get anything.' In such a situation, an employer must be able to trust his employees.

A second common way to obtain dependable and skilled employees is to train them yourself, to internalize the supply of labour: '... internal recruitment reduces the heavy costs of recruiting, screening and training technical and managerial staff' (Whalley, 1986: 61). Joshua, for example, has paid higher education abroad for two of his brothers. With prior work experience, they assumed high positions in his conglomerate of companies. Joshua uses a similar approach for non-family employees. He trains them in-house and sends them to attend courses overseas. The general idea is to favour those who have worked with the company for some time. Factory managers are in most cases long-time employees, which means 'in one way or another we were involved in training them'. During this process, Joshua has been able to learn about their personal characteristics. He is concerned about three factors: their confidence, competence and commitment. 'At least two of the qualities will always be there. For me, I tend to believe that commitment and confidence come up with very good management', Joshua explains. He downplays the role of competence in favour of both confidence and commitment.

So how do the entrepreneurs try to ensure that the trusted employees can actually remain trusted? Simply put, they pay them well and extend paternal care toward them, reminiscent of that existing in the extended family system. In smaller companies, where financial resources are particularly scarce, the entrepreneur often tries to establish a relationship where the employer proclaims a willingness to assume responsibility for at least the subsistence of his workers in return for their commitment to work. They 'push together', as Isaac expressed it. While it may not be common, there are even instances where employees work for free during the first year or so, with the understanding that they will be compensated as soon as profits start to accrue.

Larger companies often require a class of higher ranking officers which are harder to find and generally pay higher wages. They have usually found their market segment and have a steady influx of cash. Charles provides evidence of this:

> For example the engineer, we give him two hundred dollars per month and free for house. Free for electricity, free for water and two children to school in Tanzania. Medical check-ups and when he's feeling ... we give him free.[4]

Jacob also claims to give the professional and technical staff extra incentives like medical care:

Sometimes we even subsidize the school fees of their children. In order to retain him, we might even purchase vehicles. I prefer this way rather than high salaries, because somebody may be a drunkard. We take care of them in a way like family. Sometimes we subsidize their food.

In general, the idea is to make trusted employees part and parcel not only of the company, but in a sense, also of the family. Although few entrepreneurs explicitly go as far as Edwin, who even used the word 'dependents' for his employees, most indicate that they take on a certain degree of paternal obligations toward their employees. Charles, in speaking about one of his long-term employees who is going to Dar es Salaam for a 'big job', illustrates this:

I've been with him for a long time. He gets a salary, but he is like our family now. When he has been like ten years here he is like your family. Because his son and your son they have to play again. Many times you have to assist.

Since Tanzania lacks a general welfare system the entrepreneurs build their own little welfare nuclei. Members of these communities are primarily their trusted employees, but the other workers are included to varying degrees as well.

Employing Relatives

Since the well-being of the company would seem to be closely correlated to the well-being of the whole family unit one would expect family members to be ideal employees. However, it is not quite as simple as that. Marris and Somerset's 1971 study of business activities among the *Kikuyu* in Kenya provides an important contribution to our understanding of the intricacies of being a business person and provider the same time in East Africa.

The major basis for social security and belonging in most African societies is the extended family. The extended family operates on the basis of a number of more or less clearly stated rules of conduct, that also define what one may expect from one another. In this sense, the extended family may be considered an integral part of the informal institutional framework. However, this often works as an impediment to enterprising activities:

The East African family is, then, characteristically under too great a strain, too poor in resources, and too bound by the principle of sharing out to offer a system of relationships readily adaptable to the organization of a business. The family estate is not a corporate interest, but an entitlement from which each, in due time, can claim his portion. A father's duty is not to rule, but to provide. So the intrusion of kinship into business confuses managerial authority by claims to equality and independence. Unable to meet these demands, the employer provokes jealousy and insubordination, and faces the embarrassing task of disciplining his kinsmen. He would prefer not to become involved with family at all, or at least make sure that any relative who joins him understands the relationship as a business arrangement.

Marris and Somerset, 1971: 148

Below, we will see that the situation of Tanzanian entrepreneurs in the mid-1990s is little different. Employing extended family members is a problematic issue for many of the entrepreneurs.

Among the 26 entrepreneurs interviewed there were nine who explicitly voiced a preference for 'outsiders' instead of extended family labour. Three of them employ *only* 'outsiders', while others are cutting down on the number of extended family members – 'chasing them out', to use Noel's term. Noel has had enough bad experiences, he says:

> If somebody comes from outside the extended family you can command him, but if they are for example your brother they are reluctant. They take money, 'give me money', anything can happen – you pay them salary, allowances, still . . . so it's better to have somebody else who's not extended family.

While Noel does not want to keep any extended family members as employees, there are some who only speak of chasing out distant relatives, not the closest family members. At least four of the nine who prefer outsiders rather than extended family as employees, explicitly make such statements. The three who employ only outsiders explained also that they would like their sons to join them in future.

In contrast to the nine entrepreneurs who prefer to employ outsiders, there are two entrepreneurs, Jacob and Samuel, who speak explicitly in favour of employing members of the extended family. Samuel's explanation is that 'it is our somewhat cultural habit that you somehow don't trust so much people from other extended family'. Jacob explains that there are four people in the company from the extended family that are employed just because they are extended family: 'but for the rest, I have just people who are capable to do it'. He adds:

> Rather than doing that [*employ outsiders*] it's better you train some-body from within the extended family. So that he becomes part and parcel of the business and then becomes easy to control. Rather than somebody from the outside, you can't control him easily.

The remaining 15 entrepreneurs are ambivalent and look at each indi-vidual case; like Ali who notes: 'Some of them, they take advantage of being the member of the extended family. Therefore, they are not serious, some of them. [The] advantage on the other side is that you can expect them to be honest on the job'. Some entrepreneurs like Peter state that the only important factor is 'merit', or competence. If two persons of equal merit, one extended family and one an outsider, approach Peter for a job, the extended family member will 'of course' be favoured. Given the willingness to assist members of the extended family, why is it that the entrepreneurs often employ outsiders rather than extended family members? Why is there such an ambivalence? The answer is partly about control and partly about the quality of work.

Samuel and Jacob claim it is easier to 'control' extended family, while others think it is easier to control 'outsiders'. This raises the question of whether the two groups are talking about 'control' in the same sense. On the one hand, entrepreneurs like Jacob appear to be talking about cre-ating a relationship of mutual benefit to employer and employee. To create such a bond, outsiders must be given greater financial incentives than extended family members. Otherwise, they may abuse the trust given, and run off with company assets. Even if the case is taken to court, the offender can bribe his way out of it. This particular concern is voiced by Samuel, but other entrepreneurs have also mentioned their lack of confidence in the legal framework.

On the other hand, there are entrepreneurs who prefer 'outsiders' for 'control' purposes. They have a slightly different conception of control. It does not seem to be a matter of making sure that their employees do not steal company assets. Instead, the issue of control is related to the fact that outsiders can be sacked almost at will. Extended family members, in contrast, are very difficult to get rid of, even when they misbehave gravely. Samuel suspended his brother-in-law two times for embezzling before firing him the third time.

Among entrepreneurs who prefer 'outsiders', they are seen, as Maria says, as 'more professional'. They are simply better workers. Unfortunately, she says, it is not easy to get this kind of people to work in peripheral areas like Bukoba: 'they have to be poached'. Maria has had such problems with the bookkeeper position in her company. She has already had two bookkeepers leave the company because of the location: 'Nobody reasonably well educated would want to come here', she thinks.

Charles also attests to the importance of professionalism. He says that 'outside family they work better, they work harder than those who belong to our extended family'. Charles is a man who has large extended family obligations, from which he has no intention of shying away. He employs several members of his extended family. Therefore, he says, 'we have to mix all of them. For three, you take one which belongs to extended family, he goes with them, and they have to share the commission'. Charles is referring to making employees work in small teams, where all depend upon each other. By placing extended family members in a minority among outsiders, Charles counts on the outsiders to force the 'insider' to perform to desired standards.

It is evident that the issue is up-bringing and/or inadequate education in the view of most entrepreneurs. Mark for example says: 'Such people who feel they are part and parcel of your family, to work in industries, unless they are exposed to good education, they can't see the sense.' Similar concerns are voiced by Victor, who is very reluctant to take on relatives. He says he has no problem taking in brothers and sons: 'I have groomed them myself, so I know they are good.' In the same manner, Isaac contends: 'they [relatives] don't see what you want to promote...maybe some because they are luxurious people...some because they don't understand, because of maybe lack of education. Those who can understand more. Those who can visualize the things...'. Joshua, one of those who is reluctant to bring in extended family members, said he selected a few of his brothers for further higher education abroad, to have them come back into his company and occupy high-ranking positions. Jacob and Nathan also try to provide a good education for their dependents, especially their own sons, so they can run the companies in the future. However, education is not emphasized primarily for purposes of having sons taking over the entrepreneur's company, but for giving them a head start in life, and 'make him independent,' as Thomas puts it. In fact, Charles even explains that of his own children:

I need half of them to get a very, very high education. But the big one [the first-born son], and I think three of them, are needed to get low education because it will...help the business. If he has high education he cannot do this....He cannot bargain, when he is educated. So I need

half of them to go high and I need half of them to stay with me. . . . For
the girls it's better to go high in education [even up to doctorate].

To Charles, placing the children in higher education is important to
prepare them for a life outside business. In fact, most entrepreneurs
think that providing education for their children is the most important
gift that they can give. Isaac even calls it the 'solution of life'. However,
education has side-effects. Traditional values are questioned and new
affiliations, not necessarily based upon a common descent or geographic
origin, are forged.

Obligations to Extended Family Members

All the male[5] entrepreneurs feel they have obligations toward their
extended families. This also applies to those entrepreneurs who are
not first-born sons. Virtually all of the entrepreneurs take care of such
responsibilities. Some extended family members, primarily close family,
receive monthly allowances. The entrepreneurs also pay for the education of sons and daughters of extended family members. The entrepreneurs who engage in family support report having recurring monthly
contributions of anything from TSh 10,000 to well over TSh 500,000 per
month. This can be compared to the minimum wage at the time which
was TSh 10,000 per month.[6] In the upper ranges of this interval, most of
the expenses can be attributed to school fees for children in the
extended family. In the lower ranges, expenses are mostly related to
subsistence needs for close family, i.e., mother and father and whoever
takes care of them.

On top of the recurring expenses, virtually all entrepreneurs provide
ad hoc finance to extended family members – paying for hospital fees,
for example. Entrepreneurs who live in urban areas are often requested
to house and feed children of rural extended family members who go to
school in town. They are also expected to bring gifts when visiting their
home villages and pledge generously in ceremonies such as weddings
and funerals. Another common *ad hoc* expense is money lent or given to
help extended family members set up a venture of their own. Virtually
all entrepreneurs provide such loans interest-free. The majority do not
even think of it as a loan, rather as an expense. Thomas explains:

Well, I would give him in terms of a loan, but I wouldn't bother him
if he's faring fine. I wouldn't ask for it. But it's better you make him
understand it's a loan, which he's supposed to return. That will make

him work much harder. And so that he will not use it for other things and then come back and ask for another loan.

Financial assistance for venture creation may amount to substantial figures. On the other hand, as Thomas points out, if successful, it allows the relatives to stand on the own feet.

However, many entrepreneurs contend that the financial burdens placed upon them through supporting the extended family are heavy. Like John says about being first-born: 'It's just giving me more problems.' Yet few seek to avoid these obligations, and virtually everyone thinks of them as something that they just have to take care of. Only three entrepreneurs stay away from their obligations entirely, and they can do that either because the family is far away, or because most of them are even better off.

Some entrepreneurs, like Edwin, are happy to cater for extended family members. Edwin is proud of his capacity to shoulder the responsibility:

> I was born in a very, very extended family. I used to stay with my grandfather who was married to two wives. Of course we lived together including my father, until later when my father shifted from my grandfather's house to do his own business. So I'm very used to an extended family like that. So when I feel responsible, I'm responsible for that. I just feel proud ... our custom if the father is not around, and I'm the eldest son I take charge of everything on behalf of my father. So I'm almost this man, so I'm responsible for everything. All those who were dependent on him ... I have different dependents, of different kinds of course. There are those who are working under me, and those who are under me directly as members of the family, and close relatives. So in fact I need a lot.

Edwin likes to think of himself as being responsible for the welfare of others, and it makes him proud to be able to do so successfully. There are several entrepreneurs who are not as enthusiastic about shouldering their extended family obligations. Mark, for example, states: 'It not only makes me work harder, but it also puts me in some financial problems. ... If I had my own family sphere, my seven children and us we would be nine, we could be sitting at one table. But now if you have fifteen or sixteen people you have to sit at two tables.' He continues to talk about his sister: 'she had some children. I don't know how she got them, but it's all right, that's my lot.' There are also 'so many' relatives who come to him for help. Of course, he usually tries to help: 'You see, in the African tradition...you deny help to someone, although you have good reasons, very few understand, and in fact the larger the family, the more assistance you must give. Because they think having a big family is due to economic strength, which is not the case.'

Summarizing, most entrepreneurs support their extended family in one way or another. For the majority, however, extended family obligations are problematic. They find it difficult to shoulder them and at the same time keep their company operating well. A quote from Moses summarizes the general understanding of extended family obligations. In response to my question about the extended family being a burden for company operations, he says:

> Well, if you see it from the Western point of view, you feel that it [*the company*] is economically not being helped, but from an African point of view you're proud of it. Now, these two cultures they are fighting in between. You can have some people saying now that it's not my duty to help.

Larger numbers of Tanzanians today find that they can make money on their own. Their operations are however affected by their personal relations to extended family members. Entrepreneurs who want to expand their operations in the future, and retain good relations to their extended families, are finding it difficult to make a trade-off between satisfying the short-term needs of family members and seeing to the long-term benefit of the company. To surrender to the pressure and accept tradition is the easiest way out. Only a few entrepreneurs refuse to take that way.

Concluding Discussion

In the analysis above I have analysed the complex problems facing Tanzanian entrepreneurs, and identified two strategies: generating resources internally, and establishing relations of trust. Rather than seeking collaboration and collective efficiency gains through involvement in various production networks, the overwhelming majority of the entrepreneurs preferred to integrate their production activities and thereby control as much as possible of their production themselves.

I have emphasized the role of inter-personal relations and trusting, or not trusting, other economic actors. There is not much confidence among entrepreneurs that the formal institutional framework will ensure economic exchange without loss and/or bottlenecks and I have shown that the entrepreneurs in many instances instead seek to create personal relations. The essential content of such relations is 'trust', widely defined.

However, such social relations can be both supports and obstacles, particularly when trust is extended to kin. Related to this problem are the obligations that entrepreneurs have toward their extended families and the practice of employing extended family members as a way of taking on these obligations.

However, there are indications that changes are in the offing. An increasing number of entrepreneurs are limiting their involvement in the extended family and they are investing quite heavily in the education of their children. Whether the basis for trust in this process will change, from being ascribed to being earned, cannot be said with any certainty, but the evidence makes this likely. If that happens, Tanzania will become a more modern capitalist economy where formal, rather than informal, institutions shape economic transactions.

Notes

1. As spelled out in the Arusha Declaration of 1967. There are many publications addressing the developments during this 20-year period. See, e.g. Kiondo (1989) and Havnevik (1993).
2. The central aspects in a definition of 'trust' are that: 'someone, a *truster*, believes something about someone else, a *trustee*. The truster has a belief about the trustee's ability to do something, about her/his character, etc. This belief is somehow important for the truster who may be at odds if the trustee does not live up to what the truster expects him/her to do or be' (Sanner, 1997: 53)
3. Thomas is not his real name. None of the names mentioned in this chapter is authentic.
4. $200 is equal to approximately TSh 100,000. That is ten times the minimum wage.
5. Male entrepreneurs are emphasized because they traditionally have the burden of being the provider for the family. Maria only has family obligations for her two adopted children.
6. It should be noted that this salary was not sufficient even for the basic needs of an urban single male. See Tripp (1989).

4
Financing Small and Medium-sized Enterprises in Eastern Europe

Debora Revoltella

This chapter focuses on small and medium enterprises in transition economies and analyses the specific problems they face in obtaining external funds. The financial structure of Czech firms is analysed and it is shown that small and medium-sized enterprises rely much more on internal resources than large ones, probably due to higher interest rates and transaction costs. These results are in line with what has been found by Mayer (1990), concerning developing countries and Corbett and Jenkinson (1994), concerning developed countries. This chapter goes on to study whether there are specific inefficiencies in credit and capital markets in transition economies in eastern Europe, which affect financing opportunities for small and medium-sized enterprises. The focus is on legal frameworks regulating credit and capital markets, and on the information contexts of small and medium-sized enterprises in transition economies, and their underdevelopment.[1]

The Role of Small and Medium-sized Enterprises in the Three Economies

An analysis of the problems facing small and medium-sized enterprises in the three economies discussed here is complicated by the fact that the same definitions are not in use everywhere. The cut-off points, according to labour force, which are most commonly used for non-agricultural enterprises, are listed in Table 4.1.

With all due reservations because of the different definitions, the share of registered small and medium-sized enterprises in the total labour force is shown in Table 4.2.

Table 4.1 Definitions of small and medium-sized enterprises

	Small	**Medium**
European Union	Less than 50 workers	Less than 250 workers
Poland	Less than 50 workers	Less than 250 workers
Czech Republic		Less than 500 workers
Hungary	Between 11 and 50 workers	Between 51 and 250 workers

Table 4.2 Share of small and medium-sized enterprises in the total labour force

	Poland	**Czech Republic**	**Hungary**
1994	16.3	3.2	9.7
1995	15.2	2.9	9.3

Source: ECE, 1996.

Figure 4.1 Small and medium-sized enterprises by sector in 1994

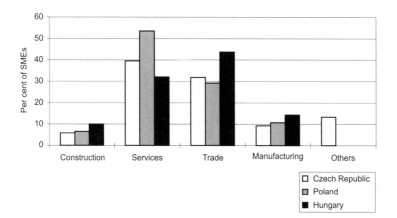

Source: ECE, 1996.

The overwhelming majority of small and medium-sized enterprises in the three countries is in trade and services. Manufacturing enterprises only comprised around one-tenth of small and medium-sized enterprises in each country (see Figure 4.1).

Financing Firms' Investment in the Czech Republic: a Firm Level Analysis

In order to analyse financial choices of enterprises during the process of transition to a market economy, a sample of more than 600 enterprises listed in the Czech capital markets for the 1993–94 period was studied. First their behaviour is analysed on an aggregate level. They are then classified as small, medium and large enterprises, and it is shown how size affects financial choices.

For the analysis in this chapter, balance sheet data were used and the analysis distinguished between the following sources of funds: self-financing, new equity, bank debt and other kind of debt. Self-financing is the sum of all internal resources which are not provided by partners or by de-investment. It includes non-distributed profits, changes in funds and depreciation. Due to the lack of information concerning distributed dividends, the overall change in reserves plus depreciation is used instead. Equity financing has been calculated as the change in own capital, while bank debts are new credits (of the short and the long type) from banks. Other kinds of debt include commercial debt, public debt, etc. Following one of the basic accounting equations:

$$I^* = \Delta \text{Banks} + \Delta \text{Other credits} + \Delta \text{Equity} + \text{Self-financing} \qquad (1)$$

By definition, change in the firm's assets (total gross investment, I^*) equals change in firm's liabilities plus depreciation (change in bank debt – ΔBanks, plus change in other debt – ΔOther credits, plus change in equity capital – ΔEquity, plus Self-financing). The following analysis is in terms of flows. The increase or the reduction in the use of each source of funds is considered and thus the importance of different agents in financing investment is evaluated.

Figure 4.2 shows the results of the analysis for Czech enterprises in the 1993–94 period on an aggregate level.[2] It is interesting to note the importance of self-financing compared to other sources of funds. This could be a consequence of higher costs of external resources and of constraints in credits and capital markets. More generally, both asymmetric information and agency models (Harris and Raviv, 1990) predict the prevalence of this form of financing. The form of financing which is second in importance is new equity but this is probably overestimated, due to the privatization process. New debt (bank and non-bank) finances represent 11 per cent of total investment in 1993–94.

This aggregate analysis shows that Czech enterprises prefer internal resources and use debt and equity financing only to a limited extent.

Figure 4.2 Financing enterprises in the Czech Republic in 1994: a flow analysis (calculated from balance sheet data)

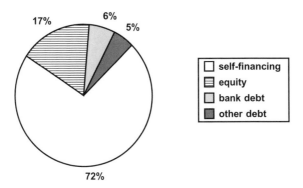

This attitude could be a consequence of general inefficiencies of credit and capital markets, affecting all kinds of enterprises, mainly related to the legal framework. This point is discussed later on in this chapter – but it is interesting to detect the relationship between firms' size and financial choices in order to highlight the different conditions and costs that small and medium enterprises face in seeking for external funds.

As a first attempt, the correlation between self-financing and an index of enterprise size (the natural logarithm of total assets in 1994) was calculated and a weak negative correlation was found. This means that the smaller the enterprise the larger is the share of self-financing and vice versa. In order to obtain a more detailed picture, the sample was divided into three classes, according to the European Community definition of small and medium enterprises, based on total assets. The first class includes enterprises with less than ECU 5 million in total assets (small businesses), while in the second class there are firms with a level of total assets in the range between ECU 5 million and ECU 27 million (medium). The third class includes all the enterprises with more than ECU 27 million in total assets (large). Following this definition, 265 enterprises in the sample are small, 246 medium and 147 large.

The data presented in Table 4.3 highlight some important features, concerning the change in the use of different sources and thus the relevance of each one in financing investment. Although all enterprises use primarily internal resources, this source is more relevant for small and medium firms. The importance of equity financing increases with the size of the firm, while the change in bank debt is positive for

Table 4.3   Change in the use of sources of finance, 1993–94, by firm size (calculated from balance sheet data)

	Small	Medium	Large
Equity (%)	10.18	15.25	30.11
Self-financing (%)	82.54	71.80	54.67
Bank debt (%)	−8.91	15.94	14.01
Other debt (%)	16.17	−2.94	1.05

Table 4.4   Firm size and financing through debt in 1994: stock analysis (calculated from balance sheet data)

	Small	Medium	Large
Debt/total assets (%)	26.53	31.96	35.88
Bank debt/total assets (%)	10.21	16.97	16.47
Short-term debt/total assets (%)	21.48	24.64	26.17
Long-term debt/total assets (%)	5.05	9.05	10.74

medium and large enterprises but negative for small ones, in 1994. This could be a consequence of either demand or supply factors.

By developing a stock analysis of the relationship between leverage ratios and size of the firm, the main conclusions of the previous flow analysis are confirmed (see Table 4.4).

Large firms generally have a higher level of indebtedness, which could testify to an easier access to credit markets. This result may also be a consequence of the strong link existing, in transition economies, between the size and the age of a firm; large firms are generally older and thus they have accumulated greater indebtedness. However, by distinguishing between different forms of credit, it is found that the long-term debt ratio is higher for large and medium enterprises, probably due to the inheritance from the planned economy. Short-term debt is of primary importance for all three groups of enterprises; this is definitely a consequence of the prudence adopted by creditors. Short-term debt, by requiring frequent re-negotiation, implies an higher control of the creditor over the debtor, and is widely used in transition economies. When bank debt is considered, we can note the low indebtedness ratio for the smaller enterprises, in line with the previous observations.

What variables influence debt ratios? In order to answer this question all possible causes were considered together, rather than testing a specific model. As a dependent variable, the leverage ratio in 1994 is used, which is calculated as total debt over total assets (*DTA*) in equation 3 and as bank debt over total assets (*BDTA*) in equation 4. The following independent variables are considered: tangible assets plus inventories, divided by total assets (*IGPTA*) as indicators for the collateral value of assets, profits over total assets (*PROTA*) as indicators for profitability and the logarithm of sales (*lnsal*) as indicators for the magnitude of activities. The estimated equation is:

$$DTA = a + b_0 PROTA + b_1 lnsal + b_2 IGPTA + e, \qquad (2)$$

where a is a constant, b_0, b_1 and b_2 are regression coefficients and e is the error term.

The result is as follows: (*t* test in parenthesis):

$$DTA = 0.293 + 0.013 lnsal - 0.689 PROTA - 0.177 IGPTA \qquad (3)$$
$$(7.522) \quad (5.679) \qquad (-6.531) \qquad (-4.077)$$

In equation 3, a highly significant and positive value for the parameter of the sales variable (*lnsal*) confirms at the firm level that size influences indebtedness (and thus financing) decisions. The coefficient of the Profitability variable (*PROTA*) is significant and negative, showing that the most profitable firms use external sources of finance to a lesser extent. Theoretically this result can be explained by considering the high costs of external funds, due to asymmetrical information and agency problems. The negative sign of the asset variable (*IGPTA*) contradicts our hypothesis; it can be explained by considering the heritage of financial practices in planned economies. In particular, before the transition, firms used to finance their investments in fixed capital through new equity issues, while debt was used to finance working capital. A slight reduction of the positive correlation between fixed assets and equities in the last years shows that this link is still present. Furthermore, this result suggests that enterprise debt is not fully guaranteed, thus creditors would not be fully protected in case of default of the debtor.

The results of the regression do not change if the leverage ratio is specified as the ratio between bank debt and total assets (equation 4); the only relevant change concerns the sign of the parameter of the asset variable (*IGPTA*), which is now positive. This means that enterprises' indebtedness with banks depends on the collateral value of assets, thus showing that banks allocate credits according to established and prudential rules (*t* test in parenthesis):

$$BDTA = 0.043 + 0.005 lnsal - 0.277 PROTA + 0.053 IGPTA \qquad (4)$$
$$(1.684) \quad (3.276) \qquad (-3.935) \qquad (1.856)$$

Generally speaking, the empirical analysis shows that internal funds are the first source of finance for all Czech enterprises, while debt and equity are residual forms of finance. Furthermore, by tabulating sources of finance by firm size category, an indirect relationship between size and use of internal resources was detected. The stock analysis showed that small firms consistently have a lower debt ratio, when compared to medium and large ones. This is true for every form of debt (bank debt, short-term debt and long-term debt). Finally, when considering the determinants of enterprise debt structure, size has been detected as one of the relevant explanatory variables. All these pieces of evidence show that small and medium enterprises are less involved in credit markets. In the next section the reasons for this will be investigated and possible solutions will be suggested.

Credit, Capital Markets and Small and Medium-sized Enterprises

The first form of finance considered is bank debt. One of the main problems affecting enterprise financing in transition economies, is the persistence of non-economic practices in credit allocation, which depend on delays in the transformation of the banking system. In the Czech Republic, as well as in Poland and in Hungary, however, the restructuring of the banking sector, in spite of radically different strategies, is now starting to achieve good results. Some problems still persist in the Czech Republic. However, generally speaking, political influence on banking activities is infrequent, while credit policies in all the three countries mainly follow market rules. If we want to be more precise concerning the new bank credit policies which are arising in transition economies, we should note a movement towards short-term financing, prevalently directed to large enterprises, while high spreads on interest rates persist. The availability of collateral and other sources of guarantees represents a neccessary precondition of access to credit markets.

Given these general conditions, the limited role of bank debt in financing small and medium enterprises needs to be explained. From the supply side, the inability of banks to evaluate different enterprises and monitor their behaviour can create, in the case of small and medium enterprises with an unknown past, a real failure of credit markets (Akerlof, 1970; Stiglitz and Weiss, 1981). In Hungary for example, a government policy was applied in 1994, in order to finance a series of investments in small and medium-sized firms, channelling funds via the banks. This policy was intended to provide fresh capital to enterprises in the short run, and also to create a link between banks and small enterprises, in the hope of facilitating better information and a reputation effect for small productive units. However, due to a high percentage of unsuccessful credits, banks definitely lost confidence in small and medium enterprises. Since then banks have developed and applied an unwritten rule, by which no loans are granted below a certain sum. In 1996, the share of bank credits directed to small and medium enterprises was still quite limited (less than 10 per cent, while the share of small and medium enterprises in the labour market approximated 24 per cent). Similar problems exist in the Czech Republic and in Poland. Because small and medium enterprises have not established reputations with the banks and because of scarce information on their profitability, access to the credit market is impossible or very expensive. In addition, a general lack of collateral, widespread use of informal, non-registered forms of financing and institutional inefficiencies make banks reluctant to finance this kind of enterprises.

From the demand side the limited role of bank debt in financing small and medium enterprises can be explained in terms of high interest rates. By comparing bank interest rates on credits to the best and to the worst clients in Hungary (small and medium enterprises usually fall in the latter category), the differential treatment is evident (see Figure 4.3).

When speaking about financing through equities, we should distinguish between the transformation of the firm in a public structure and the recourse to venture capital. Problems connected to the first form of

Figure 4.3 Bank interest rates on credits to best and worst clients in Hungary

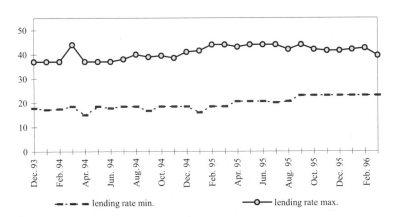

Source: Hungarian National Bank, *Monthly Bulletin*, various issues.

financing for small and medium enterprises will be analysed in the next paragraph, being essentially connected to the costs of selling and publishing information, thus to the institutional context. However, we can note that generally, small and medium enterprises avoid equity financing for three reasons. Firstly, due to agency costs and limited information, selling of their equities is generally difficult and implies discounts. Secondly, before being listed, firms must satisfy strict conditions and finally, having a new equity holder means losing control over activities and major decisions. Overall, going public is feasible only for the medium-sized and large units.

All these financing problems are shared by enterprises all over the world. However, in transition economies, the limited size of capital markets is a further constraint to the financing of small and medium enterprises. An exception is the Czech Republic. The coexistence of two forms of capital markets, a traditional Stock Exchange and a Securities Exchange,[3] allows the listing of a greater number of enterprises (1750 at the end of 1995) and a wider participation of smaller enterprises than elsewhere in the Securities Exchange System, in fact, listing costs are reduced and it is possible to exchange all equities registered in the Security Centre, while direct access is allowed to everyone. However, the operations in this capital market are mainly related to the privatization process.

The advantages connected to financing through venture capital depend on the direct link which arises between the firm and the financier. Problems are connected to the difficulties of finding interested investors in a context in which information is scarce. It is thus important to have appropriate institutions that allow enterprises and financiers to meet. Among these are the project *Poland and Hungary: Aid for the Restructing of Economies* (PHARE), varied World Bank initiatives and the Joint Venture Programme, which aims at creating joint ventures between Central and East European enterprises and Western European ones. In transition economies this form of funding is extremely relevant, especially when a foreign partner is considered.

General Inefficiencies Connected to the Juridical and Institutional Context

The inefficiencies of credit and capital markets in transition economies, highlighted above, are linked to the underdevelopment of the legal framework, which at the time was not always able to protect financiers, granting them a fair return for their investments. For this reason, financiers preferred less risky activities, thus neglecting funding of enterprises. In this section the main limitations of the legal framework in 1994 are discussed as well as the steps that have been taken in order to solve them.

As to financing through debt, the main problems are linked to the inefficacy of collateral and bankruptcy laws, which do not fully guarantee repayment to the creditor in case of insolvency. This implies a higher risk for creditors and therefore, less financing is available for enterprises. The most frequent problems connected to collateral laws are: lack of registration rules, unclear lines of priority in case of default, high costs and a poor secondary market for mobile and immobile goods. All these problems reduce the expected value of collateral well below its nominal value. As a result of this creditors require guarantees for 150 per cent of the value of the credit and enterprises, due to their poor capitalization, face enormous problems in satisfying these demands. This situation leads to forms of credit rationing – profitable projects are not financed because enterprises promoting them do not have sufficient capital to provide collateral. This problem is particularly relevant for small and medium enterprises, especially the newest ones, which are insufficiently endowed with capital.

Direct government interventions have an important role in this context. Guarantee funds, by region or by sector, have been created, in order to relax the financial constraints due to lack of collateral, while reducing, at the same time, the risk for creditors. Programmes of this kind are found in the Czech Republic (financed by the Ministry of Economy, through the Czech and Moravian Bank of Guarantee and Development), in Hungary (Hungarian Fund for Promotion and Development of Small and Medium Enterprises) and in Poland (Fund for Promotion and Development of Small and Medium Enterprises, which has been created following the new policy for small and medium enterprises of the 6 June 1995). However, in all the three countries the government is developing appropriate legal measures. In Hungary and Poland, in particular, new regulations, in 1996 and 1998 respectively, provide a uniform system of registration of non-possessive pledges against movable property.[4]

Bankruptcy legislation, as well, has been inefficient, which discourages creditors. In Hungary, a new bankruptcy law is in force since January 1992, and was amended in 1993. In Poland the 1934 bankruptcy law was reinstated, with several amendments, in 1990. It was complemented with specific provisions for banks and insurance companies and with temporary laws for the joint restructuring of banks and enterprises and for the transformation of state companies, which provide for an extraordinary judicial procedure to resolve insolvency situations in these cases. In the Czech Republic a bankruptcy law was adopted in 1991, but was not enforced before 1993.

Generally speaking, in transition economies, legislation regulating bankruptcy under the form of reorganization or liquidation has been implemented to resolve the problem of inefficient resources allocation by favouring the use of strict market restraints on the workings of firms and making debt governance easier, thus enhancing capital flow to enterprises, but at the same time avoiding too much damage to the economic system. Given these objectives there has been a trade-off between benefits deriving from a greater flexibility and those deriving from a greater rigidity in the application of the law. On the one hand, flexible laws may lead to the continuation of soft budget constraints attitudes while, on the other, rigid laws might lead to liquidation of enterprises that are only temporarily insolvent and the real value of which is higher than that realized through liquidation. The efficiency of legislation depends on the solution to this trade-off.

The 1991 Hungarian bankruptcy law was strictly based on principles of rigidity. The automatic trigger[5] and the requirement for unanimity among creditors in the decision to implement reorganization have been used as an instrument to obtain an enhancement in the financial discipline of enterprises. The rigidity of this approach most definitely guaranteed an immediate disciplinary effect as testified by the number of proceedings for bankruptcy (in 1992 and 1993 there were 17.133 liquidation trials and 5,156 cases of reorganization) but perhaps at too great a cost, in terms of chain dissolution of commercial relations. Amendments to the Hungarian law in 1993 attempted to re-establish equilibrium between rigidity and flexibility of the law by eliminating the automatic trigger and unanimity of agreement among creditors for reorganization.[6]

In Poland and the Czech Republic bankruptcy legislation has followed more flexible principles. Governments in these countries have preferred to guarantee better protection for enterprises, avoiding interference from bankruptcy rules in privatization and the liquidation of enterprises temporarily insolvent because of inherited debt through trade arrears. In the Czech Republic the fear of chain bankruptcy has caused lengthy delays in the implementation of legislation and exemptions for several sectors[7] even beyond 1993. This extremely flexible approach has certainly had a price. It has limited creditors' incentives to monitor enterprises and has allowed the continuation of soft budget constraint attitudes. In Poland as well, the application of legislation has been flexible, and protection of enterprises has been guaranteed through the Arrangement Proceeding Law, but at the same time, more care has been taken over creating incentives for restructuring and the adoption of hard budget constraints (temporary law on the joint restructuring of banks and firms). In general, however, although great differences exist among the three countries, long delays testify to the inefficiency of the legal framework.

When financing through equities is considered, problems connected to the institutional and legal framework seem to affect firms more than financiers. This form of financing is, in fact, theoretically available for every kind of enterprise. However, it is expensive to be listed, which makes this form impractical for small- and medium-sized enterprises. The legislation in all the three countries requires the firm which wants to be listed to publish certain information concerning its activities, profitability, its degree of indebtedness, etc. Public authorities do not check for the quality of the information and do not provide judgements concerning the opportunity of investing in a certain firm. They only control that the information disclosed is sufficient to allow financiers to evaluate the firm. All this discourages medium and small enterprises. This is even more true, considering the possibility that an equity issue is unsuccessful, which is still high. Summing up, the transformation of a medium-sized enterprises into a public company implies high costs and is therefore infrequent. In the Czech Republic, the possibility of financing a firm through the Securities Exchange is a good alternative, due to lower costs and information requirements. This alternative is not available in Hungary and in Poland.

Lastly, there is the legal framework concerning financing through venture capital. Managers seeking investment funds try to find external resources in exchange for the promise of future profits. The investors, however, do not have specific rights of restitution of the invested funds, but gain the right over future profits, secured by the right of vote in the decision-making process of the firm. From a legal point of view, this right is secured by the Civil Code and by the Company law, which specify the juridical form of a firm and all rights connected to capital. Specific laws protect foreign capital investments, by granting the opportunity of profit rescue.

Leasing is widely used to enlarge or restructure productive activity, rather than the perhaps more conventional methods discussed above. Advantages connected with leasing are great: enterprises do not face liquidity problems and do not need to provide collateral; creditors, who continue to hold property rights on goods, face lower risks. In terms of asymmetric information and agency problems, leasing contracts represent a good solution, granting a strong creditor control over debtor. For all these reasons, leasing is becoming the most important form of finance for small and medium enterprises and in all the three countries leasing activities are widespread.

Conclusions

The analysis developed above allows us to highlight a direct relationship between the size of a firm and its opportunities for access to external resources. Although this relationship exists both in developed and in developing countries, it is noted that some special features of the transition process can explain the severe character of the financing problems faced by small and medium enterprises in the Czech Republic, Hungary and Poland. In particular, it is shown that the underdevelopment of credit and capital markets, as well as the ineffective legal framework regulating them, can exacerbate information asymmetries and agency problems. Financiers do not feel adequately protected and therefore reduce their financing to the less secure firms, the small and medium sized ones.

From an economic policy perspective, the relationship between size of a firm and access to external resources provides a rationale for the development of an active support programme for small and medium sized enterprises. In the Czech Republic government intervention in their favour is regulated through the act 299/1992, which supports the development and formation of this kind of productive units through advance credits and guarantees. In 1995 the Ministry of Economy has adopted eight sub-programmes. In Hungary the effort to sustain small and medium sized enterprises has always been much more fragmented, due to the lack of a unified law, until 1996. Support has usually been provided through the allocation of credit and guarantees. In Poland, the legislative framework this respect is also quite incoherent. In addition, both in Poland and in the Czech Republic an officially sanctioned definition of small and medium enterprises does not exist. This limits the intervention opportunities and the efficacy of different actions.

Notes

1. For a review of the issues, see Gray and Hanson (1993), Mizsei (1994), Steinherr (1993), Berglof and Roland (1995); Pohl *et al.* (1995), Singh (1995), and Shleifer and Vishny (1996).

2. About developments in the Czech Republic, see *inter alia* Capek (1995), Coffee (1996) and Zeman (1996).
3. This is a separate capital market which was intended to serve directly small stockholders and has numerous regional outlets.
4. See further Berglof and von Thadden (1994), Baer and Gray (1995), Bonin and Schaffer (1995), Gray and Hendley (1995) and World Economy Research Institute (1996).
5. Automatic opening of bankruptcy proceedings after 90 days of a firm's insolvency. Insolvency may be for any sum and towards any type of creditor.
6. Dittus and Prowse (1995) disagree with this. Although they recognize the excessive rigidity of the law as it initially was, they feared that eliminating the automatic trigger would be a step backwards inasmuch as the incentives to financial discipline were still insufficient to guarantee the timely activation of bankruptcy proceedings.
7. The main exemptions have been conceded to the agricultural sector.

Part II
Industrial Clusters and Networks

5

Structural Adjustment and Cluster Advantages: A Case from Peru

Evert-Jan Visser

It is generally recognized that spatial clustering yields advantages for SMEs, not only in European 'industrial districts' but also in developing countries (Visser, 1996). However, the issue is what *type* of clustering advantages enhance SME competitiveness. As SME clusters emerge in dissimilar market and technology settings, the logics of various clustering processes are diverse. In addition, clustering advantages shape producer preferences and their perceptions of alternative business styles, and therefore, their response to competitive crises.

This chapter analyses how clothing producers in the Gamarra cluster in Lima have responded to a competitive situation brought about by free trade policies. The primary question is whether the advantages associated with spatial clustering in Lima become greater or smaller in the context of increased foreign competition. A secondary question is what producers can do to develop the advantages of being located in the cluster.

A large literature on European 'industrial districts' and SME clusters in developing countries focuses inter-firm co-operation as a source of collective efficiency (e.g. Goodman and Bamford, 1989; Pyke, 1992; Schmitz, 1992; Nadvi and Schmitz, 1994; van Dijk and Rabellotti, 1997). From a learning point of view, two factors can be identified in order to understand better how inter-firm co-operation facilitates growth in clusters. First, strategic co-operation among clustered firms facilitates the effective processing of novel business information, thereby enhancing innovation. Secondly, a change in the perception of the costs and benefits of co-operation can induce an increase in co-operative links between producers and traders. The latter – a change in perceptions – is a necessary condition for the former – increased inter-firm co-operation and innovation.

In this chapter, the concept 'mental model' (Denzau and North, 1994) is used to deal with the gap between perception and reality with regard to the expected costs and benefits of co-operation between SMEs. The concept is thus useful to explain a lack of co-operation between SMEs, even if they are clustered, which would reduce the transaction costs of co-operation. Whether or not SMEs co-operate, depends, in this view, on the *perceived* balance of the costs and benefits of inter-firm co-operation. This is in turn influenced by the historical lessons learnt in a cluster, expressed in a collective mental model of how to run a business successfully. Over time, the traditional advantages of clustering become tacit components of this model. Hence, the type of clustering advantages is crucial for how producers reflect upon past experiences.

The next section provides a conceptual framework for analysing the relationship between a process of clustering and SME competitiveness. This includes defining clusters, classifying clustering advantages, and identifying – from a learning point of view – the hurdles that hinder the move from mere coexistence to active co-operation within the cluster and the evolution of collective efficiency (Schmitz, 1992, 1997). The history of the Gamarra cluster in Lima, including the general demand and supply environment in which it emerged and grew, is narrated in the following section in order to throw light on this issue, and the empirical evidence concerning the type and magnitude of clustering advantages is summarized. Recent changes in the market environment of the Peruvian clothing industry are analysed next, and empirical evidence regarding the performance of clustered firms in the new market context is summarized. The responses of clustered producers towards a trend of decreasing sales and the resulting change in multilateral co-operation networks are also discussed. In conclusion, it is argued that in coping with a changing market environment, clustered producers may be at a disadvantage compared with dispersed ones. This risk appears to be real in cases where passive advantages of clustering have historically been important, as in Gamarra (Visser and Távarra, 1995).

Conceptual Framework

Clustering contributes to the capacity of SMEs to compete: 'clustering opens up efficiency and flexibility gains which individual producers can rarely attain' according to Schmitz (1992: 64–5). The beneficial impact of clustering for SME competitiveness was first stressed by Marshall (1890), and further elaborated in the literature on 'industrial districts' in industrialized countries (Goodman and Bamford, 1989; Pyke and

Sengenberger, 1992). This literature provides a model of clustering in which five characteristics stand out:

- inter-firm division of labour based on vertical specialization and subcontracting;
- a mix of co-operative and competitive interactions between firms;
- socio-cultural embeddedness of economic transactions;
- institutional development enhancing the supply of business support services;
- entrepreneurial dynamism.

In SME clusters in developing countries these properties cannot be taken for granted (cf. Nadvi and Schmitz, 1994; van Dijk and Rabellotti, 1997). For instance, the feasibility of vertical division of labour between firms depends on the trade-off between market incentives and transaction costs, the outcome of which varies across different market situations and institutional settings. In addition, subcontracting occurs in varied forms depending on the characteristics of the relevant market and the technological environment. A third point is that a process of spatial clustering of SMEs in developing countries may be largely a defensive and local phenomenon, and the business information available to firms of local origin. Producers' perceptions are then mostly based on local business experiences. Under these circumstances, path and context dependence may produce the 'entropic death' of the local entrepreneurial milieu (Camagni, 1991: 140).

In empirical analysis of SME clusters in developing countries, it is important to avoid mixing their features with the stylized facts of European industrial districts. A first step in this direction is to define clustering on the basis of the known common denominators of SME clusters around the world, namely, as a process of spatial concentration of economic activities within a certain sub-sector and at a location where industrial experience has been built up for a number of years.

It should be observed that according to this definition, clustering is a dynamic process and therefore, it is neccessary to assess the dynamic capabilities of clustered producers, preferably through repeated observation. In addition, a range of driving forces can stimulate a process of spatial clustering, resulting in different sources of SME competitiveness. However, there are two main models of clustering processes. On the one hand, clustering can be due to a few common denominators behind the once-only location decisions of entrepreneurs. This is the case where the principal goal of locating in the cluster area is to passively benefit from some favourable location factors. Examples are the availability and quality of transport and wholesale facilities, and of physical infrastructure. The presence of a multitude of competitors implicitly influencing each other in investment and commercial decisions (and thus reducing short-term commercial risks as well as long-term uncertainty associated with investments in fixed capital) is another example. Clustered producers automatically enjoy these advantages, that is technological externalities and pecuniary effects (cf. Scitovsky, 1954; Mishan, 1971). Schmitz (1997: 9) refers to these as the 'passive' advantages of clustering. They are available to anyone working in the cluster area, and also accrue to producers visiting the area, e.g. for the purchase of inputs.

However, clustering may also result from a collective process including the developing of complementary and co-operative linkages with other SMEs. Competition compels producers to upgrade their ties with suppliers, clients, competitors, banks and research centres in order to offset the disadvantages that characterize most small- and medium-sized enterprises (SMEs), e.g. high cost of information and cognitive constraints to innovation (Visser, 1996: 25–32). In other words, producers aim at finding solutions to competitive problems on the basis of co-operative learning (technical, managerial and entrepreneurial) and innovation (with regard to products, processes and organization). Process innovations may, for example, result from a technical/commercial dialogue between users and producers of intermediary products (vertical linkages), while quality improvements are but one result of co-operation between producers making similar products (horizontal linkages). Schmitz (1997: 9) calls this 'active collective efficiency'. According to this model, active collective efficiency arises at the level of networks of functionally interdependent producers, and may then spread across the cluster and even attract outside firms to the cluster.

The difference between the two models is inter-firm co-operation, which is not needed for passive collective efficiency but essential for active collective efficiency. This distinction is very important in the empirical analysis of SME clusters in developing countries. If a performance gap between clustered and dispersed firms is observed, the question then follows whether this is (mainly) due to passively or actively acquired advantages.

In addition, passive collective efficiency works in a top-down direction, from the cluster (meso-) level to the micro-level of individual firms. Active collective efficiency works in a bottom-up direction, from the responses of individual firms to competition, through inter-firm linkages and business networks, and up to the cluster level.

There are at least four reasons why SMEs co-operate with other firms: asset-specificity and indivisibilities; information asymmetries and measurement problems; externalities and public goods (Yong-Il and Wilkinson, 1994); and, in a dynamic approach, cross-firm learning effects (Lambooy, 1994; Nooteboom, 1994). At times of trade liberalization, learning effects are of particular importance. Learning is a condition for innovation which, in turn, enhances the chances of survival at times of competitive shocks and lays the basis for sustained competitiveness over time.

Learning is not a rational process, however. This is due, firstly, to standard problems that give rise to transaction costs, such as opportunism on the side of suppliers of business support services, and a limited width, depth and variety of data collection capabilities in SMEs (cf. Nooteboom, 1992: 287, and Visser, 1996: 26, 28). Secondly, this is due to bounded rationality as observed by Simon:

> If we accept the proposition that both the knowledge and the computational power of the decision-maker are severely limited, then we must distinguish between the real world and the author's perception of it and reasoning about it. That is to say we must construct a theory . . . of the process of decision, [which] must include not only the reasoning processes but also the processes that generated the actor's subjective representation of the decision problem.
>
> North, 1994: 362

The 'mental model' concept makes it possible to analyse the gap between perception and reality. It refers to one's perceptions, the preferences that people have for these perceptions, and the control they exert over these preferences. In his discussion of the nature of learning, North (ibid.) argues that the direction of the learning process depends on 'the expected payoffs to acquiring different kinds of knowledge [while] the mental models that the players develop shape perceptions about the payoffs'. Nooteboom (1992: 285) adds that people hold preferences with regard to their expectations and perceptions of the utility of different kinds of knowledge. Hence, they select information in line with their mental model, so that preferences persist over some time (cf. Philips, 1988: 12). In terms of bounded rationality, this means that people not only lack computational power but may even be unwilling to compute.

Reversing the argument, learning requires an act of will – a conscious decision to deviate from one's preferences, and start to collect and interpret divergent and challenging information (after having disregarded it for some time). Strong will is indeed required, when taking into consideration the mechanisms that enable people to adhere to existing preferences and perceptions, neglect divergent and challenging information, and preserve a particular mental model. In this regard, Simon stresses the role of emotions in filtering information, especially in threatening situations, while Heiner assigns this function to norms and values (Nooteboom, 1992: 289).

Cognitive categories are a third factor that enables or limits learning processes. As stated by Nooteboom (1993: 286–7): 'perception, interpretation and evaluation are performed on the basis of categories that condition knowledge in the double sense of enabling and limiting it'. Once acquired, knowledge may sink to the level of tacitness,[1] while cognitive categories may harden into epistemological obstacles, as suggested by Bachelard (Nooteboom, 1992: 289). The implicit nature of tacit knowledge makes it difficult to monitor, communicate and transfer and, therefore, obstructs (self) criticism and learning. Cognitive categories give rise to cognitive conservatism, which in its extreme form induces people to stubbornly neglect information that does not fit with their existing perceptions and preferences.

So far the emphasis is on factors that constrain learning: an inert mental model. The question arises what offsets these factors and thus triggers learning. The answer is new experience, either of a physical, social, cultural, spiritual, economic or personal kind. Once this experience is sufficiently challenging, people will need to change their preferences and perceptions about acquiring or accepting new types of knowledge. This, ideally, results in awareness taking the place of tacit knowledge, while new information is collected, analysed, incorporated and applied. Hence, path-dependent behaviour is replaced by change.

This framework is useful for addressing the issue of the learning and innovation potential of (dispersed and clustered) SMEs. A first point is that individual SMEs acquire a substantial part of their know-how through learning-by-doing[2] (Malecki, 1991: 146), making tacit knowledge common for SMEs. Next, the personality of the owner–entrepreneur (in terms of, e.g. stubbornness and self-reliance) also influences the capacity and willingness to deal with new information. A third point is that SMEs generally have disadvantages in resources (Visser, 1996: 20–33). Hence, a lack of staff limits the scope of data collection, a relatively low level of education limits the depth of data processing, and the dominant position of owner–entrepreneurs reduces variety in perception and interpretation (Nooteboom, 1992: 289). As a result, dispersed

SMEs are more easily trapped by cognitive conservatism, which limits the capacity to select, process and assimilate external information and the willingness to invest in new directions. This has negative consequences for their capacity to learn, upgrade and innovate.[3]

In this regard, clustered SMEs have an advantage over dispersed ones because of local circulation of information about best business practices, products and markets. Clustered SMEs are less dependent on internal cognitive resources. However, this advantage is path and context dependent, making business behaviour largely subject to local influences. Once change is required due to non-local developments, for example in the aftermath of trade liberalization, the mental model shaped by the local collective experience may actually hinder development in the cluster (cf. Meyer-Stamer, Chapter 2, this volume).

Conversely, competitive crises can stimulate cluster development under the right circumstances. Clustering *facilitates* SME development by lowering the transaction costs associated with networking.[4] In turn, co-operative action in networks is crucial for collective decoding, interpretation, assimilation and application of new information.[5] Networks, in other words, help small entrepreneurs to tackle the cognitive hurdles of tacit knowledge, path and context dependence and cognitive conservatism. Successful networks will not go unnoticed in a cluster setting, and set new terms of reference for the performance of non-participating firms. In terms of the learning model, SME networks provide non-participating entrepreneurs with external experience that challenges the existing mental model of how to run a successful business.

From this follows that the principal issue in empirical research on SME clusters in developing countries can be formulated as follows: To what extent does inter-firm co-operation in business networks promote cross-firm learning and innovation? This issue is particularly relevant in a setting of trade liberalization. Schmitz (1997: 10) argues that cluster capacity to respond to opportunity and crisis requires 'shifting gear from passive to [active] collective efficiency'.

However, whether this happens depends on the trade-off between the *perceived* benefits and costs of inter-firm co-operation: market incentives and transaction costs respectively. A positive balance facilitates inter-firm division of labour and co-operation in business networks; a negative balance prevents entrepreneurs from moving in these directions. In a situation where the clustering process has, for a long time, been based on predominantly passive clustering advantages, the local mental model may work against inter-firm co-operation in business networks. Market incentives will be misunderstood and transaction costs overestimated, resulting in a negative trade-off between the perceived benefits and costs of inter-firm co-operation, leading to lock-in and stagnation.

The Gamarra Cluster

The Gamarra cluster is located in La Victoria, one of the 43 municipal districts of Lima. The city has the largest market potential of all cities in Peru, both in terms of demand for consumer goods and when supply of inputs is considered. The municipal district of La Victoria has a long history (since the 19th century) of various industrial activities: textiles and clothing, metalworking, automobile repair services, woodworking and several final consumer products.

The cluster location is also close to a wholesale market for staple food crops, the first to be established in Lima. This market was built in 1945. It attracted traders from all over Peru and triggered the urbanization of the surrounding hills, on the basis of land invasions organized by migrant traders. Later waves of migrants also settled on the slopes of these hills, some of them participating in garment making. These pioneers in the clothing business sold their products in the neighbourhood of the wholesale market, where they were later asked to come nearer to a bus-stop for long distance busses. This bus-stop was located in Gamarra street, and became a meeting point for traders who sold agricultural products to the growing capital city and distributed manufactured products to regional and rural markets. Hence, the industrial path of La Victoria merged with an increasing trade in consumer goods. This has been crucial for the later role of the cluster in connecting the centralized supply of textiles and clothing products in Lima with geographically dispersed demand in rural areas and intermediate cities.

Using the main roads surrounding the cluster as its physical limits, the cluster comprises 60 housing blocks (Ponce, 1994: 100), of which, in October 1995, 35 were used by traders and producers. The cluster is steadily expanding, however, through, for example, 'immigration' by street vendors from surrounding areas and the construction of new shopping centres. What was once a quiet neighbourhood has now grown into a commercial area, with real estate prices of US$5,000 per square metre. Garment producers daily flood the neighbourhood, along with traders (of inputs, equipment and final products), suppliers of services (e.g. repair and maintenance, book-keeping and related services, food and beverages, etc.), and individual consumers shopping for inexpensive clothes.

In August 1993, the cluster comprised more than 150 shopping centres and it has continued to grow since. In July 1997, several new shopping centres were under construction. According to an August 1993 estimate, 6,800 firms were then active in the cluster area: 50 medium-sized and 1,950 small clothing firms; 4,100 traders of cloth fabrics and accessories; 300 restaurants; and 150 companies selling equipment and components (Ponce, 1994: 100–1). These figures exclude the numerous street sellers and informal micro-businesses operating in and just outside the cluster (on the slopes of surrounding hills). In 1993, the tax administration estimated that the total number of firms in the cluster was 8,000, together generating an annual turnover of US$800 million. Although impressive, this last figure may still underestimate the real numbers. An extrapolation of the survey data for 1993 suggests that the annual turnover of the 1950 small clothing firms amounted to US$280 million alone.

What then fuelled the expansion in the number of firms and the total turnover of clothing and textiles businesses in Gamarra? Four general trends appear to have influenced the cluster's evolution:

- The modernization of the Peruvian countryside and highlands, during past decades, enhanced the demand for cheap and fashionable garments (e.g. T-shirts, shirts and jeans) at the expense of artisan production.
- The widespread impoverishment of the Peruvian population, during 1975–92, assisted in increasing the domestic market for cheap garments by including the population of intermediate cities and of the relatively well-off capital city, Lima.
- The negative impact of import-substitution policies on the efficiency and flexibility of established large, clothing firms (Vega-Centeno, 1988) contributed to their inability to compete in the emerging but dispersed, difficult-to-reach and variegated rural markets, as well as in metropolitan and urban markets for cheap garments.
- The persisting flow of migrants to the capital city of Lima, looking for safety, food, shelter, education, medical care, work and income combined with the rudimentary equipment, production methods, organization, labour skills, management, and product information required to compete in the domestic clothing market led migrants to start clothing businesses, one after another.

To conclude, before the implementation of free trade policies there were many business opportunities for domestic firms who made cheap fashion goods. Migrant entrepreneurs seized these opportunities, taking advantage of low barriers to entry. However, the type of clustering advantages driving the development of the Gamarra cluster were shaped behind protective barriers, and when they came down, the sustainability of the cluster was endangered.

Cross-section data collected in February/March 1994 reveal that clustered firms performed better than the ones outside the cluster, due to factors that are external to individual firms and specific for the cluster area (i.e. clustering advantages). In terms of employment size, clustered firms were, on average, larger than dispersed firms due to higher volumes and forward integration. In terms of employment growth, clustered producers expanded employment to such an extent that they were no longer micro-firms (according to the Peruvian definition), whereas dispersed firms normally added one or two workers to the initial workforce and, hence, remained in the micro-firm category.[6] Further, unpaid family labour is (relatively) rare in clustered firms. The average monthly pay per worker in 1993 was, on average, 30 per cent higher in the cluster.

In terms of monthly average gross sales per worker in 1993, clustered firms do better than dispersed producers, the gap being particularly large for the smallest firms. Clustering thus enables small producers to exploit cluster advantages that help them to overcome resource disadvantages at the firm level. In contrast, 'big is better' for dispersed firms. The better sales record of clustered firms does not necessarily imply a higher income for the entrepreneur, because rents and real estate prices are relatively high in the cluster.

But what type of clustering advantages explain these differences, active or passive collective efficiency? In the cluster, inter-firm division of labour is limited to finishing activities (yielding some cost advantages). Dispersed firms are more involved in subcontracting and also in capacity contracting. The conclusion is that clustering advantages at the level of production (including learning through subcontracting) are too weak to explain the performance gap between clustered and dispersed firms. Labour productivity is higher in the cluster, however, which is partly a result of easier access to experienced workers.

In planning production, information spill-overs from several sources are helpful. It is common practice in the cluster to purchase and disassemble competitor's products, analysing and assimilating the strong points. Sometimes, this boils down to straightforward copying of goods. Most producers lack formal technical knowledge of pattern making, standard sizes, and other basic skills and the products of competitors become their technical guides. Designers are rarely hired, but some producers have attended a training course. But it is more common to see them walking around the neighbourhood, scanning fashion trends and the market penetration of new products. If a novelty appears to be very popular, it is purchased and copied. Thus, the diffusion of still-tacit knowledge and work-in-progress through direct observation is facilitated by the high density of clothing activities in the cluster.

In transacting goods and services, buyers enjoy low costs of search and matching, while sellers realize economies of scale in distributing activities. The costs of using the market mechanism are lower in the cluster on both sides because proximity makes linkages with suppliers of inputs and buyers of output, wholesalers, retailers, and final consumers, easier to maintain.

These advantages are important for small firms which, from an individual point of view, face diseconomies of scale and scope in their transactions. The evidence thus is that clustering advantages which facilitate product planning and lower transaction costs are largely responsible for the observed performance gap, in every size category, between clustered and dispersed producers. These advantages, however, accrue relatively effortlessly to the producer. It is passive collective efficiency which creates an advantage for the producers in the Gamarra cluster.

The Response to Trade Liberalization

As stated earlier, a major purpose of this chapter is to answer the question whether passive collective efficiency can sustain SME competitiveness when protective barriers are lifted, or whether a history of such advantages negatively influences the ability of clustered producers to respond.

In October 1995, a second survey was carried out comparing clustered and dispersed producers. The objective of this survey was to trace the development of the performance gap, to observe changes in the behaviour of firms (regarding the various business processes and with special attention to the possibility of enhanced inter-firm co-operation), and to assess the strategic decision-making capabilities of selected producers (case studies).

Earlier, Peru passed through a long period of economic stagnation and instability. During 1975–92, income per capita fell by 32 per cent. In 1992, per capita income was equal to the 1960 level (Banco Central de Reserva del Perú, 1995: 135). Inflation has been above 10 per cent since 1974, reaching an all time high of 7,650 per cent in 1990, when Alberto

Fujimori was elected president. 1990 was a year of drastic changes in economic policy (Visser, 1996: 83). Import tariffs were lowered from an average of 63 per cent in 1985 to 16 per cent in 1994 (Banco Central de Reserva del Perú, 1994: 175). Strict tax policies increased revenues from approximately 1 per cent of GDP in 1989 to 11.1 per cent of GDP in 1994 (op. cit.: 88). Other measures were a drastic reduction of the public sector and the elimination of direct and indirect subsidies.

Until 1990, the cluster's development had been marked by the construction of shopping centres and the gradual growth of the cluster in terms of the number of firms and domestic sales. The cluster enjoyed a short period of improved business conditions during 1986–87, when president Alan Garcia applied protectionist, populist and demand-led growth policies.

Meanwhile, clothing imports have been rising. This is also felt in the Gamarra cluster, where producers complain about increasing trade in imported garments (July 1997). These garments are relatively cheap and Peruvian consumers want to pay the lowest price possible. The fact that the imported goods are not made using superior Pyma or Tanguïs cotton varieties (only grown in Peru), does not prevent domestic firms from losing ground in their home market.

The challenge is thus to enhance quality, speed, flexibility, design and sensitivity to fashion requirements elsewhere, in addition to making products at low unit costs. Firms in the Gamarra cluster have to compete with Los Angeles' garment district, for instance. 'The [LA] clothing manufacturers have developed a system of flexible production that allows them to respond to subtle changes in fashion, faster than their Latin American competitors. They also have easy access to a group of trend-setting Californian designers (*The Economist*, 9 August 1997: 19).

The Peruvian clothing industry, however, consists of a small part that is internationally competitive and a large group of firms that have great problems competing with foreign producers.[7] Firms in Gamarra generally belong to this last category. A few producers in the cluster have exported to countries other than Bolivia or Ecuador, but none with success (some even went bankrupt, see Visser, 1996: 165–8).

Survey data for 1995 indicate that, for the group of clustered producers, the monthly average sales per worker decreased by 27 per cent after adjusting for inflation and the appreciation of the Peruvian Sol against the US dollar. According to most clustered producers, the cause of decreasing sales was increasing competitive pressure from new low-cost producers, of both domestic and foreign origin. Traders demanded compensation for the high prices in the form of improved product quality and design. A few producers accordingly invested in new equipment. However, most clustered producers adhered to more routine responses to maintain sales (purchasing a new sales outlet in the cluster area, or undertaking sales promotion trips to the countryside). Some have entered the 'low road to industrialization': cutting costs and prices by firing personnel, stripping products of any decoration and relocating to cheaper but unsafe areas outside the cluster.

These responses do not match the competitive challenge of improving product quality and design and enhancing efficiency. Purchasing new sales outlets implies that scarce financial resources are invested in bricks and cement. Undertaking journeys to regional markets implies high opportunity costs, in addition to revealing a preference for self-reliance instead of co-operation with specialized traders. Cost-cutting responses lead to poverty. On the other hand, there is no sign of the development of more co-operative linkages with suppliers of inputs, specialist producers or established marketing agents capable of finding and exploiting new markets.

Local Business Groups

With regard to multilateral co-operation, in networks or task groups focused on specific business goals, 1995 was a special year. A total of five initiatives to form such groups were recorded in the cluster. Case-study evidence shows that the mutual acquaintances among local producers helped in establishing the task groups. By the end of the year, one group with the name 'Sociedad de Consorcios de Exportación de Gamarra' (SCG Gamarra) already had 150 members.[8] Below the performance of these groups is reviewed on the basis of fieldwork in 1995 and a visit in 1997.

Multilateral co-operation between a number of producers has awareness-raising effects, making it a potentially important mechanism for clustered producers losing ground in their home market and willing to fight back, although they may not know how to. Among independent producers, it normally takes a respected colleague to question someone's convictions, to discuss strengths and above all weaknesses, and to propose solutions. Owners of small firms tend to be self-confident and stubborn, and this is the case in the Gamarra cluster as well, where producers are part of a long history of learning-by-doing and learning-by-imitation (Visser, 1996: 214, 216). Hence, the awareness-raising effects of multilateral co-operation depend on the extent to which cognitive obstacles to learning are overcome.

Multilateral networking also enables producers to make additional investments, insofar as externalities can be incorporated, indivisibilities avoided, and information problems resolved. Groups and co-operative networks are also better able to contact external agents such as large firms, research and training institutes, banks and authorities, thus transcending the lack of such linkages in the history of the cluster (Visser, 1996). Finally, once small-firm networks manage to achieve a breakthrough in terms of markets, products and skills, the lessons will spread, particularly in a cluster setting.

However, in 1997 SCG Gamarra suffered internal organizational problems that inhibited its intended functioning. The group had anticipated these problems, however, by requesting advice in the fields of international marketing, technological upgrading and management. This assistance was to be supplied by an international development organization but the expert involved became immersed in the socio-cultural differences, mutual prejudices and misunderstandings that have been dividing the Gamarra cluster from its surrounding environment for decades. To outsiders, the producers in the cluster are 'opportunistic' and 'individualistic', while the outsiders, are seen by the cluster members as 'inflexible' and 'academic'. The expert was unable to bridge this divide.

Another group, the GAPOOL (Gamarra T-shirt makers' Consortium) network, was involved in exports to the USA and Canada right from the beginning but without success, however (Visser, 1996: 216). High costs of inputs (fabrics), inappropriate labour skills, insufficient finance and organizational errors were the main problems. Here, a lesson may be to acquire experience with export markets by means of subcontracting arrangements with large firms before becoming involved in independent but potentially painful export ventures.

A third example is APEGA (Gamarra Association of Small Enterprises) (cf. Visser, 1996: 215). The leader of this association claims to represent the interests of small producers renting or owning a workshop in one of the shopping centres in the cluster. (A major source of conflict is that street-sellers do not incur any costs for renting or buying shops.) APEGA also organizes business-oriented activities like weekly training sessions (with guest trainers), trade fairs (in hotels around Lima), and meetings with experienced engineers. APEGA has among other things handled exports to Venezuela, Colombia and Bolivia. A total of 2800 producers participated in one of the above events, while a few hundred are regular visitors and considered as active members. The more direct and active approach to problems with competitiveness which characterizes APEGA has thus been successful so far.

There are at least three reasons why efforts towards multilateral co-operation in the cluster did not meet the high expectations of 1995:

- the organizational inexperience of both leaders and group members;
- the gap between market requirements (e.g. in export markets) and current capabilities (financial, technical, managerial, entrepreneurial and cognitive);
- the wider socio-institutional environment does not favour co-operation.

Let us now consider each in turn.

The division of tasks between different groups is an initial problem that has to be solved by the leaders. Some groups compete on the basis of a large membership, at the expense of internal coherence and strength. Case study evidence indicates that as many problems appear simultaneously, this provokes intense discussions among the members who are unwilling to compromise, however.

The gap between requirements and capabilities is partly due to the inability of owners of small firms to delegate functions to specialized staff, a problem which is particularly acute in the Gamarra cluster, where learning-by-doing and learning-by-imitation has been way to master the technical and commercial aspects of the clothing business. Many producers consider themselves capable of performing any task. They select inputs, purchase and repair machines, hire and fire workers, transact inputs and output, supervise production, monitor subcontractors, make investment decisions, recover loans, pay creditors, and follow fashion trends. As a result, they have had trouble in performing well due to time constraints. This negatively affects the performance of the groups.

However, cognitive bottlenecks are more important. The competitiveness of firms in Gamarra was based on passive forms of collective efficiency that long reinforced standard behaviour among producers in the cluster, which expressed the local mental model of 'best business practices.' Among the main elements of this model is a preference to invest in one of four areas, namely:

- vertical integration (internalize finishing activities);
- the expansion of sewing capacity leading to underutilized machinery;
- additional sale outlets in the cluster area;
- the construction of shopping-centres (in co-operation with other producers).

Additional elements are a preference for simple mass products (T-shirts, track-suits, underwear), satisfaction with unstable, price based, links with traders and a reliance on kinship ties for co-operation. Generally, local sources of information and know-how were considered satisfactory as well.

Self-reliance (as opposed to co-operation), individualism (as opposed to trust) and quick actions and responses ('andar mosca') as opposed to strategic thinking are the key attitudes of this mental model. These attitudes are reinforced by the passive advantages of clustering. However, this model hinders the further development of the cluster and these old attitudes even harden whereas change is highly required because of trade liberalization. This suggests that when clustering is largely based on passive collective efficiency, it may slow down rather than facilitate small-firm development under free trade regimes.

There are also cultural obstacles to building up effective grass-root organizations in Peru. As one thoughtful producer put it in 1997:

> The problem of SCG Gamarra is the problem of all other associations in Peru... We live in a culture of opportunism: taking advantage of each other and of situations. Members of a group are suspicious from the moment they join. They expect that everyone will be "smart". This is in contrast with the norms of honesty that characterize our family, our education and the regions where we were born. It is therefore difficult to build up effective task groups in Gamarra.

This problem manifests itself in particular in the relationship between entrepreneurs in Gamarra and the citizens living in the city surrounding the cluster. This last group often argues that too many migrants have invaded their city during the past decades, and despise the changes that have taken place as a result. Behind this attitude is a clash between Indians (the 'cholos' from the highlands) and Latinos (the 'costeños' or 'Limeños' living in coastal areas). Much of the discussion about the failure of the producer groups to live up to expectations smacks of the usual mutual accusations between the people making a living in Gamarra and a suspicious and sometimes even hostile socio-cultural environment.

Concluding Remarks

The historical mechanisms which earlier enhanced the performance of producers in the Gamarra cluster shaped a local mental model that hinders close inter-firm co-operation. This slows down the process of adjustment to new competitive threats requiring new responses.

The evidence reviewed above concerning the evolution and performance of the Gamarra cluster shows that passive advantages of clustering were sufficient to be successful against dispersed producers before 1990, when trade liberalization started. Since then, however, the clustered producers have been unable to cope with foreign competition. Their responses are based on past experience and business practices that have long been important to thrive and survive, but which have quickly lost relevance in the face of new requirements. However, the clustered producers have created co-operative business networks in order to enhance competitiveness, learning and innovation, but with mixed results.

This evidence thus indicates that clustering may hinder, instead of fostering, small-firm development. A long period of relying on passive advantages of clustering tends to induce a situation of functionally disconnected small firms enjoying the fruits of a one-time location decision. This then becomes the local mental model of best business practice. In this situation, co-operative interactions between producers do not arise spontaneously from clustering, despite the observed reduction in search and monitoring costs; in fact, this effect easily is more than offset by a local opportunism, perceived and real. In addition to the underdevelopment of internal networks within the cluster, local lock-in also hinders linking up with the external environment of the cluster (at the urban, regional or international level). Hence, non-local information and know-how is not imported, reducing the likelihood of enhanced, timely and continuous learning, of innovation, and of the diffusion of innovation.

On the whole, we can therefore conclude that in Gamarra, the advantage of clustered firms compared to dispersed producers turned into a disadvantage as protection was lifted, because the cluster was largely based on passive forms of collective efficiency.

Notes

1. Polanyi (according to Nooteboom, 1992: 289) distinguishes between focal and subsidiary awareness. Much knowledge is tacit in the sense that it is outside the focal sphere of awareness.
2. For a discussion on different types of learning processes, see Visser (1996: 30–1).
3. With regard to innovation, Camagni (1991: 126) distinguishes between a competence-decision gap (the 'impossibility of ... assessing the outcomes of

  alternate actions') and a control gap (in the sense that 'the outcomes of present actions depend on the independent actions of many actors on which the firm has by definition a minimum control'). These two gaps are relatively wide for SMEs.

4. The high density of related economic activities facilitates screening and selection on the basis of local information and reputations. Also, proximity between agents facilitates monitoring.

5. Insofar as one entrepreneur explains a matter over and over again to a colleague so as to convince the latter that a certain adjustment in business practices or some investment is necessary *vis-à-vis* an external event or trend, local meaning is given to the – perhaps rather incomprehensible – external data. So, dialogue cements network linkages and defines their essence: the building-up of a mutual preference for complementary competence and the joint reduction in dynamic uncertainty associated with innovation.

6. We refer to employment growth over time. Hence, the relatively large employment growth among clustered firms may be due to the age factor.

7. The country is not an important player in the world textiles and clothing market. Its share in world trade has been on a downward trend since 1978 and oscillates around 0.10 per cent. Garment exports have been on the rise from US\$14.6 million in 1983 to US\$172 million in 1994, but so has also the denominator of the value of world trade in apparel products. Fifteen large firms account for the bulk of garment exports (Monitor Company, 1995; Visser, 1996: 91–2).

8. This sharp increase in membership was also due to the decision of 'Banco Latino' to start providing working capital to firms in the cluster, with the condition that these be member of a group.

6

Innovation in Roof Tile and Copper Craft Clusters in Indonesia

Henry Sandee and Piet Rietveld

There is increasing evidence that clusters matter in developing countries. This is very true for Indonesia, and especially its densely populated provinces such as Central Java. Klapwijk (1997), using a definition of a cluster as a group of at least five industrial enterprises belonging to the same sub-sector that operate in one village, estimates that there were some 4,400 rural industry clusters by 1989 in Central Java. Together, these clusters contain 675,000 workers, which is around 30 per cent of the total manufacturing labour force. In some districts of this province clustering is very significant: some 75 per cent of the villages in the semi-urban Klaten district contain small-scale or cottage industry clusters. It must be noted, however that the majority of these clusters are dormant or 'pockets of poverty'. They consist of poor household enterprises which operate with traditional technology and aim at low-income markets.

Now that it is widely recognized that clusters matter, attention in the literature is shifting towards cluster dynamics. A main issue is whether dormant clusters can change into more vibrant entities. Some authors use the concept of 'trajectory of cluster development' in the discussion on cluster dynamics (Humphrey, 1995; Knorringa, 1998). This chapter intends to contribute to this discussion while focusing on the process of innovation adoption in two distinct small industry clusters in Central Java, namely roof tile and copper handicraft manufacturing. In our cases, innovation adoption implies technological change which allows enterprises to make better products that can be sold to higher income market segments. Our study illustrates that innovation adoption is highly facilitated by clustering of enterprises. It provides first adopters with flexibility which is of crucial importance for successful cluster transformation. In addition, our case studies show that innovation adoption requires collaboration among small-scale producers to render technological change feasible.

Our first case concentrates on a roof tile cluster located on the outskirts of a small town. Traditional tile production is upgraded with adoption of so-called hand-press technology which, due to indivisibilities, cannot be profitably run by individual producers at the early stages of the transformation process. Our second case focuses on a copper handicraft cluster where innovation adoption leads to a new situation in which producers do no longer manufacture basic household utensils but concentrate on 'modern' products such as vases, mural decorations, lamp shades, and other handicrafts. The new market is highly dynamic but unstable which has stimulated early adopters to develop flexible employment strategies and certain traditional producers become their additional wage workers during peak periods. The innovation adoption process is in this case characterized by the introduction of new designs and gradual upgrading of equipment allowing step-by-step improvement of the quality of output.

The second section discusses a framework to assess transformation of traditional clustered enterprise. Our case studies are presented in the subsequent sections. Data and information were collected within the framework of different research projects and this clearly limits our attempts to compare the innovation adoption process in both clusters. The third section presents the characteristics of the clusters prior to the start of innovation adoption. In the fourth and fifth sections we discuss and compare innovation adoption and diffusion processes in both clusters. We find that there are still many producers who have not (yet) adopted the new technology and in the sixth section we look at the constraints on innovation adoption. Conclusions are drawn in the last section where we consider the implications of our cases for cluster dynamics, and discuss different approaches to innovation adoption and diffusion in clustered enterprises.

Transformation of Clustered Enterprises

Prospects for small industry clusters are likely to differ as they belong to distinct manufacturing sub-sectors which each have their specific characteristics with regard to the importance of scale economies in production and marketing, price and income elasticities of demand, and the related significance of market segmentation (Nadvi and Schmitz, 1994). The possibilities for cluster transformation should be viewed, of course, for each manufacturing sub-sector separately. In general, however, it requires significant changes in both production and marketing systems. In order to survive and expand their businesses, small-scale producers need to look for new markets in which relatively rich consumers are found. These markets are frequently not served by their traditional agents and intermediaries, and it becomes necessary to channel the output in new ways. Given the complex nature of technological change, cluster transformation through innovation adoption is limited to the most promising traditional clusters (Sandee *et al.*, 1994; Sandee, 1998).

Cluster transformation may be viewed as a multi-dimensional process which leads to many changes: new technology is introduced which requires new inputs, new skills, new production processes, new equipment, and the opening of new marketing channels. It may lead to establishment of new producers and/or service units in the cluster. Skills need to be upgraded, and it may no longer be possible to rely on family labour and relatives only. Furthermore, and very importantly, the introduction of new technology may not be possible without changes in the business relations *among* producers. The new technology package is often not tailored fully to the traditional organization of production and marketing, and it is likely to disrupt traditional practices (Sandee, 1995).

Transformations do not come about by themselves but they need to be initiated by actors who function as agents of change. A distinction can be made between producer-driven and buyer-driven initiatives to trigger innovation adoption. In the former case, the producers themselves are the key actors who introduce new technology in the cluster. In many cases, however, producers lack the access to information and funds to initiate change, and intermediaries from outside, such as traders, lead the introduction of new ideas, designs, and technology in the cluster.

Our distinction is rather similar to Knorringa's classification of cluster trajectories. According to Knorringa (1998) there are two trajectories that capture the development of 'top segment' traditional clusters in developing countries. Either a basic cluster of small enterprises becomes a 'satellite' district in which firms produce for actors outside the cluster, such as wholesale traders or retailers, or the transformation is initiated by actors inside the cluster. Selected producers can take the lead and with time, they will be increasingly surrounded by smaller units that supply them as subcontractors or supply to other, usually less attractive, market channels.

This latter form is particularly relevant to understanding the cases presented here. We therefore focus on producer-driven innovation adoption and argue that technological change requires collaboration among firms to develop into more explicit co-operation, with specific purposes and based on explicit arrangements (Schmitz, 1997: 10).

Characteristics of Traditional Tile Production

The roof tile cluster in the village Karanggeneng is located on the outskirts of the small town Boyolali in Central Java. In 1987, tiles from Karanggeneng were known as high-quality traditional output. Thanks to good transport facilities, the producers in this cluster have access to wide markets, compared with surrounding clusters. In 1987 there were some 120 tile producers in the cluster.

In traditional tile production, preparing clay is done through feet pounding while simple moulds are used for printing. A kiln is used for firing tiles. There are both male and female producers in this cluster. Producers in Karanggeneng make use of both family and paid labour in the production process. There is a clear division of labour within the enterprise and also between enterprises and suppliers of inputs and services. Female workers are mainly employed in printing tiles while men are dominant in the other stages of the production process.

The majority of traditional producers in Karanggeneng did not sell directly to final consumers. Some producers sell exclusively to traders and their production sites are on land owned by traders, who also control a number of clay pits in the village. Purchase and transport of inputs and outputs are then generally taken care of by the traders. Another category sell their tiles exclusively to building materials shops. They work on contract for specific shops, which provide them with regular orders and down payments. There are also producers who receive their orders from other producers in the cluster whenever the orders they accept exceed their own production capacity. In contrast, there are traditional producers who sell directly to final consumers. In these cases, they organize the transport of tiles to the customer by truck drivers.

Table 6.1 presents a comparison of tile producers selling their tiles through different chains. Table 6.1 shows that traditional producers with direct access to markets do not only sell more tiles than the others

Table 6.1 Traditional tile producers and marketing chains in Karanggeneng (dry season 1987, approximately 6 months)

	Sales to intermediaries ($n = 23$)	Direct sales to customers ($n = 11$)	All producers ($n = 34$)
Tile output (number)	62,400	67,100	63,900
Average tile price (Rs)	20.4	29.5	23.3
Industrial capital (Rs 000s)	264.6	659.7	392.4
Age of owner (years)	32	47	38

but also sell tiles at higher prices. It also shows that these producers have invested more in their business. They are also older than the others suggesting that producers build up their enterprise gradually through the years.

The advantage of clustering in this case is that it allows co-operation in the execution of large construction projects, such as the production of tiles for schools or market shelters. Out-contracting of work is, in such cases, very common. In Karanggeneng, family ties are very important and most producers can easily point out a number of relatives who are also involved in tile production. Out-contracting of work takes place mostly within such kinship networks and this provides opportunities for business expansion that would be absent in the case of dispersed enterprises. There is also frequent exchange of workers among enterprises belonging to the same extended family and some producers work occasionally for relatives. Relatives are also an important source of working capital. Leaders provide advice on quality of output, and they offer apprenticeships to their extended family. Clustering makes it also possible to develop a specialized casual labour force for clay processing and firing tiles. Individual producers do no longer have to allocate their own resources to these services, but can buy them on the market. This narrows the scope of distinct tasks for individual producers which may increase their efficiency.

Characteristics of Traditional Copper Craft Production

The village of Tumang is located on the slopes of the mountain Merbabu in Central Java, relatively isolated from main urban centres. In the past, the isolated location of the village was even more pronounced as there was no asphalt road leading to the cluster. Tumang has a long tradition in copper manufacturing. There are some 400 producers in the cluster. Traditionally, the industry in the cluster is small-scale with output mainly consisting of kitchen utensils with pots being the most important item. A substantial part of the market is in rural areas; the copper pots produced are suitable for cooking with firewood, which is still a main source of energy in rural Java, as opposed to urban Java where paraffin is used. During the 1980s, traditional copper kitchen utensils have faced increasing competition from aluminium and plastic products which are very popular. They are considerably cheaper, but less durable than copper and cannot be recycled easily. Traditionally, copper manufacturing is done almost exclusively by men, and most enterprises rely on family labour only.

Table 6.2   Traditional copper craft producers in Tumang, 1985

	Weekly output average (Rs 000s)	Industrial capital average (Rs 000s)	Average age
All producers (*n* = 27)	36	89	38

Sources: Rietveld and Gorter, 1990; Yuwono, 1993.

Table 6.2 presents basic data on traditional copper production in the Tumang cluster. Weekly output is so low that copper manufacturing was unlikely to be the only source of income for the producers and their families. Industrial capital is limited which makes it possible to exit copper production at low costs. In 1985, all producers sold their output at the local village market where traders and other buyers gathered almost every afternoon.

The main advantages of clustering in this case are associated with acquisition of inputs and marketing of output. Copper sheets and other raw materials are purchased jointly by producers at city markets which are some 75 kilometres away. Suppliers of inputs visit the market in Tumang. This market is also the main outlet for the traditional kitchen utensils as various types of intermediaries collect the output and bring it to many cities in Central Java. Production linkages among firms were rare, and there is little evidence of out-contracting. Producers did not produce for specific customers but, instead, they produced for the village market where they bargained daily with buyers.

Comparing Traditional Tile and Copper Craft Clusters

The clusters show common characteristics which are typical features of cottage industry clusters in Indonesia and many other developing countries. They consist of household enterprises which are still firmly embedded in the rural household economy. The labour force is mainly family. They operate with traditional technology that has not changed substantially for many decades. Both clusters are well embedded in regional networks. Inputs are not only acquired locally, and output is aimed at supra-local markets. Inter-firm linkages are generally under-developed and concern out-contracting jobs only. External economies are confined mainly to joint acquisition of inputs and marketing of output.

A main difference between clustering of traditional tile and copper handicraft enterprises concerns the production cycle. Tiles are produced in batches and a full cycle lasts some 4–5 days, while copper handicraft producers bring their traditional pots to the local market every day. Initial investment is higher in tile production and profits as well.

Innovation Adoption and Leading Actors

When we now look back, we can conclude that the basic condition for cluster transformation and technological change in Karanggeneng and Tumang was satisfied. Tiles of better quality, so-called pressed tiles, and artistic copper products were in great demand, and producers in both clusters were aware of this. Neither Karanggeneng nor Tumang were among the poorest and most isolated traditional clusters. Their producers have relatively well-developed skills and the clusters are embedded in regional trade networks and not exclusively oriented to local customers. However, innovation adoption will not take place without *actors* who take the lead under uncertain circumstances when the advantages of new production methods and marketing channels have not yet been proven.

The process of innovation adoption in both clusters was *producer-driven* with local entrepreneurs as the leading agents of change. This contrasts with buyer-driven innovation adoption where customers or intermediaries are the primary agents of change.

Early Diffusion of Hand-press Technology in the Tile Cluster

In the case of Karanggeneng, adoption of hand-press technology was initiated by a small group of leaders from families with long-term involvement in traditional tile production. Successful pioneer adoption in the tile cluster is explained primarily by two factors. First, traditionally leading producers got access to information on more productive technologies. Initially, they knew about pressed tiles but had not had the opportunity to 'see and feel' the new equipment. It took a trip co-financed by producers, local government and a nearby university to give them a chance to actually see the hand-press technology with their own eyes, and assess together whether they were technically and financially able to adopt it. Secondly, leading producers were able to step out of their traditional networks and develop joint action together with their competitors. This required flexibility and willingness to explore new strategies. Joint action worked because local leaders saw clear economic advantages.

Hand-press production contains the same phases in the production process as the traditional technology. The main difference is that printing is done with presses instead of wooden moulds. Pressing such tiles requires a better clay mixture, which is obtained through introduction of a diesel-driven clay mixer. In addition, it also requires the purchase of better-quality wood to reach higher temperatures. All pioneers financed the purchase of the hand-press out of their funds.

An essential (and the most expensive) element of the hand-press technology package is the motorized clay mixer. Since one mixer can be used in combination with about six hand-presses an indivisibility problem emerges in the first phase of adoption. This was solved by one of the pioneer adopters who bought the clay mixer after receiving assurance from the other pioneers that they would buy presses and use the services of the mixer. A new network was formed among the pioneers as a necessary condition for producer-driven adoption of new technology with indivisible elements.

Relations among these pioneers were mutually beneficial and based on economic calculations. Orders for pressed tiles were shared, the mixer was used in turns, and the new output was promoted jointly. Pioneers also co-operated to create a supportive infrastructure, including credit for working capital and repair services. All pioneer adopters belong to the group of producers that were previously selling their traditional tiles directly to consumers. They continued to do so after adoption of the hand-press technology.

Early Innovation Adoption in the Copper Craft Cluster

In the copper craft cluster innovation adoption was an incremental process. In contrast with tile production, technological change in the copper handicraft industry is a gradual process which allows producers to purchase new equipment piece by piece in accordance with their financial means. Further, innovation adoption in the copper handicraft cluster does not encounter technological indivisibilities which require collaboration among adopters. Small investments and basic skills upgrading are sufficient to start making products according to new designs. However, as we discuss below, there are advantages (scale economies) associated with manufacturing new products on a larger scale which may explain why there are so few adopters in Tumang compared with Karanggeneng.

Innovation started after 1979 when the local branch office of the Ministry of Industry organized a series of training courses in the village which focused on both technical and managerial skills needed for innovation adoption. As a follow-up, selected producers of Tumang took up apprenticeships in workshops in Yogyakarta and Bandung which improved their technical skills enormously. Moreover, the apprenticeships were very useful to develop marketing networks: later on we see that these workshops contract out orders to adopters in the Tumang cluster. In general, marketing new output was indeed a barrier that had to be overcome since new products could no longer be marketed through the local village market. Consequently a much more active approach is required to reach new groups of urban and, occasionally, international buyers.

Diffusion of Innovations

We have access to data on innovation adoption in both clusters in 1993. In that year about 50 per cent of the tile producers in Karanggeneng had adopted the hand-press technology while only some 3 per cent had switched to new designs in Tumang. This gives the impression that technological change has been much more successful in the tile cluster compared with the copper handicraft cluster. We will argue below that this conclusion is not necessarily true. The clusters show very different patterns of transformation. In the tile cluster, firms have remained relatively small and increasing demand for new products has been accommodated through growth of the number of adopting enterprises. In Tumang, demand for new products has resulted in the emergence of a limited number of relatively large and flexible firms. Innovation diffusion cannot be understood without noting patterns of inter-firm linkages. In Karanggeneng, technological indivisibilities are the key to understand the deepening of these linkages, while in Tumang the emergence of traders and large firms, which are placing large orders, have stimulated the development of a flexible but skilled labour force to accommodate periods of peak demand. In both clusters, adopters have been able to develop their enterprises on a scale that would not have been possible if they had not been embedded in a cluster of small firms.

The cluster Karanggeneng was regularly mentioned in the regional newspapers during the period 1990–93. Problems regarding the negative environmental impact of tile manufacturing were temporarily solved, because the local government allocated additional sites for clay digging. Urban expansion of nearby Boyolali city resulted in a diversion of heavy traffic which is no longer allowed to pass through its main street. Instead, the traffic passes through Karanggeneng, and this makes the tile cluster even more accessible to buyers. Both developments have stimulated further adoption of the hand-press technology. There were

Table 6.3   Logit regression analysis for adoption in Karanggeneng, 1993 (sample of 29 press and traditional producers)

Variable	coefficient	*t* value
Age entrepreneur (years)	−0.05	−0.47
Education (years)	1.93	1.84
Gender (dummy)[a]	3.01	0.85
Social network (dummy)[b]	4.30	1.92[c]
Trade network (dummy)[d]	−3.21	−2.45[c]
Output 1987	−15.05	−1.51
Constant	−0.01	−1.41
Log likelihood[e]	−6.51	

Notes:
[a] The sample group included only 3 female producers. They are underrepresented in the group and this may have been the reason why gender has no significant impact on innovation in the logit analysis.
[b] If a producer considered himself/herself to be a relative of a certain identified pioneer adopter the dummy score was one, while the score was zero otherwise.
[c] Significant at 0.05 level.
[d] When producers sell through traders the dummy score is one, while the score was zero otherwise.
[e] The log likelihood is a measure of the average fit often used in logit models (see for example, Cramer, 1991).
Source: Sandee (1995: 125).

some 50 adopters by 1993 while the annual number of new adopters levelled off in 1992 and 1993.

Logit regression analysis was carried out to analyse which variables explain innovation adoption for a limited set of producers.[1] Table 6.3 summarizes the main results.

Table 6.3 shows that specific characteristics of individual entrepreneurs, such as age and education, are of limited importance when it comes to adoption. We see, however, that the networks in which producers operate need to be taken into account. Collaboration among pioneer adopters did gradually fade away in favour of the re-emergence of traditional forms of co-operation which are structured around kinship networks. Once the risks and uncertainties of technological change were reduced, traditional production and marketing patterns were upgraded to incorporate the new technology. Power-driven mixers are now shared by pioneers and their relatives. The logit regression analysis shows that the social network in which producers operate matters. Adoption is facilitated if there is a family relationship with a pioneer adopter as the latter is interested to upgrade and expand profitable hierarchical networks. To the new adopters, the arrangement guarantees indirect access to markets as orders are provided through subcontracting linkages. Equipment is bought with the assistance of the pioneer, and technical and financial assistance are provided for innovation.

Table 6.3 also indicates that producers who sell exclusively to traders are in a disadvantageous position with regard to innovation adoption. Traders link the producers in Karanggeneng to rural households, and this market segment shows little interest in buying pressed tiles. With this small number of observations, no significant impact could be found for gender although we know that women producers face stringent barriers to innovation adoption in this tile cluster. Successful traditional producers were expected to find it easier to deal with the risks of innovation than others, and, consequently, feature prominently among the early adopters. However, the coefficient for output in 1987 is negative: the introduction of the innovation has led to a rather different distribution of income among producers. We found that this development can be understood, on the one hand by the occurrence of technological indivisibilities in innovation adoption, and, on the other hand, by the obligation felt by pioneer adopters to turn first to their relatives when they intend to diffuse the handpress technology in the cluster.

Traditionally, this tile cluster is characterized by unequal access to markets with some producers being able to sell to whoever they want while others mainly produce for specific producers, traders, or other intermediaries. The pioneer adopters in Karanggeneng were producers who were key actors in the production and marketing of traditional tiles. Innovation adoption required collaboration to overcome technological indivisibilities. First, this was done through collaboration with other pioneers, later, through upgrading of traditional networks. The enterprises of local leaders have grown throughout the years in terms of capital investments and number of workers. There are however both physical and economic limits to growth of individual enterprises. In Karanggeneng it is an exception to find adopting firms with a labour force of more than seven workers. Tile production uses much space, especially for drying the tiles prior to firing, and in densely populated Karanggeneng the expansion of individual firms will not be possible without taking over the production sites of neighbours. In addition, the production cycle cannot be shortened without significant new investments in kilns and additional space constraints. Consequently, the transformation of the cluster shows an expansion of upgraded traditional networks and a growth of the number of adopters. Thus local leaders grow not so much through continued expansion of their own production but rather, due to their favourable access to markets, by means of intensified out-contracting of orders to their network of adopters.

In the copper handicraft cluster in Tumang, producers are not either adopters or non-adopters. Rather, the share of new types of products ranges from 0 to 100 per cent. In 1985 there were eight operators who had started the adoption process.

Four possible determinants of the degree of adoption have been distinguished: age, education, participation in specific training courses organized by government agencies, and output as an indicator of the scale of the enterprise (Rietveld and Gorter, 1990). The age of the entrepreneur and education play significant roles in the decision to follow courses. Older producers and those with little education are less interested in courses on new designs and production methods compared with their younger, more educated counterparts. A different picture holds, however, for innovation, the results for which are shown in Table 6.4. Age and education do not play a role in innovation adoption. Further, innovation is not limited to course participants.

These findings are rather similar to what was found in the tile cluster in Karanggeneng where we also found that pioneer adopters do not have specific age or educational characteristics. In the tile cluster, we found that pioneer adopters were leaders of specific traditional networks who

Table 6.4   Regression with innovation adoption as dependent variable in Tumang, 1985 (sample of 35 copper firms)[a]

Variable	coefficient	*t* value
Constant	−3.27	−0.59
Age	−0.09	−0.73
Education	−0.17	−0.45
Output	0.36	2.19[b]
Participation in courses	0.45	1.14
$R^{2\,c}$	0.71	

Notes:
[a] Rietveld and Gorter (1990) also carry out ordered logit regression while adjusting for the fact that while all semi-and full adopters are represented in the sample, only some 20 per cent of the non-adopters were sampled. We do not present those results here as the findings do not differ significantly from the findings presented in Table 6.4.
[b] Significant at 0.05 level.
[c] R^2 in an indicator of the fit of the model. In this model 71 per cent of the total variance in the dependent variable (innovation adoption) is explained.
Source: Rietveld and Gorter, 1990: 14–16.

were willing and able to take the risks associated with technological change and cluster transformation. To some extent, it seems that the same holds true for Tumang. Table 6.4 indicates that the output level, an indicator of firm size, is a significant determinant of the adoption of innovations.

A new research project found that there were 12 adopters in the Tumang copper handicraft cluster in 1993, compared with 8 adopters in 1985 (Yuwono, 1993). The number of adopters was still very small given the fact that there were still more than 400 traditional producers in Tumang. Innovation adoption in this cluster requires new skills, new designs, new investments to purchase a range of new equipment, and new marketing skills. The obstacles to upgrading production and marketing seems to be larger in the case of the copper handicraft cluster than in the tile cluster.

We can distinguish between two groups of innovators in Tumang. First, there are adopters who sell their output mainly to selected buyers. These buyers include, on the one hand, large firms that have subcontracted specific orders to producers in the cluster. Output from Tumang is frequently processed further in these large firms as the necessary equipment, for so-called finishing, is expensive. On the other hand, this group includes a variety of large government and private institutions and firms that participate in the official 'Foster Father' subcontracting scheme which aims at improving the links between small and large enterprises in Indonesia. The scheme includes activities such as assistance in marketing output, technical training, general training, and provision of subsidized credit lines. Secondly, there are producers who sell the output themselves at markets in nearby cities like Solo, Yogyakarta, and Semarang, while they also receive orders from visitors to Tumang. There are examples of occasional visitors from Hong Kong and Taiwan who have spotted Tumang products at exhibitions and come down to the cluster. Recently, the introduction of mobile phones and faxes in the cluster has stimulated the contacts between buyers from Jakarta and Surabaya and from overseas.

Table 6.5 provides a comparison between some characteristics of the two groups of adopters in the copper handicraft cluster. Producers who have institutional consumers as their main market outlet operate on a larger scale and their firms are bigger. They have higher turnovers and employ more workers. Their profit margins are lower than those of their counterparts, who sell exclusively to final consumers, because bargaining with institutional consumers, who are mainly larger firms, is likely to be difficult compared to dealings with final buyers who do not

Table 6.5   Innovators selling to institutional consumers and final consumers (each group consists of 6 producers)

	Institutional consumers	Final consumers
Labour force (persons)	13.7	4.8
Turnover last month (Rs)	590,000	210,000
Profit margin (%)	31.6	42.3
Percentage of output sold to institutional consumers (%)	70	0

represent firms or institutions. Thus the main advantage associated with access to institutional markets is a large turnover and high income albeit at lower profit margins compared with those selling directly to final consumers. Table 6.5 indicates further that even the producers selling to institutional buyers sell part of their output to households through which they can generate higher margins.

Innovation adoption in Tumang has not given rise to the emergence of inter-firm linkages and collaboration as in the tile cluster in Karanggeneng. Adoption of the new technological package has been individual. There were no technological indivisibilities that required joint action. Individual firms have built up their new capital stock gradually through regular small investments whenever profits allowed them to do so.

Access to higher income market segments, especially foreign customers, required access to expensive finishing equipment which is characterized by significant technological indivisibilities. These indivisibility problems were overcome by means of collaboration with large firms outside the cluster. The need to gain access to such equipment is a key in understanding the development of subcontracting relationships between institutional buyers and Tumang adopters.

One may be inclined to conclude that in Tumang innovation has not resulted in significant cluster transformation given the limited number of adopters throughout the years. However, there have been substantial changes in the copper handicraft cluster which are not revealed by focusing exclusively on the number of adopters. In Tumang adopters have developed their business on a much larger scale compared to Karanggeneng. Their firms have grown from household enterprises to small firms with a growing paid labour force. Physical expansion of firms in this cluster is much more feasible than in the tile cluster where it would require taking over the production sites of neighbouring producers. Moreover, larger production units in the copper handicraft cluster generate substantial scale economies as a consequence of a gradual but steady growth of capital goods and access to a large but flexible labour force.

Demand for modern copper handicraft products is rather unstable throughout the year as it depends on the number of specific construction projects, festivities, etc. Adopters in Tumang have developed a strategy to accommodate demand fluctuations which would not have been possible without the nearby presence of non-adopters. Adopting producers employ traditional producers on a large scale as wage workers whenever there are large orders. It does happen that specific orders require the services of more than 100 traditional producers who then become casual workers. Technological change in Tumang has given rise to the development of large and flexible networks which allow adopters to enter profitable but unstable market segments.

Constraints on Innovation Adoption

In both clusters there are still traditional producers who have not (yet) adopted upgraded technology. We cannot fully understand their behaviour by means of an approach which focuses on individual entrepreneurs only. Innovation adoption is not only a matter of individual producers comparing costs and benefits of technologies, but also a matter of access. In both clusters, there are clear indications that certain producers are not allowed direct access to the new technology by the leading adopters.

After the very dynamic year in 1989, the annual number of new adopters in Karanggeneng decreased although there appeared to be sufficient benefits which would justify further innovation adoption in the cluster, as shown in Table 6.6.

Table 6.6 shows that adoption of the hand-press technology leads to multiplication of turnover and an almost 100 per cent increase in the

Table 6.6   Comparison of traditional and press tile producers, census data, 1993

	Traditional producers ($n = 53$)	Press producers ($n = 49$)
Seasonal turnover (Rs 000s)	1,880	9,184
Age producer (years)	46.8	44.0
Education (years)	3.0	6.2
Labour force (persons)	3.2	6.0

labour force. It shows further that traditional and press producers do not differ with respect to age, although there are some differences with respect to education.

We need to understand the strategies of network leaders to fully understand the constraints on complete adoption. From the viewpoint of network leaders there are three strategies for accommodating the increase in demand for pressed tiles. They can produce more tiles themselves, they can contract out more jobs to existing adopters, or they can stimulate more traditional producers to innovate. We note that the first and second strategies are popular but that certain groups of traditional producers are excluded from innovation adoption. Constraints on adoption are particularly felt by female tile producers. By 1993, no female entrepreneur had adopted the press technology although they constitute some 25 per cent of all producers in the cluster. Access to press networks and dissemination of information on the new production technique is limited to men. In general, we see in Karanggeneng that female producers are confronted with norms which do not stimulate adoption (Wahjana, 1994). Such an effective exclusion mechanism also applies to specific groups of male producers. These groups consist primarily of traditional producers who sell their output through local leaders and intermediaries. They are embedded in networks where they have the specific task of producing traditional tiles. The Karanggeneng cluster remains an important centre for traditional output, and both local leading producers and intermediaries are reluctant to stimulate further innovation diffusion. Thus stimulating innovation diffusion in the tile cluster was especially relevant in the early years because there was a need to share the risks, tackle technological indivisibilities, and arrive at a 'critical' level of production which put Karanggeneng on the map as a centre for production and trade in press tiles. Consequently, specific traditional networks were upgraded and geared towards pressed tile production. These networks become the focal point for generating scale economies and growth of demand for pressed tiles are now met in the first place through more production and investment in the existing press tile networks.

We do not have recent survey data on traditional producers in the Tumang cluster, and, consequently, our assessment is based on qualitative observations made during several visits. The majority of producers in Tumang continue to produce traditional output which is still sold locally to rural consumers. The decision of certain entrepreneurs to innovate has not disadvantaged the traditional producers. Their position may even have improved since the size of competitive output is reduced.

In addition, the new production lines of the adopters have created opportunities for casual labour for traditional producers.

Thus it seems that the low adoption rate in the copper handicraft cluster is related to the following factors. First, scale economies have emerged which make it increasingly difficult for traditional producers to catch up with the quickly expanding adopters. Current adopters dominate contacts with buyers which may limit innovation adoption. Secondly, traditional producers are no longer completely dependent on the production of basic utensils as a source of income, but they are now also earning wage income through flexible involvement in the production processes of modern producers.

Conclusions

In this chapter, we have compared innovation adoption in two clusters previously studied in separate research projects. In both cases, technological change can be characterized as producer-driven product innovations leading to process innovations. In both cases innovation adoption leads to the production of new output which can no longer be sold through traditional marketing channels.

Innovation adoption and the (lack of) diffusion among clustered producers cannot be fully understood when we focus on individual producers only. We need to take account of inter-firm linkages while explaining technological change. In tile production, clustering facilitates collaboration among producers because of technological indivisibilities. We found, however, that collaboration will only last as long as it is relevant for leading producers. In the tile cluster there are physical limits to enterprise expansion in a densely populated area. This has stimulated the increasing emergence of subcontracting relationships. In the copper handicraft cluster, we saw that adopters expand their enterprise to generate scale economies and aim at dynamic market segments. The flexible nature of the demand for modern copper products has been accommodated by means of a flexible labour force which retains a foothold in traditional production.

Finally, we show in this chapter that cluster transformation through innovation adoption should not be approached solely by focusing on changes in the number of adopting enterprises through time. We have shown that additional insights into technological change processes in clusters may be acquired when we look at other factors as well. For example, in the tile cluster many adopters are, in fact, subcontractors who are firmly embedded in specific networks which are headed by specific pioneer adopters, while in the copper handicraft cluster, many traditional producers are also involved in modern production albeit as wage workers. We conclude that assessments of cluster transformation reveal that innovation adoption is not only a matter of individual choice but it is also a matter of participation in networks.

Note

1.   We refer to Sandee (1995) for a discussion on the specifications of the applied logit regression analysis.

7
Light Engineering Networks and Structural Adjustment in Zimbabwe

Charles M. Halimana and Árni Sverrisson

This chapter analyses the light engineering sector in Zimbabwe and the effects of structural adjustment.[1] We argue that these effects are heterogeneous and depend on the location of companies within the structure of the light engineering industry, and on how managers and proprietors perceive the effects of structural adjustment. The chapter is based on material gathered by the authors in Zimbabwe over a number of years in surveys and interviews. First, an outline of the recent history of light engineering in Zimbabwe is presented and its basic structure outlined. We proceed to summarizing the evidence on sector level, and then we discuss the strategic options which are currently available to enterprises in the light engineering sector in Zimbabwe. In this discussion we focus on how social networking impacts on technology and vice versa, and how the options were perceived by our interlocutors in the context of adjustment, drought and political turbulence.

Light Engineering Before Independence

Elsewhere, Halimana (1995) has presented a detailed picture of the light engineering sector in Zimbabwe, and we shall only recapitulate the main highlights here. During the Unilateral Declaration of Independence (UDI) period, 1965–80, economic sanctions and the strict import regulations imposed by the government worked in effect as protective measures for Zimbabwean industry.

However, import regulations and sanctions also made machine imports difficult. Therefore, industries in Zimbabwe generally use very old machinery. This is also the case in the light engineering industry as can be seen in Table 7.1 which shows the vintage percentage of machinery in operation (formal sector only) in 1990 (Halimana, 1995:

Table 7.1   Age distribution of machines in
light engineering firms in 1990

Vintage	Percent
1880–1889	1.0
1890–1899	1.0
1900–1909	0.0
1910–1919	1.9
1920–1929	5.8
1930–1939	3.9
1940–1949	7.7
1950–1959	15.4
1960–1069	20.2
1970–1979	20.2
1980–1989	23.1

75). A large number of general purpose engineering firms were therefore established during the UDI period, based on the production of spares and various rehabilitation and rebuilding work and the imitation capability, which had been established earlier, was dramatically expanded. In addition, companies manufacturing different types of equipment for other industries grew in number. This activity, fairly sophisticated by African standards, had started to spread during the sixties, but grew rapidly in the seventies, after the UDI (Ndlela, 1986:46). A similar pattern can be observed in the production of equipment for agriculture and mining, two mainstays of the Zimbabwean economy. Military operations during the seventies also created local demand for engineering products.

Light Engineering after 1980

After the liberation of the country in 1980, many old companies in the light engineering sector were closed, and new took their place. Of the companies studied by Halimana in his 1990 survey, 43 per cent had been established in the 1980s (Halimana, 1995: 27). If we add to this the companies which changed hands during the 1980s or just before 1980 it is clear that at least half of the current owners of formal sector companies in the light engineering industry in Zimbabwe entered the field in relation to the inauguration of majority rule.

Before 1980, educational policies reserved training for skilled work to white (and occasionally coloured) youths. Further, in large factories and manufacturing establishments such as light engineering companies, machine shops and foundries, skilled workers usually acted and act as supervisors and effectively ran the production side of the companies. A large number of semi-skilled workers most of whom were black and trained at their current place of work performed the actual work. One consequence of this is that the skilled white workers were able to develop contacts with customers while working for others, contacts which then formed the basis for their own businesses later on or success-ful take-overs of existing companies. This type of social capital could not be accumulated easily by black workers, and was in particular much more difficult to acquire than technical skills per se. As a result, the new owners of formal light engineering companies were almost all white persons: light engineering workshops owned by black persons in Zim-babwe were then and are still mainly confined to the so-called informal sector.[2] These latter workshops are mostly limited to making metal structures and household utensils, and other cutting, welding and bend-ing activities (cf. Zwizwai and Powell, 1991; Jeans, 1995). Machining (turning, planing, etc.) is rarely found.

Table 7.2 shows the *volume of production indices* for clothing and footwear, wood and furniture, metal and metal products and all manu-facturing.[3] The cyclical patterns of the different indices are similar. If we compare metalworking with the aggregated index, we can see that both reached a maximum in 1991, and thereafter volumes fell dramatically. We can also observe that the growth in metalworking after 1980 is much less than in all manufacturing, in contrast to the pre-1980 situation. If we compare the numbers for metalworking with wood and furniture and clothing and footwear we see that these latter activities have fared much better over the post-1980 period as a whole.

In the early 1990s, the context of manufacturing, including the light engineering sector, changed with the introduction of structural adjust-ment policies, or ESAP (Economic Structural Adjustment Programme). The protection afforded local industry through a quarter-century of sanctions, import substitution and foreign exchange regulations came to an end. The effects of this show up in Table 7.2. The indices for all manufacturing as well as for clothing and footwear turn down, whereas wood and furniture appears to thrive.

The wood sector sells most of its finished products locally and does not have to contend with significant import competition. It is, in other words, inwardly oriented. In contrast, the clothing and footwear sector, which boomed after Independence behind protective barriers, now competes with cheap imported products, and also competes with foreign buyers for local raw materials. It was and is therefore very

Table 7.2   Volume of production indices, 1970–94

Year	Clothing and footwear	Wood and furniture	Metals and metal products	All manufacturing groups
1970	78.7	71.7	60.3	66.5
1971	83.8	77.3	69.9	72.6
1972	91.5	82.6	80.1	81.4
1973	92.0	88.3	91.0	87.4
1974	96.3	94.1	99.3	93.8
1975	90.8	84.4	98.6	91.6
1976	86.1	76.9	91.1	86.0
1977	82.9	72.4	78.9	81.2
1978	75.3	76.9	78.1	79.2
1979	83.7	86.2	89.7	87.2
1980	100.0	100.0	100.0	100.0
1981	128.4	103.4	104.8	109.4
1982	118.6	85.8	96.4	108.7
1983	109.2	82.3	94.8	105.8
1984	99.9	81.6	89.4	100.7
1985	111.5	82.5	100.5	112.2
1986	106.6	86.5	98.2	115.4
1987	119.5	80.9	95.1	118.1
1988	120.2	95.3	100.4	123.9
1989	137.7	84.5	106.2	130.9
1990	145.0	89.9	111.4	139.1
1991	148.9	101.2	113.5	143.0
1992	124.5	105.9	100.6	129.9
1993	127.7	95.3	82.3	119.3
1994	129.0	107.0	93.2	132.3

Source: Central Statistical Office; *Quarterly Digest of Statistics*, Dec. 1989, table 14.5; Mar. 1995, table 16.0, Harare.

vulnerable to the impact of structural adjustment policies. Metals and metal products also suffered as the perennial problems of the industry with acquiring inputs and capital equipment from abroad were relieved.[4]

This is apparent from Table 7.3 which shows imports of selected categories of machinery (at 1980 prices). The categories shown are those in which local industries can conceivably compete with imports. The aggregate of the selected categories has changed since independence: from a low point in 1984, imports increased steadily up to 1990, whereupon there was a sharp rise followed by a fall in 1993. Comparing with Table 7.2 we can see that production volumes fell already in 1992, i.e. one year earlier.

There are two possible explanations for this. One is the increase in interest rates which followed on ESAP. Interest rates fluctuated around

Table 7.3 Imports (value) of selected categories of machinery, 1981–93 (1980 prices based on building materials index)

Category Year	Artisans Hand Tools	Farm machinery	Textile and leather	Food-processing machinery	Electric machinery apparatus	Heating/cooling equipment	Metal-working machinery	Total
1981	3,235	14,888	11,087	2,756	12,870	2,689	1,785	49,311
1982	3,545	12,729	13,127	1,545	12,719	1,880	1,849	47,393
1983	1,371	16,869	5,842	1,741	9,535	5,082	2,748	43,188
1984	1,140	8,154	3,624	1,707	9,476	3,560	2,453	30,115
1985	2,799	7,208	8,398	1,580	5,804	1,654	2,390	29,834
1986	3,480	9,046	13,587	2,088	7,964	2,600	5,913	44,678
1987	3,838	9,359	9,733	2,997	7,905	3,345	4,548	41,725
1988	4,940	10,836	15,817	3,139	9,494	5,257	8,032	57,514
1989	5,502	11,290	19,737	3,034	10,137	6,468	10,349	66,517
1990	5,061	9,917	19,425	2,513	9,060	6,316	10,360	62,652
1991	6,629	20,562	30,425	2,949	15,647	10,830	14,157	101,198
1992	6,239	27,334	25,579	8,654	7,947	31,289	15,145	122,187
1993	6,414	13,183	12,976	4,275	8,082	8,342	9,268	62,540

10 per cent p.a. (depending on the form of the loan) in 1990 but in 1992–93 they fluctuated around 30 per cent p.a.[5] This tends to discourage investment in new machinery. However, Zimbabwe also suffered from a series of droughts in the early 1990s which have affected agriculture adversely, and in consequence, the entire economy. According to our interviews, the effects of the drought loomed much larger in the evaluation of managers and proprietors of the situation than ESAP. Further, ESAP does not strike all sectors with equal force as we saw in Table 7.2. Engineering firms which relied on work for sectors which are hard hit by ESAP and drought simultaneously have suffered in particular (cf. Asmussen, 1993; Pedersen, 1994).

The bottom line is that rehabilitation and maintenance of old equipment still constitutes a significant source of work for many firms, in spite of the deregulation of imports of machines and machine parts, and is likely to continue to do so in the immediately foreseeable future.[6] However, within this general continuity ESAP has created both opportunities and problems.

Options in the Light Engineering Industry

As structural adjustment has gained momentum, light engineering firms in Zimbabwe have been forced to reconsider earlier choices, based on the protective environment which then prevailed. A number of options is open in this regard, and in this section we analyse the structure of opportunities and the possible consequences for the future development of light engineering in Zimbabwe on the basis of interviews with managers and proprietors. We want to bring home the point that opportunities of firms as well as their possibilities to take advantage of them are not defined simply by key macro-economic variables, but rather depend on how the firms are inserted in local production and distribution networks and on the internal technical and social structure of the firms, both of which are the results of company history or 'company biographies'. Together, the opportunity structure and the potential of individual firms or firm owners create specific conditions for entrepreneurship, which is therefore seen as a process in which opportunities are created or closed, and not just as a process in which opportunities are identified and developed.

The concept 'company' or 'firm' is problematic because a company usually includes many different activities which are networked with the company environment in different ways. As a result of this internal heterogeneity, unified 'company action' is the result of a process in which the integration and orchestration of different activities is constructed and established. In small- and medium-sized companies, closely controlled by their owners, this problem is relatively manageable on a face-to-face basis, however, and does rarely lead to the development of explicit, durable, structures of co-ordination that go beyond conventional accounting. For the purpose of this chapter we will therefore assume that companies are the relevant actors (Morgan, 1986; Sverrisson, 1993). Each company faces networking opportunities and constraints in their environment, and taken together they form a set of options which does not determine unequivocally neither the development of the industry as whole nor the trajectories of individual companies, but are frameworks within which problems are defined and (largely contingent) decisions are made by proprietors and managers. However, it is possible to identify a number of patterns in how the opportunities which present themselves are interpreted from the viewpoint of individual companies, in the light of the technical, financial and social resources at each proprietor's disposal (cf. Trulsson, Chapter 3 and Meyer-Stamer, Chapter 2, this volume). Each pattern can be seen as a *possible* strategy for proprietors facing turbulent and insecure business environments. In the following, we summarize the patterns identified on the basis of our interviews, in the form of relevant strategies pursued by at least some light engineering firms.

Developing Separate Ventures

Developing many separate ventures is a well-known strategy all over Africa, as a means of hedging against uncertainty, and also found in this case. One owner of a light engineering firm had for example developed a stone-cutting business on the side, another was involved in a bus operation and tourism.

In the former case, the company specialized in spares for agricultural machinery. Business in this area was slow because of the droughts. However, there exists a demand for cut and polished stone, for high class buildings such as luxury hotels, for gravestones, etc. (the latter rising because of HIV, which in opposition to drought and famine does not only shorten the lives of the poor). Due to his existing contacts with landowners, on whose land the appropriate rock could be quarried, this entrepreneur was able to acquire his raw material.

Saw blades used for stone-cutting need to be replaced at fairly frequent intervals, because the mixture of cooling water and dust, which is produced at the point of contact with the stone, wears down the cutting edges rather quickly. Earlier, acquiring a steady supply of these blades was a complicated process. After structural adjustment and import deregulation these blades were suddenly easily available through an importer in the vicinity. The skills needed in purchasing, making, maintaining and occasionally, rebuilding machinery for stone-cutting already existed in the company, and workers with the requisite operating skills as well.

In the latter case, the company was also specialized in spares, but this time mainly with customers in industry and transport activities, and prospects were uncertain because of deregulation. The opportunity for the bus company existing alongside the light engineering operation was, in contrast, created by the deregulation of bus services. The vehicle maintenance competence needed had been built and developed partly through the light engineering history of the proprietor but also through the 'safari' part of a tourist service, which had been started earlier on the basis of family connections after sanctions had been lifted and European tourists started to flow in during the 1980s. One of the less glamorous aspects of 'safari' operations is, after all, the somewhat heavy and frequent maintenance which off-road vehicles demand. However, these maintenance-related connections were of relatively little consequence, because there are few services which are so easily and frequently provided by competent outsiders as vehicle maintenance. The main connections were instead financial and family based: in effect, the owners were investing money earned in contracting business niches in opportunities for other, younger, family members in growing business niches.

Developing Technically Related Ventures

Another strategy is to develop ventures related through component provision and subcontracting. One light engineering company, for example, was a part of a conglomerate with a significant share of transactions (around 30 per cent) conducted with other firms in the conglomerate. In a sense, the light engineering activities had originally been conceived as supporting activities related to the other, major, activities of the conglomerate. However, the light engineering activities here were of two very different kinds: on the one hand, metal furniture components (hinges, legs, frames, etc.) were manufactured in large batches, with welding and bending technologies, and then incorporated into the products of a furniture company in the conglomerate, which in this way had gained a competitive advantage in furniture niches where metal components are a significant part (office furniture, school furniture, medical supplies, industrial applications). The advantage had less to do with prices than security of delivery: by controlling the supply of metal components the furniture manufacturer could take on large contracts tendered by the public authorities and not least, large corporations, and avoid the deductions routinely applied to such contracts in case of late delivery. In addition, this part of the light engineering operation made a variety of products and sold components to other furniture manufacturers.

The other light engineering activity was a machine shop, which is a more skill intensive activity with lower tolerance levels. This machine shop would take care of any maintenance needs arising within the conglomerate, and provide the same service to a number of other companies as well. A particularly important aspect was the making of moulds for the manufacture of plastic containers, toys, lids, pipes, etc. This had originally started as a service to others. However, the deregulation of trade had opened the opportunity to expand local production of plastic artefacts, as the flow of the raw material, that is plastic pellets, was ensured, and the neccessary machinery suddenly could be acquired by anyone. Again, by ensuring the reliable supply of a critical component, the moulds, which have to be made according to the specifications of the customer for each product, the conglomerate possessed significant advantage over the competitors, who depended on unrelated or even competing enterprises in this regard.

Expanding the Product Range through Complementary Ventures

The most common form of this strategy was to expand a machining operation by adding the assembly steps, welding, bending, and bolting together, etc. In this way the range of potential products was widened, often on the basis of designs adapted to locally available equipment, skills and materials. Most importantly, however, this made it possible to make products sold directly to end users, eventually through a retailer, and de-link from the fortunes of other companies, particularly those which now became competitors. Thus, for example, one engineering company was launching a new product, playground toys, aimed at a small but lucrative niche, based on the middle-class group which thrives when trade opportunities grow. This company had earlier focused on providing machining services to a large variety of customers, mostly other companies, but the general decrease in demand for such services and the extreme competition that followed had led the owner to look for new ventures.

Focusing Diffuse Demand Through Niche Strategies

Market niches can be analysed from two points of view, from the output side or from the input side. They can, in other words, be seen as constituted by customer groups who demand particular products, or by the utilization of a particular resource or a group of suppliers (Burt and Talmud, 1993). Most of the resources used by light engineering firms in Zimbabwe, except human and social capital (Burt, 1992), are of a general character, and therefore, niches tend to be socially defined.

A nice example of this is the production of bull-bars. Bull-bars are extra fenders fitted on the front of vehicles in order to minimize damage from collisions with wildlife or livestock. They are made by bending and welding techniques which are widely in use and a large number of workshops can provide them. However, an entrepreneur had standardized design and made ready-to-go bull-bars for all major makes of vehicles, with bolt-holes and fastening clamps as appropriate to each model. He could therefore offer a wide range of bull-bars which could be fitted within the hour, instead of the owner leaving his vehicle for several days while a custom designed bull-bar was being fitted. Through contacts with importers the entrepreneur both provided bull-bars to be delivered with new trucks, and attracted the attention of prospective private customers. As a result, he became the main provider of this particular item in the town.

In this case, existing but diffuse demand was channelled through contacts and combined with design and production capabilities to create a niche out of an activity which had earlier been distributed among a large number of workshops on a one-off basis. By standardizing design, lowering prices and establishing marketing channels, the entrepreneur in question focused this niche on his products, and transformed it from an area of general welding and bending into a specialized activity, without any change in the technology used.

Another company was benefiting from increasing crime rates and specializing in heavy iron gates. In this case, demand was focused through another company owned by the same family which installed alarm systems.

Getting Better at What You Are Good at

A different strategy is to expand within a niche in which the company has already established a strong presence, at the expense of competitors. This could be done for example by focusing on quick and timely delivery, lowering prices, or by developing new outlets and contacts to customers. A company which specialized in spares for heavy lorries had opted for this strategy. It acquired computer-operated machinery which shortened production time which is an essential consideration in the case of spares which are not kept in stock, enhances quality and minimizes throwaways to virtually nil. Through building more effective supplier networks, this company also tried to remain competitive in the assembly of standard pneumatic brake components and hydraulic valves and couplings. In addition, a major part of the strategy was to develop distribution channels, through spares retailers, and in this way, widen the customer group. This active marketing was necessary to be able to sell the increased output.

The bull-bars maker above competed with a multitude of general purpose workshops, and his main competitive weapons were standardization and specialization leading to niche creation. The maker of spares, which is a comparatively skill-intensive activity, only had a handful of competitors and he combined technological change, increased marketing efforts and reorganization of input networks in order to gain an advantage within his existing niche. The difference in competitive strategies between the two is largely explained by the organization of their respective markets. Hence, the effects of structural adjustment on particular segments of the light engineering industry largely depend on the previous organisation. Activities which were the province of flexible general purpose workshops become specialized, activities in which this specialization has already taken place become candidates for technological change.

Connecting to Brokers

The last strategy in response to structural adjustment to be discussed here is connecting to brokers. Brokers should here be seen as a category of operators who mediate between customers and producers. They are different from traders in that they channel orders and help establishing subcontracting relationships, rather than buying and selling on their own account. One example of this strategy was a company which made components for the subsidiary of a British company producing on licence in South Africa. Earlier belonging to the large category of general 'jobbing' workshops, this company had established a specialized production line for this purpose, and acquired additional machinery in order to be able to take on these orders. However, rather than dealing directly with the British/South African company, the owner dealt with the broker. Moreover, orders were placed for the components from one month to the next, and a more stable subcontracting relationship had not evolved, although competition from other local companies was in this case theoretical rather than of any practical consequence, due to the relationship with the broker. However, frequent re-negotiations of prices took place, and although the owner obviously had benefited from his relationship with the broker he had little leverage.

Although such brokerage relations could be observed in a variety of cases, as when car importers directed customers to a particular fitter of bull-bars or a security firm directed customers to a particular maker of iron gates, these were usually activities which facilitated expansion rather than its very basis as in this case. Well aware of the fragility of the relationship the owner had consequently maintained his customer network in the vicinity, which mainly consisted of vehicle repair workshops who needed machining services now and then.

Development Trends

None of the options outlined above implies or leads to mass-production. Although quasi-mass-production is possible if orders are steady and the customer networks well established (and preferably tied by written or oral preferential supplier contracts) fully fledged mass production implies that the entire company is oriented towards a particular product or a small subset of the potential product range and all the process steps, that is the entire internal production network of the enterprise, is integrated and tuned to this purpose. This had not happened in any of the light engineering companies we visited, nor is it likely to happen in the foreseeable future. Rather, what we observed was specialization with retained possibility for a wider product range, which at least now and then was drawn upon to support the cash flow generated by the main activity or to change orientation in response to observed demand, or what has come to be called 'flexible specialization' (Piore and Sabel, 1984; Schmitz, 1989).

In other words, we have two extremes here. On the one hand there are companies which continue to get most of their work from regular customers each of whom places orders relatively rarely (maintenance-related work, etc.). However, the companies visited in this category were trying to develop niche products and specialize in those in order to get a significant share in that niche. On the other hand we have companies which were specializing in a limited product range, but given the opportunity were willing to take on a varied range of products on a one-off basis. In one sense the difference here is merely one of degree, i.e. the percentage of cash flow generated by 'manufacturing' or 'jobbing' respectively. On the other hand, the implications of each option for the structural transformation of the Zimbabwean light engineering industry are quite different.[7]

This becomes clear if we consider the consequences of each strategy for the reconfiguration of technical networks on the one hand, and for the development of customers' and suppliers' networks on the other.

The wide scope strategy builds on the types of multipurpose machinery hitherto so typical of most light engineering firms, whereas the specialization strategy implies importation or local construction of specialized machines, or at least the reorientation of the internal production organization to a single focus. This in turn makes the technical network in each company more rigid, and their location in the total light engineering network more determinate. This latter possibility, specialization, leads to the following scenario: From a light engineering network predicated on maximal flexibility where maintenance related work, copying of spares and rehabilitation of machinery plays the major role, the Zimbabwean light engineering industry as a whole tends to coagulate (relatively speaking), as an increasing number of firms try to establish and defend niche positions or focus on specialized components. This in turn places light engineering firms in a mutually quasi-dependent relationship to particular customers, and these customers (e.g. assembly firms, wholesalers) become more dependent on or are even tied with contracts to particular suppliers.

The wide scope strategy leads, in contrast, to the continued existence of highly flexible firms oriented towards repair, maintenance and rehabilitation. These firms can and do compete with in-house workshops in large firms either by possessing better or specialized machinery or by being cheaper. Although a tendency for larger firms to farm out their repair and maintenance work to small contractors was reported to the authors, it is too soon to say if this becomes a permanent feature of the light engineering network in Zimbabwe. However, it is clear that as firms pursue either strategy, or try to combine them, homogenization of the light engineering sector in technological terms is unlikely and any policy measures will therefore have indeterminate effects on companies in the industry.

An additional aspect of the flexible specialization scenario is the management of customer networks and the inverse problematic, how user-producer network structures influence product choice and establish the parameters within which choice of technology is exercised (cf. Stewart, 1978).[8] Two of the companies visited were in this sense typical of how network connections or their absence can guide the direction of specialization rather than issues of competitiveness per se. One company was extending its current product range, and introducing state-of-the-art technology in order to serve its existing customer network better and increase its share in their purchases. The other had chosen the opposite direction: built a new customer network, but on the basis of elementary techniques. Two other companies studied exemplify a different distinction. The former was tied to a production network through a broker and working as subcontractors within that context where as the latter operated an extremely loose customer network based on reputation rather than regularly repeated transactions, but both were specializing, if in a somewhat different fashion.

Conclusion: Technological Networks and Enterprise Networks

Generalizing, we can observe that companies are very heterogeneous technically, and the scope of their activities varies. In the same line of business it is not unusual to find highly specialized companies which focus on a small section of the production chain (and in extreme cases, a single technical function), whereas other companies are involved in a large section of the sequence, or even combining several interrelated sequences under one roof. Hence, the company structure of an economic collective (such as a branch or industrial area) tends to be superimposed on the technical structure, and the two are generally not isomorphic. Analytically, one can and should therefore distinguish the production network, i.e. networked sequences of practices which are linked together (cf. Berkowitz, 1988), from the company/enterprise/ establishment concept and the analysis of commercially organized links that keep companies together in networks.

The two types of networks are to a large extent governed by different dynamics. In the case of the technical structure, innovation processes, training networks, diffusion networks and the resulting state of technological sophistication largely determine the typical relations that apply between people and things, between things and between people, whereas credit, finance, prices and power determine the relations between companies. The relations between technical and company networks are indeterminate insofar as company strategies referring to the short and medium term are concerned, as we have seen above. The range of possible combinations is practically infinite. Hence, the technological consequences of macro-economic policies tend to be indeterminate as well, and macro-economic policy cannot be substituted for a technology policy which directly addresses issues such as innovation facilitation, training and design development.

Notes

1. Comments by B. M. Zwizwai, A. Sibanda, L. Masuko, N. Wekwete, L. Sachikonye, W. J. Ascough, M. Dziruni, Prasada Reddy, R. Swedberg and M. P. van Dijk helped shape this chapter for which we are grateful. Financial support from the University of Zimbabwe and Sida (Swedish International Development Agency) is gratefully acknowledged. Many thanks also to the managers and owners of Zimbabwean light engineering companies as well as the trade unionists, NGO workers and spokesmen for industry organisations who generously gave of their time to discuss their activities with us.
2. As the saying goes, the informal sector is hard to define but easy to recognize once you encounter it. We are using the term here in this general descriptive sense, according to conventional colloquial usage (cf. Sverrisson, 1990).
3. Zwizwai and Powell (1991: 13) imply that one company, ZISCO (a parastatal steel mill) accounts for close to half of metal and metal products output.
4. This had in particular affected small and medium sized enterprises. See Sverrisson (1992: 112ff).
5. Central Statistical Office; *Quarterly Digest of Statistics*, Mar. 1995: 48.
6. Further details can be found *inter alia* in Ndlela *et al.* (1990).
7. For a general discussion of the strategic options for industry in Zimbabwe see Rasmussen and Sverrisson (1994).
8. Stewart later edited two anthologies pursuing this problematic from an economics point of view: Stewart (1987) and Stewart *et al.* (1990).

Part III

The Economic and Political Environment

8

A Macro-perspective on Small Enterprise Growth in Southern Africa

Poul Ove Pedersen

This chapter looks at the small enterprise/informal sector from a macro-perspective: Does the sector expand or contract, and when and why does it expand or contract? Macroeconomics tend to focus only on the formal sector and therefore generally have little to say about the informal sector. The small enterprise literature has more to say, but provides many, different and often conflicting interpretations and conclusions about development trends. These are difficult to test, because almost all our knowledge about small enterprises and the informal sector is based on cross-sectional data or at best a few (rarely more than two) comparative cross-sections, which are usually not strictly comparable. Models and theories of small enterprise development are therefore inferences from cross-section data and not really based on solid empirical knowledge. This becomes a problem, when we attempt to draw conclusions about the effect of events such as structural adjustment, because we cannot know whether the observed changes are a result of short-run policies or long-run structural changes.

A second problem is that until recently most empirical studies have been based on fairly small samples, often less than 100 enterprises and seldom more than a few hundred. Most studies have therefore focused on only a part of the small enterprises (e.g. a specific sector (manufacturing more often than trade), the smallest, the medium-sized, the urban, the rural, the poorest, or the most successful) or treated the small enterprises as if they were a homogeneous group. One of the results has been endless discussions about the definitions of small enterprises and the informal sector, rather than about the diversification and development of the sector. Another result has been that different theories and models of small enterprise development have been seen as alternative rather than complementary.

Surveys with much larger samples have been carried out in a number of African countries recently and in some countries even two consecutive surveys, which permits a more disaggregated analysis and in some cases also a more detailed analysis of the dynamics. I attempt here such an analysis of small enterprise dynamics, based on data from Zimbabwe on small enterprises at three points in time. This one-country analysis hides, however, the large national differences existing in the structure of small enterprise sectors, and I therefore also compare the small enterprise sectors in Zimbabwe, Kenya and Botswana.

As a starting point I outline four different theoretical explanations of small enterprise or informal sector development, which result in rather different expectations of the development of small enterprises. I then use the discussion of these different explanations to structure the empirical analysis which follows.

Four Explanations of the Development of the Small Enterprise Sector

Small enterprises develop in between agriculture and the formal, primarily urban economy and thus depend on the development of both. However, most theories of small enterprise development tend to focus either on the urban informal sector and relate it to the short-run swings in the formal urban economy or to focus on rural non-agricultural activities and relate them to the long-run structural changes in the rural economy resulting from processes of commercialization, industrialization and urbanization.

The different theoretical explanations also differ in what they see as the major driving force, namely either an excess labour supply which cannot be absorbed in the formal sector and is therefore forced into the informal sector and small enterprises in spite of poor pay, or a demand for goods and services which is not satisfied by the formal sector (or which it supplies at prices which are unattractive to some consumers) and therefore creates a potential market for small enterprises.

The four different theoretical explanations presented below combine these two characteristics in different ways.

Labour Supply Theory

The small enterprise sector is in labour supply theory assumed to develop in response to the growth in unemployment and to function as a place of last resort for people who are unable to find employment in the formal sector. Therefore the urban informal sector will grow in periods of crisis when the formal sector contracts or grows too slowly to absorb the labour force, in spite of its inefficiency and the generally low income generated. However, in periods when formal employment grows, the small enterprise sector is assumed to contract again and thus develop in cycles opposite those of the formal economy. A large part of the literature has taken this position in interpreting the growth of the informal sector after structural adjustment (see e.g. Daniels *et al.*, 1995; Brand *et al.*, 1995; Meagher and Yunusa, 1996).

Although there are undoubtedly certain elements of truth in this explanation, studies based on this theory suffer from a number of empirical problems.

First, empirical studies pursuing this argument tend to limit their sample to the poorest and smallest enterprises and eliminate the more 'modern', successful, capital and knowledge intensive enterprises beforehand. When they argue that small enterprises are inefficient and earnings low this is such cases an artifact of the sampling, not a finding.

Secondly, due to lack of time series data, growth estimates are often based on information on the year of establishment of the enterprises gathered in cross-section surveys. However, given the short life of many small enterprises, such data are likely to give a completely wrong picture of the growth in the number of small enterprises, because we cannot know how many enterprises have gone out of business before the time of the survey and, therefore, do not know whether the registered enterprise-establishments are a result of rapid replacement of enterprises or of real growth in the number of enterprises.

Thirdly, even if growth in the number of small enterprises can be identified in the period after structural adjustment, the argument would require that the informal sector did not grow, or at least grew more slowly before adjustment, and without time series data this is impossible to show and as we shall see below this is doubtful.

Fourthly, if the informal sector is to function as a place of last resort, it must be easily accessible. However, many studies show that this is only the case for a small part of the informal sector. It is sometimes argued that small informal businesses concentrate on trade because this is supposed to require less capital and knowledge than production. While it may be true that production requires more investment capital than trade (when we talk about very small-scale producers even that may be doubtful), small-scale trade is likely to require more working capital in order to secure a certain income than small-scale production, partly because the value added is lower for the trader than for the producer, and partly because in small-scale production the customer will often be required to pay for the materials in advance, while the small-scale trader will have to give credit (even more often than large formal retailers).

Scoones *et al.* (1994) have studied the development of non-agricultural activities during the drought in a drought-stricken area in Zimbabwe. He shows that while many people started to operate small non-agricultural activities in the beginning of the drought, most had to stop again as the crisis tightened, partly because they had eaten their working capital, and partly because their customers had no money. Therefore, the informal sector plays only a limited role as a place of last resort during crises. Instead, people rely on family networks and patrons.

Output-demand Theory

The argument in this theory is that a market for the products and services of small enterprises is the driving force in their development. Therefore, the small enterprise sector will tend to develop cyclically concurrently with the economy as a whole. However, the small enterprises will also develop in competition with the large enterprises in the formal sector, and their development will be constrained by formal sector monopolies. Structural adjustment policies which limit such monopolies and attempts 'to create a level playing field' will therefore be an advantage for the small enterprises, because it may allow them to conquer market shares from the large ones. Proponents of structural adjustment tend to base their arguments on this theory.

Empirical studies based on this theory tend to focus on the upper end of the informal sector, often the manufacturing enterprises and the larger, more resourceful and successful small enterprises, which have a potential to grow into the formal economy (see e.g. the different sampling procedures in the two Nigerian studies made by Meagher and Yunusa, 1996 who adhere to a labour supply theory and Dike, 1997 who adheres to an output demand theory). They often show a special interest in the possibilities for strengthening small enterprises through mutual networking or clustering or through the creation of linkages between small and large enterprises, such as sub-contracting or franchising. However, due to low levels of trust in the business community and poor infrastructure such arrangements have in general been little developed in the African countries (see e.g. Liedholm and Mead, 1991, 1993; Grierson and Mead, 1995; and McCormick and Pedersen, 1996), and are unlikely to develop in crisis situations where the large enterprises operate at a low capacity utilization. Instead, enterprises appear to integrate vertically as much as possible in order to be independent of the unstable environment (Trulsson, 1997). This clearly reduces the efficiency of the large enterprises and the market access of small enterprises to services and inputs.

Based on survey data, Daniels (1994) shows that enterprises in high-profit sectors tend to behave as expected by the output-demand theory, while enterprises in low-profit sectors rather follow the labour supply theory.

Commercialization of Rural Areas and Non-agricultural Activities

Most African countries are still predominantly rural with a large share of agricultural production being non-commercial subsistence production. However, as a result of increasing commercialization and urbanization they are gradually being drawn into the money economy. This increases the demand for cash and urges people to engage in cash-earning non-agricultural activities. At the same time, increasing cash among people creates a growing market for rural non-agricultural goods and services. Therefore, even if the economy as a whole stagnates, increased commercialization may in itself lead to an increased rural market primarily for non-agricultural products, but also to some extent for the informal and formal sectors in the urban areas, which supply the rural areas. This is the thesis of the theory of agriculture-led industrialization (Mellor, 1976; Adelman *et al.*, 1989; Haggblade and Hazell, 1989).

Contrary to the output-demand theory, which linked the informal sector to a cyclical urban economy, this theory links the informal sector to long-run rural development, and the generally irreversible trends of de-agrarianization and urbanization (see e.g. Bryceson and Jamal, 1997). It is supported by the large share of the informal sector which in most low-income countries is located in the rural areas.

Parallel to the labour surplus theory presented above, which related labour surplus to formal sector employment, at least part of the new literature on de-agrarianization relates the development of rural non-agricultural activities to the rural labour surplus, which either migrates periodically or permanently to the urban areas or finds employment in non-agricultural activities supplementary to agricultural production (Bryceson, 1996; Bryceson and Jamal, 1997).

The prediction of such a theory would be pretty much the same as of the theory of commercialization of the rural areas, namely continuous growth in the small enterprise/informal sector, although the rural labour surplus variant would also focus the development of the urban informal sector as a result of rural-urban migration.

Industrialization and Small Enterprise Development

According to both traditional Marxist and classical economic theory, small enterprises are expected to be ousted by 'modern', large-scale industry and thus gradually disappear as a result of industrialization and economic development. These expectations were based on empirical findings that small enterprises tended to be less efficient than large ones, because the large enterprises achieved either scale economies or monopoly powers. Many studies of small African enterprises in the 1960s and 1970s expected this development (see e.g. Müller, 1980), and after independence most African governments (and many donors) tended to see the small enterprises as a result of a stagnating formal industry and a sign of under-development to be suppressed.

Clearly some sub-sectors, like tailoring, do compete with industrial products (whether nationally produced or imported) and have been forced to reduce their level of activity or restructure. However, in general, small enterprises have disappeared neither in the industrialized nor in the developing countries. The problem with the argument and most of the empirical studies of scale economies is that the small and large enterprises are assumed to be doing the same thing in direct competition. However, the small enterprises generally do not do the same as the large ones. They tend to find niches in the input or product markets where the large enterprises cannot exploit their scale economies and therefore cannot compete. Or they specialize in distribution to peripheral or low-income areas where the distribution costs of the large-scale sector are prohibitive. Therefore many enterprises specialize in trade. Even those small enterprises which we traditionally classify as producers mostly sell their products retail and often use a larger part of their time and earn a larger share of their profit as retailers than as producers. Where the small enterprise would not be able to compete with the industrial producer it may be able to compete with the local retailer selling the industrial product. There will of course be an indirect competition between the formal and the informal producers, but not a complete subordination as assumed, e.g. by theories of petty commodity production. Therefore Müller (1997) could find that Tanzanian blacksmiths whose doom he had prophesied in the 1970s were still in operation and innovating in 1994.

A Composite Theory of Small Enterprise Development

The expectations for small-enterprise development for each of the four theories presented above are shown in Figure 8.1. The four theories of small enterprise development have generally been seen as alternative explanations, although they are usually applied to partly different segments of the small enterprise sector. Therefore I shall argue here that the different explanations should rather be seen as complementary theories, depicting simultaneous processes which influence different segments of the small enterprise sector with different weights. I would thus expect different parts of the small enterprise sector to develop differently over time. Taking the different theoretical explanations at face value I would expect:

- that activities with easy access and functioning as a place of last resort would expand during crisis and contract during upturns in the economy (Theory I in Figure 8.1);
- that market responsive activities would expand during an upturn in the economy and contract during crises (Theory II in Figure 8.1);
- that activities developing as a result of long-run processes of commercialization and monetization in the rural economy would expand both during crises and during an upturn in the shorter cycles of the economy (Theory III in Figure 8.1);
- that especially manufacturing activities operating in direct competition with the formal sector would contract both during crises and an upturn in the economy (Theory IV in Figure 8.1).

Such a composite theory would be in correspondence with the findings of my analysis of small businesses in small rural towns in Zimbabwe that even during the deepest crisis in 1992 some sectors benefited from the crisis at the same time as others suffered (Pedersen, 1997).

To investigate such a composite theory requires ideally time series of disaggregated data for the development of the small enterprise/informal sector. Such data are hard to come by. However, in Table 8.1 we present data for the sectoral composition of rural non-agricultural activities in Zimbabwe in 1986, 1991 and 1993, respectively. Here the first period 1986–91 represents a period of relative economic progress, while the second period 1991–93 was a period of economic crisis, where the introduction of structural adjustment measures and a serious drought coincided in 1992, and led to rapid price hikes and dramatically falling purchasing power for the majority of the population.

Figure 8.1   Predictions of theories of small enterprise (SE) development

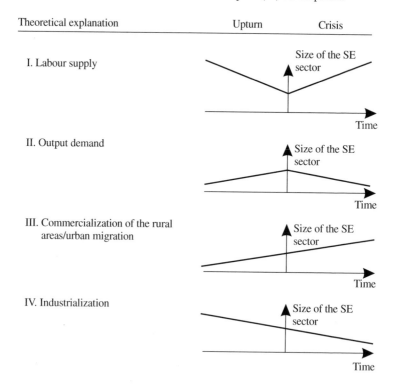

All the data are based on a complete count of the number of small enterprises (employing 0 to 50 persons) at all addresses in a stratified random sample of rural and urban enumeration areas. The expanded figures should thus in principle represent a complete picture of the population of small enterprises. In practice there has, of course, been some differences in the sampling procedures especially between the first and the two later data sets (see the note to Table 8.1). However, we still believe that the data are sufficiently comparable to give a crude indication of trends.

Unfortunately, similar data are not available for the small urban enterprises in 1986, but only for the years 1991 and 1993. These data are also shown in Table 8.1. They show that the urban small enterprises only make up 30 per cent of the total. They will be analysed in more detail below.

Small Rural Enterprises in Zimbabwe

In comparing the three percentage distributions of small rural enterprises in Table 8.1 it should be remembered that the total number of small enterprises has increased dramatically between the three years, both because the rural population has increased by around 3 per cent a year and because the average number of small enterprises per household

Table 8.1   Sectoral distribution of small rural and urban enterprises. Signs show the direction of change during the period*

Sector	Rural			Urban	
	1986	1991	1993	1991	1993
	(Helmsing, 1991) (excl. small towns)	(Daniels, 1994) (incl. small towns)		(Daniels, 1994)	
Flour milling	0.7	+1.0	−0.4	0.0	+0.2
Beer brewing	6.3	+8.2	−2.9	0.0	+0.1
Tailoring + dressmaking	13.9	−5.8	−3.2	14.9	−11.8
Knitting	10.4	−9.2	−7.3	18.2	−15.1
Crocheting	6.9	+7.5	+12.4	16.4	+19.5
Shoe works and repair	2.4	−1.0	+1.1	0.9	−0.1
Grass and cane	11.1	+20.0	−16.4	1.0	−0.6
Wood carving	5.8	−5.1	−4.6	1.0	−0.6
Carpentry	2.1	+2.4	+2.6	1.7	−1.0
Pottery	6.7	−2.5	+3.6	–	–
Brick making	1.7	+2.6	−1.9	0.0	+0.1
Tinsmithing	1.7	−1.3	−1.2	0.3	−0.2
Welding and other metal work	5.9	−0.6	+2.4	1.4	−1.1
Other manufacturing	4.9	+6.7	+7.4	10.7	−8.5
Total manufacturing	82.0	−73.9	−67.4	65.7	−58.5
Construction	7.6	−5.5	−3.8	1.4	−1.1
Trade	8.2	+18.1	+25.5	28.6	+35.6
Services	2.1	+2.8	+3.3	4.3	+4.8
Total	100	100	100	100	100
Total sample size	288	1815	–	3760	–
Estimated no. of enterprises		598,000	686,000	238,000	256,000
Growth in no. of enterprises		7.1%		3.6%	

* The 1991 and 1993 data are drawn from the GEMINI studies (Daniels, 1994) and the 1986 data from Helmsing (1991). All three data sets are based on household interviews in a random selection of rural areas in the county. There are however a number of differences in the sampling procedures used in the GEMINI and Helmsing studies, which means that a comparison can, at best, give a crude indication of trends. For instance, while Helmsing's study covers only the rural areas proper and is based on simple averages, the GEMINI study includes the small rural centres and is based on population weighted averages. Exclusion of the small towns from the 1991 and 1993 data would narrow the gap between the 1986 and 1991 data a little, but without changing the structure of the data.

has increased. Helmsing (1991) cites a survey from 1983/84 showing that 15 per cent of all rural households were operating non-farm activities then, while the GEMINI study (McPherson, 1991) found that around 40 per cent of all rural households operated at least one non-agricultural activity. This corresponds to an annual change in the percentage of rural households with non-agricultural activities of about 3–3.5 per cent and an annual increase in the number of non-farm activities of about 6–6.5 per cent, compared to 7.1 per cent in the period 1991–93. Thus from 1986 to 1991 the number of rural non-agricultural activities is likely to have increased by 50–100 per cent, while it increased by 12 per cent between the 1991 and 1993 surveys. Thus only sub-sectors for which the percentage figure for 1991 is at least 50 per cent below the 1986 figure are likely to have experienced an absolute decline, and those with larger percentage figures are likely to have increased by more than 50 per cent in absolute terms.

A comparison of the pattern of change in the main sectors shows that the direction of change is the same in the two periods, i.e. a relative contraction of manufacturing and construction and an expansion of trade and services. This speaks in favour of a structural theory of type III or IV. However the speed of change seems to be larger during the crisis period, which proponents of the labour supply theory might see as a sign in favour of theory I.

If we look in more detail at the sub-sectors within the manufacturing sector, the upper part of Table 8.1 shows that the small manufacturing activities are highly concentrated in a few sub-sectors: beer brewing (8.2 per cent in 1991), dressmaking and tailoring (5.8 per cent), knitting (9.2 per cent), crocheting (7.5 per cent), grass and cane products (20 per cent) and wood carving (5.1 per cent). In total these six sub-sectors comprise 56 per cent of all the enterprises.

Although manufacturing activities as a proportion of all rural non-farm activities decreased in both periods, this pattern does not hold for all sub-sectors. Only tailoring and dressmaking, knitting, wood carving, and tinsmithing decreased during both periods, dropping from 32 per cent to 16 per cent of all non-farm activities. Especially tailoring and dressmaking, which dominate the group of sub-sectors, have decreased rapidly probably in both relative and absolute terms during both periods. On the other hand, knitting and wood carving have decreased more moderately and have probably experienced a small absolute increase especially during the first period. These sub-sectors face less severe competition from formal industry and imports than tailoring, because they more often produce high quality compared to the industrial substitutes.

They also have access to tourist and export markets. That especially tailoring and dressmaking are hit by the long-run structural decline depicted in theory IV corresponds to our expectations. It has been argued that the opening for imports of second-hand clothes as part of structural adjustment should hit tailoring and dressmaking hard. However, the figures hardly support that view as the sub-sector appears to have contracted even more rapidly before structural adjustment than after.

The sub-sectors crocheting, carpentry and other manufacturing have grown in relative terms in both periods, from 13 per cent in 1986 to 22 per cent in 1993, thus corresponding to theory III. That 'other manufacturing' has grown in both periods corresponds well to our expectations, as we would expect a gradual diversification as part of the structural transformation of the economy. It is more surprising to find crocheting here, which is the most important sub-sector in the group. It grew especially rapidly during the second period, probably because crocheting work has been used for barter in the informal import trade from Botswana and South Africa, which has increased rapidly after the initiation of the structural adjustment programme (Brand *et al.*, 1995).

Food processing, grass and cane products and brick making expanded their share of production during the upturn and contracted during the downturn. This could be an indication of a cyclical market orientation à la theory II. However, for both food processing and grass and cane products, the contraction during the drought is likely to be caused by lack of raw materials rather than lack of market. The drought relief provided for the rural areas came in the form of mealy meals which had already been processed in the large urban mills, and therefore led to growth in retail trade rather than in milling.

Finally, pottery, welding and shoe works and repair have contracted during the upturn and expanded during the downturn. They thus seem to follow the labour supply theory of type I. This is, however, not very logical as neither welding nor pottery can be said to be easy entry sectors. Both require considerable technical knowledge and welding in addition requires relatively large investments. Shoe repair could be considered an easy entry sector, but it only grew very slowly during the crisis period.

Small Urban Enterprises in Zimbabwe

For the small urban enterprises I only have data for the crisis period 1991–93 (see Table 8.1). These data show that the small urban enterprises make up less than 30 per cent of all the small enterprises, which is still an over-representation relative to the total population, of which only 25 per cent is urban.

The number of small urban enterprises grew by only 3.6 per cent per year during the period. The number of people working in small urban enterprises appear to have increased even less (Daniels, 1994). This is, however, less than half of the growth in the number of small rural enterprises (7.1 per cent), and probably also less than the increase in the urban population during the period. This does not appear to support the hypothesis that increased urban labour supply during the crisis should have led to a growth in the number of small enterprises (theory I).

Although there has been a tendency to contraction in the formal sector, especially in the public sector part, in many African countries, as a result of structural adjustment, this has in most cases led only to a stagnation in formal employment but seldom to a large absolute decline in formal urban employment. Therefore, the number of formal employees actually retrenched is small relative to the national labour market. It is of course more important in terms of the urban labour market, but even here it is so little that only empirical studies based on very large samples will be able to register it. Studies of small enterprises after structural adjustment therefore generally do not find retrenched employees among the small-scale entrepreneurs (see e.g. Brand *et al.*, 1995). The large number of urban youth and rural migrants entering the urban labour market every year, whether there is a crisis or not, is much more important for urban unemployment. And the falling real wages in the formal sector are likely to be a much more important reason for employees or their wives to start a small enterprise than retrenchment; but that fall in real wages is not just a result of structural adjustment, but started much earlier.

The data in Table 8.1 on the sectoral distribution of the small urban enterprises show that the urban enterprises are much more concentrated in a few sectors than the rural enterprises. The urban enterprises are especially concentrated in petty trade, which comprised 28.6 per cent of all the urban enterprises in 1991 growing to 35.6 per cent in 1993, and, within the manufacturing sector, in tailoring, dressmaking, knitting and crocheting, which together comprised 49.5 per cent of all the enterprises in 1991, but had fallen to 46.4 per cent in 1993. However, of the four sub-sectors only tailoring and knitting went down, while both crocheting and dressmaking increased rapidly. Thus in the urban areas there has been a concentration of small enterprises into low income easy access sectors during the crisis, which might speak in favour of the labour supply theory. The dominance of these sectors already before the crisis indicates, however, that the growth in the low income sector in the crisis period is a continuation of more long-run processes of urban migration and the increasing participation of women in the urban labour market which has taken place especially since independence. This also corresponds to the findings of Brand *et al.* (1995) that most of the small enterprises run by women had been established well before the crisis in 1992.

These results indicate that there is a great diversity in the development of the small enterprises, by sectors and otherwise. But the results also indicate that the development of small enterprises is linked primarily to long-run (and basically irreversible) structural processes, such as urbanization and commercialization of the rural areas. This in contrast to most of the current policy debate, which tends to discuss small enterprise development in a context of relative short-term events such as the structural adjustment, droughts and cycles in the urban economy. Clearly such events have an impact on small enterprises, but the impact is likely to differ from activity to activity, and the small enterprise sector as a whole is likely to increase whether there is a crisis or not, although it may not be the same sub-sectors which are growing in different periods.

Since the 1970s, one of the main goals of rural development policies has been to increase agricultural labour productivity and rural standards of living in order to limit rural–urban migration and growth in the urban informal sector. The fallacy of this argument is, however, that a population surplus will be created in the rural areas, whether agricultural labour productivity increases or not.[1] If agricultural labour productivity does not increase, the population will have to leave the rural areas because they cannot be fed; if productivity increases, they will have to leave because there is no work for them. This is the reason why it is so difficult to stop the process of urbanization; it is also the reason why the informal sector tends to grow whether there is a crisis or not, either in the form of rural non-agricultural activities or in the form of an urban informal sector.

However, the success of agriculture does make a difference for the structure of the informal/small enterprise sector. Successful small-scale agriculture requires an efficient system of produce traders, farm input and consumer goods suppliers and other agricultural services which create a market for small and medium-sized enterprises in the rural areas. Therefore successful agriculture creates a basis for rural non-agricultural activities and the development of small rural towns (Pedersen, 1997). An agriculture with low productivity primarily leads to urban migration and an increase in the urban informal sector in the large towns.

Just as agriculture, whether it is successful or not, tends to create a rural population surplus which results in urban migration and increased urbanization, the large-scale, formal sector tends to generate small urban enterprises whether it is successful or not. The formal sector enterprises which have developed in most African countries have tended to developed into vertically integrated, closed and self-sufficient enterprises which rely on their environment as little as possible. The reason for this has been poor infrastructure and unreliable local input and service suppliers. But the closed character of the formal sector has also prohibited such small and medium-sized suppliers from developing and thus reduced the efficiency of the formal sector itself. This low efficiency has, however, permitted an informal sector to develop in parallel to the formal sector, and at least partly operate in its own parallel network. Opening the formal sector by externalizing activities will open new possibilities for the small enterprises, but it will also increase formal sector efficiency and therefore reduce the space for inefficient small enterprises. It is therefore likely to change the structure of the small enterprise sector and increase its sophistication, but not necessarily its aggregate size.

National Differences in the Structure of the Small Enterprise Sector

The above analysis indicates that the changes we are able to observe in the empirical data we have are due to long-run structural changes rather than short-run cycles and policies. However, it does not say much about what these long-run structural changes are. In a literature survey on macro-analyses of micro-enterprises in developing countries, Liedholm and Mead write that 'macro-level empirical evidence indicates that as aggregate per capita income increases there is a systematic pattern of evolution of small and medium-sized enterprises towards larger firms based in larger localities, producing more modern products' (1991: 38). Of course, such aggregate empirical evidence over the full range of development levels fits well to the classical and Marxist economics, which expect the importance of small enterprises to diminish in the course of development. It also corresponds to Adelman's generalized model of agriculture-led industrialization. However, it is too simplistic to take account of differences in small enterprise efficiency, linkages between the small and large enterprises, and changing roles of women entrepreneurs, differences in the level of education in the labour force and other socioeconomic differences. Therefore it is unlikely to be useful in understanding the differences between African countries covering a limited range of development levels.

To show this, we have in Table 8.2 compared the size and sectoral composition of the small enterprise sectors in Zimbabwe, Kenya and Botswana. Contrary to what the 'aggregate empirical evidence' leads us to expect the table shows that the size of the small enterprise sector is twice as large in Zimbabwe as in Kenya even though the per capita income is almost twice as high. This is also surprising because Kenya is known as having a policy which, at least on paper, has been favourable to the informal sector while Zimbabwe's policies have clearly favoured large industry.

Table 8.2 The small enterprise sectors in Kenya, Zimbabwe and Botswana

Sectoral distribution of enterprises (%)	*Kenya, 1995* (Daniels *et al.*, 1995)		*Zimbabwe, 1993* (Daniels, 1994)		*Botswana, 1992* (Daniels and Fisseha, 1992)	
	Urban	Rural	Urban	Rural	Urban	Rural
Food, beverages and tobacco	5.7	8.7	0.3	6.6	9.1	16.7
Textile and clothing	4.2	7.1	50.8	26.0	6.0	10.0
Wood, grass and cane	3.5	8.2	2.3	24.0	0.8	1.4
Non-metallic minerals	0.1	14.2	0.7	5.7	1.9	1.1
Metal work	1.6	–	1.3	3.6	0.6	0.7
Other manufacturing	0.4	–	1.0	0.8	1.6	0.8
Total manufacturing (without repairs)	15.5	38.3	56.3	66.7	20.0	30.7
Construction	0.4	0.5	1.1	3.8	0.2	0.0
Wholesale	1.4	–	0.1	0.0	0.1	0.7
Retail	63.4	51.4	35.0	25.5	51.4	46.8
Hotels, restaurants, bars	10.0	4.9	0.5	0.7	15.0	19.3
Services (incl. repairs)	9.4	4.9	7.3	4.2	13.6	2.6
Total	100.0	100.0	100.0	100.0	100.0	100.0
% of enterprises run by women	43		71		76	
Enterprises distributed by employment size (%):						
1 person	57		78		66	
2–5 persons	42		19		29	
6–50 persons	1		3		5	
Total	100		100		100	
No. of enterprises/1000 inhabitants	49	30	93	84	30	20
Manuf. enterprises/1000 inhabitants	8	11	53	56	11	9
Retail enterprises/1000 inhabitants	31	15	33	21	15	9

A closer look at Table 8.2 reveals that the difference between Zimbabwe and Kenya is almost entirely due to a very large number of clothing enterprises and grass and cane weavers in Zimbabwe. If they are left out of the distribution, the number of enterprises per 1,000 inhabitants is very close to that in Kenya. From a sectoral perspective this very large informal clothing sector in Zimbabwe is difficult to explain as Zimbabwe has a much larger and more efficient large-scale clothing industry than Kenya, and a clothing retail sector which is dominated by large retail chains. Thus while the clothing industry in Zimbabwe provides close to 20 per cent of the total manufacturing employment, it employs less than 5 per cent in Kenya. This must mean that in spite of the larger size of Zimbabwe's clothing industry there still remains a large clothing market which the formal sector is unable to reach.

Because of the many small clothing enterprises in Zimbabwe, two-thirds of all the small enterprises are manufacturing enterprises there, against only one third in Kenya. Correspondingly, retail trade makes up two-thirds of the small enterprises in Kenya but only one-third in Zimbabwe. However, in absolute number of enterprises per 1,000 inhabitants the sector is of approximately the same size in the two countries. Given the importance of large retail chains in Zimbabwe, this is surprising , but must be an outcome of the larger per capita income in Zimbabwe which still leaves a market for the small retailer in spite of the competition from the chain stores.

As a result of the large number of small clothing enterprises, a much larger share of the small enterprises are women-owned in Zimbabwe than in Kenya. This could be a result of the higher per capita income and a more monetized economy, which presses more women to earn cash incomes. However, the large number of small clothing enterprises is not a result of the structural adjustment policies and the drought, because their number was even larger in 1991 than in 1993.

Although the average size of the small enterprises is about the same in Zimbabwe and Kenya, the many small clothing enterprises make the share of one-person enterprises much larger in Zimbabwe (78 per cent) than in Kenya (57 per cent), and the share of enterprises with 2–5 persons correspondingly smaller (19 per cent against 42 per cent). On the other hand, there are also more of the largest group of small enterprises (6–50 persons working) in Zimbabwe (3 per cent) than in Kenya (1 per cent).

Surprisingly, the large number of small clothing enterprises in Zimbabwe also means that the small urban enterprises in Zimbabwe are smaller than the rural ones. This is contrary to Kenya and also to our theoretical expectations, because market access tends to be better in urban than in rural areas. Thus for Kenya Hosier (1987) has shown that while rural enterprises primarily produce-to-orders, urban enterprises frequently produce in larger batches for the market.

In Table 8.2 we also compare Zimbabwe to Botswana, which has a per capita income almost three times that of Zimbabwe. The Botswana data show that the size of the small enterprise sector is much smaller than in both Kenya and Zimbabwe. Thus, although the share of women-owned enterprises is larger than in Zimbabwe, the number of women entrepreneurs per 1,000 inhabitants is much smaller, and the pressure on women to earn a cash income appears to be smaller. Furthermore, the women are not concentrated as strongly in the clothing sector as in Zimbabwe. Probably due to the large share of women entrepreneurs, there are more one-person enterprises (66 per cent) than in Kenya, but not as many as in Zimbabwe. On the other hand, the number of enterprises in the largest group of small enterprises is larger (7 per cent) than in both Kenya and Zimbabwe, which, however, still means that, in absolute terms, there are fewer of these medium-sized enterprises per 1,000 inhabitants than in both Kenya and Zimbabwe.

These findings might be seen as an indication that the share of the largest group of small enterprises increases with per capita income as both the economic theories and the 'aggregate empirical evidence' indicate. However, this is not the case when we look at the absolute number of enterprises per 1,000 inhabitants. The share of one-person enterprises appears to depend more on labour market structures which are not clearly linked to per capita income but rather to different social structures, such as the participation of women in the non-agricultural labour market and the structure of the educational system, which tend to be of a long-run nature and not easy to change in the short run. We would see this as an indication that the small enterprise sector cannot be explained by simple one-dimensional models, but must be linked to the development of both the formal urban economy and the rural agricultural economy and to the development of both labour markets and the structure of the demand for small enterprise products. This lead us towards a theory of African society similar to Sverrisson's (1993) theory of technological complexes. He sees African society as consisting of three different but interrelated complexes: a state and corporate complex which is to a large extent oriented towards the urban economy, a peasant complex with its basis in the rural economy, and an intermediate complex consisting of the small-enterprise sector in both urban and rural areas (cf. Sverrisson, Ch. 10).

Conclusion

The Zimbabwe data on the development of the small-enterprise sector show that the sector is not homogeneous, but that different segments of the sector follow different development patterns. Some segments follow a long-run growth trend, some rather contract, some respond pro-cyclically to the short-run swing in the economy and some respond anti-cyclically. However, the dominant pattern for the small-enterprise sector as a whole is long-run growth, although it is not the same small enterprise activities which grow during up-turns and crises in the economy.

The explanation for this long-run growth trend is, it is argued, that the small enterprises in developing countries develop in between agriculture and the formal urban sector, but as agriculture dominates the economy, most small enterprises are established as part of the rural development process and the process of rural–urban migration. Therefore, small enterprises continue to be created whether there is crisis in the economy or not, just as the process of rural–urban migration is not very sensitive to economic crises.

A comparison of the size of the small-enterprise sector in Kenya, Zimbabwe, and Botswana shows that there is not a simple inverse relationship between the level of economic development and the size of the informal sector, as much traditional economic theory wants us to believe because a growing 'modern' large-scale industry is supposed to oust the small enterprises. Thus, Zimbabwe which has a per capita income twice that of Kenya also has a small-enterprise sector twice as large as Kenya, while Botswana which has a per capita income three times that of Zimbabwe has a small-enterprise sector which is smaller than that of Kenya.

Surprisingly, the large small-enterprise sector in Zimbabwe is dominated by clothing producers in spite of a very large and well-developed formal clothing industry. This indicates that the higher per capita consumption in Zimbabwe than in Kenya benefits not only the large but also the small enterprises.

The share of small enterprises operated by women is much larger in Zimbabwe (71 per cent) and Botswana (76 per cent) than in Kenya (43 per cent), but in absolute terms the percentage of women operating small enterprises is almost three times as large in Zimbabwe than in both Kenya and Botswana.

We cannot draw any precise conclusions from the limited data available, but they do indicate that the development and level of the small-enterprise sector cannot be explained by simple one-dimensional models, but must be linked to the development of both the formal urban economy and the rural agricultural economy as well as to the development of labour markets and the patterns of demand for small-enterprise products. However, we are still a long way from understanding the way the small-enterprise sector develops relative to the rest of the economy.

Note

1. The exception to this is where land productivity increases without a corresponding increase in labour productivity as can be the case in irrigation schemes especially when they make more than one harvest possible.

9
Good Governance and Small Enterprises in Zimbabwe

Meine Pieter van Dijk

What have several years of adjustment meant for small enterprises in Zimbabwe? In a heavily regulated country like Zimbabwe it is useful to concentrate on what deregulation and government policies have and could have achieved. In this chapter, this issue is placed in the wider context of the discussion about good governance, based on suggestions concerning the key tasks of government by the World Bank (1997). Which of the suggested elements of good governance are relevant for small enterprises and what is overlooked by this approach?

Macro-economic and Policy Context

Zimbabwe obtained its independence in 1980 and was quite successful in the 1980s, achieving an average rate of growth of its per capita gross national product (GNP) of 1 per cent between 1965 and 1988 leading to a per capita GNP of US$650 (World Bank, 1990). Zimbabwe's economic performance weakened substantially in the second half of the 1980s. Inflation accelerated and the balance of payments position worsened. Per capita income has not increased since 1989, while unemployment has grown unabated. The government budget deficit has also increased, driving interest rates to punitively high real levels in recent years, despite successive statements of intent to reduce the public sector's weight on the economy. Investments were low due to lack of confidence, limited access to and the high cost of foreign exchange.

The country was hit by a severe drought in 1992. The widespread impact of the drought was compounded by a deterioration in the external terms of trade, due to a decline in international prices for key mineral and agricultural commodities. The production of major crops declined by an estimated 50 to 75 per cent. The country faced a deficit of

1 million tones of maize and had to import maize from and through South Africa. Real gross domestic product (GDP) officially fell 7.7 per cent in 1992, while inflation rose to 40 per cent and the balance of payments deficit widened sharply (IMF Survey, 1993). The per capita GNP fell to $540 in 1995, after a period of −0.6 per cent growth of per capita GNP between 1985 and 1995 (World Bank, 1997). However, the country still has a stronger economy than most countries in sub-Saharan Africa and is more prosperous than most of its neighbours.

In July 1990 the Economic Structural Adjustment Programme was announced. In January 1991 a more comprehensive framework was brought out by the Ministry of Finance (1991). Within the country a long debate has been going on about adjustment, with a number of people resisting it, since they see it as the end of efforts to build a socialist Zimbabwe. Others worried about their living standards and whether the political will existed to do what is needed. The debate concerned the credibility of the government. It can be said that Zimbabwe 'climbed, reluctantly, aboard the structural adjustment bandwagon in 1991' (Hawkins, 1993).

In 1998 the official launch of the Zimbabwe Programme for Social and Economic Transformation (ZIMPREST) took place. In 1997 foreign investment increased somewhat, although most of it goes through the stock exchange and only concerns a limited number of companies. Domestic deregulation has been announced in the framework of ZIMPREST and the thrust of the new policy will be summarized below. The implementation of the programme has not been very successful. Political opposition surfaced in 1998 and increased when Zimbabwe started to participate in the Congo conflict.

Zimbabwe had a population of 11 million inhabitants in mid-1995. The population is growing at about 3 per cent. The manufacturing sector is second only to the South African in sub-Saharan Africa, while the agricultural sector is quite diversified, producing the necessary foods and exporting a range of commodities, particularly tobacco and cotton. Although 70 per cent of the population depends on agriculture, this sector contributed only 15 per cent of GDP. The industrial sector contributed 36 per cent of GDP, exporting in particular textiles and metal products and growing annually at around 4 per cent (World Bank, 1997). Mining is important, contributing 7 per cent of GDP and generating 40 per cent of the foreign exchange earned, from gold, ferro-alloys and nickel exports.

Population pressure and unemployment stand out as the main reasons for seeking new avenues of development: 'the traditional system cannot carry the numbers, and the educated young people who are coming on to the labour market at the rate of a quarter of a million a year' (FMB Group, 1993). The employment situation of the country has steadily deteriorated since the 1980s. It is estimated that formal sector unemployment amounted to 26 per cent in 1990 and just under 30 in 1995 (Made and Mfote, 1995). According to the same study about 150,000 people need to be absorbed by the informal sector every year in Zimbabwe.

Against this economic background the chances for the development of small enterprises are not very good.[1] On top of this the formal manufacturing sector often considers the informal sector an illegitimate competitor which should be eliminated, rather than used as subcontractors. The formal manufacturing sector accounts for about one-fourth of GDP. The largest sub-sectors are metal products, textiles and clothing, and chemical products. These three account for about 80 per cent of the gross output of formal manufacturing.

Present Policies to Promote Small and Medium Enterprises

The development of small enterprises has been discouraged by policies which favoured the development of a white-dominated, modern, capital intensive manufacturing industry. The small enterprise sector was particularly discriminated against in the pre-independence era. As a result of these policies and incentives during the period of the UDI and sanctions, the growth of the (white and formal) manufacturing sector in Zimbabwe has been quite unusual for Africa. It produces a wide range of goods reasonably efficiently, which are then distributed throughout the country. It is, therefore, extremely difficult for new small-scale or micro-enterprises to find a niche in the market and to develop. Further, financial, marketing and transportation services are tailored to the needs of the formal manufacturing and the commercial agricultural sector.

In the early 1990s, small enterprise policies and projects were still very much geared towards income generation for women's groups, usually providing only a low income to their members. In 1991, however, the Ministry of Finance announced a major effort to relax domestic controls, to increase domestic competition and thereby complement the trade liberalization programme. The Deregulation Committee was given mandate to look into rules and regulations affecting the small enterprise sector. Specific actions in the field of deregulation were announced concerning price controls, investment, labour and wage regulation and transport and other rules and guidelines which tend to impede growth. It was also noted that the requirement of permits for road transport operations has discouraged single owner-operated trucking and that zoning regulations and licensing requirements for small businesses inhibit the growth of the small scale sector.

In brief, verbal support for the small enterprises is strong, but in practice policies are not very favourable and projects have a limited impact/outreach. As noted in the *Financial Gazette* (21 August 1997, p. 2): 'Government officials stand at podiums and romanticize the small and medium enterprise sector, [but] it has become apparent that small and medium enterprises do not constitute an integral component of Zimbabwe's industrial and commercial development strategy'.[2]

Good Governance and Small Enterprises

The importance of governance issues in the country can be studied by taking government policies, rules and regulations with respect to small enterprises in Zimbabwe as the focus. This approach is followed in this chapter. The World Development Report 1997 (World Bank, 1997: 4) favours a two-part strategy to achieve greater efficiency. The first step is to match the state's activities to its capability. The second step is to improve the state's capability by reinvigorating public institutions. The main message of the report is that governments should focus on the public activities which are crucial for development. The report provides a list of fundamental tasks which lie at the core of every government's mission:

- establish a foundation of law;
- maintain macro-economic stability and avoid distortion of markets;
- invest in basic social services and infrastructure;
- protect the vulnerable;
- protect the environment.

All these five tasks are also relevant for small enterprises in Zimbabwe and will be reviewed one by one. The first two will receive particular attention, given their importance. At the end of the chapter, activities of the government which could help small enterprises, but are not included in this list, will also be discussed.

Establishing a Foundation of Law

A proliferation of small enterprises has taken place in Zimbabwe, in particular after the decline of the formal economy in 1992. Many of these small enterprises are competing with imported products and products produced by the larger scale, formal industrial sector. In this section we will analyse how laws and by-laws affect the informal sector and small enterprises and how small enterprises deal with these laws.

The legislative framework is a constraining factor for small enterprises in Zimbabwe. It is partly a leftover of the previous regime, but implemented by the present authorities. Zoning policies can be mentioned, but there also exists a whole system of licensing, for example for stalls or workshops. A small entrepreneur would first have to get a piece of land designated for his/her kind of economic activity, then obtain a permission to build and subsequently a licence for her/his business. As a result, it has been made very difficult for small entrepreneurs to develop their businesses legally. They also face problems in gaining access to facilities like training and credit (Saito and Van Dijk, 1990).

ENDA (1990) discusses in detail the legislation affecting the formal and informal sectors in Zimbabwe. The definition of the informal sector used is based on a legal criterion, namely the legal status of the activity. The possible legal status for a formal sector unit would be a partnership, a proprietorship, a registered company or a registered co-operative.[3] These legal forms are described in the company act of 1973 and the Co-operative Societies Act. The objective of the latter is to encourage the formalizing of informal sector units through registration with the Registrar of Co-operatives.

Besides these laws on the legal status of enterprises, a number of other laws (and by-laws) affect the informal sector. Among the most important are:

- The Urban and the Rural Council Acts, which empower local authorities to control and administer informal business activities through licensing. Hawker licensing in Harare and Masvingo, for example, is regulated through the Harare and Masvingo Hawkers and Street Vendors By-laws, dating from the sixties and seventies. Land allocation is also controlled by the City, Rural or District councils, which also fix market stalls rates.
- The Small Enterprise Development Corporation (SEDCO) Act.[4]
- The Liquor Act regulating the sale of liquor. It specifies types of liquor licences that the Liquor Licensing Board is empowered to issue.

A number of laws can just be neglected by micro- and small enterprises. They are relevant only if a small enterprise attempts to obtain a piece of land or a credit. In other cases much depends on the enforcement of the laws, sometimes strict, sometimes lax. Street vending in the centre of

Harare for example, would have been strictly forbidden in the 1970s and beginning of the 1980s, while it is common now. However, mobile traders in Victoria Falls have been harassed by the police, because the established shops claim they suffer from their competition.

In practice much depends on how easily a small entrepreneur can comply with the laws. It is, for example, relatively easy to get a hawkers' licence, although the conditions on where and what kind of products may be sold can be very restrictive. It is much more difficult to comply with the company or co-operatives act. Health and engineering standards can also make life difficult for entrepreneurs and the criteria used by many institutions exclude them from access to credit, training and other services. One can find almost daily examples of bureaucratic hazards for small entrepreneurs, often described in the newspapers. One example can illustrate the point.

The *Herald* of 18 October 1997 announces that 200 city vendors were arrested in Harare for breaking city by-laws by operating from non-designated points in the city centre. They had to pay a Z$25 fine. The City Council had ordered informal traders to move from the Central Business District to designated selling points in a bid to reduce congestion in the city centre. The argument used was that the Council wanted to 'maintain order and security'. The traders complain that the designated areas are at the periphery of the city, which means that they lose touch with their traditional customers. Some of these points were also too congested. Finally, some traders argue that the Z$75 levy they were paying for their place in the designated points is too high in relation to the poor infrastructure in place.

Efforts to Deregulate

Deregulation in the framework of economic liberalization should also concern the regulations hindering the development of the small enterprises. Two examples can be given. Export and import regulations are very complicated for example in the case of trade with South Africa. Secondly, as mentioned, obtaining land is very difficult. In a so-called 'growth point' an entrepreneur needed when liberalization started Z$15,000. In Harare one needed at that time twice as much. The entrepreneur needs to guarantee that she/he is able to build and has to build within one year (growth points) or 18 months (Harare and Masvingo). There is a minimum size for the plot and other restrictive regulations, particularly concerning the quality of bricks used, the way the doors open and the glass used (if chemicals are used as in the case of soap). Prices vary according to the type of land (agricultural or industrial) and ownership cannot be transferred until it is developed.

A Deregulation Project Team (DPT) was set up by the government in 1993. It has investigated legislation, policies and procedures that impede the development of the enterprise sector in the wake of the ESAP (see DPT, undated a). The report is quite unique and deals with 15 relevant subjects as follows:

1. Restrictions on hawking and street vending
2. Restrictions on borrowing powers of local authorities
3. Beer levy and excise duty on traditional opaque beer sold by local authorities
4. Monopolies of local authorities to sell traditional beer in designated areas
5. Approval of local authorities' tariff increases
6. Legislative and policy prohibitions on home industries
7. Women's and children's rights of inheritance
8. Land surveying and transfers of title to land
9. The prohibition of retail and service activities on residential properties
10. Constraints on building societies
11. Problems relating to the Liquor Act of 1984
12. Constraints on married women raising finance from banks
13. Provision of workspace for the informal sector
14. Licensing and registration of informal sector activities
15. Monitoring of new legislation

DPT (undated b) provides a follow-up, focusing on three specific issues: access to finance, constraints imposed by the tax system and issues related to physical planning and the provision of workspace to small enterprises. The perspective proposed here is an eventual graduation of informal small-sized enterprises into the formal sector. The analysis focuses on the constraints imposed by different rules and regulations to graduation.

The DPT examined legislation that appears to be an impediment to the emergence and further development of small enterprises.[5] The objective was to make recommendations to the Deregulation Committee as to how existing legislation, regulations, bylaws and statutory instruments 'can be amended with the effect that a more enabling environment for business, and in particular small enterprises, is created'. The assumption was that the capacity of the informal sector to graduate is negligible due to lack of access to finance coupled with regulatory disincentives in relation to taxes and availability of workspace. Unless these barriers are addressed, they will continue to operate as a permanent ceiling for the ambitions of most entrepreneurs.

A third report (DPT undated c) focused on the formal sector and the issues dealt with can be summarized as follows:

1. The termination of employment at the initiative of the employer
2. Specification of minimum wages and minimum wage fixing
3. Problems experienced by exporters and importers with custom procedures
4. Problems of construction contractors in doing business with the public sector
5. The development of entrepreneurial skills and business culture
6. Crèche and nursery school standards
7. The difficulties of small-scale entrepreneurs in doing business with government
8. Barriers to the setting up of professional practices

The report argues in favour of facilitating the termination of employment and of the recruitment of casual workers. It also discusses how to simplify the procedures concerning exports and imports.

The recommendations of the Deregulation Committee were accepted by the Cabinet only in 1997. In particular the following recommendations were endorsed (*Small Scale Enterprise News*, February 1997) as improvements on the current situation for many entrepreneurs.

First, the term informal trading was adopted as most appropriate to denote the activities of hawking and vending. It reflects the nature of the business activity, irrespective of whether the person selling goods does so from a fixed location, or while travelling from place to place.

Secondly, the requirements for an informal trader to hold a licence were removed and substituted by paragraphs enabling an informal trader to register and hold a registration certificate specifying areas for carrying out the informal trading and indicating penalties for operating in an area not specified in the certificate. The issue or renewal of a registration certificate cannot be denied to any person unless the denial is necessary in the interest of public safety and public morality. The local authorities should fix minimal registration fees for every trader and also pass a set of by-laws empowering the local authorities to cause informal traders to keep their trading areas clean.

By-laws that contain any provision which restricts trading to specified distances from any business premises or buildings except for reasons of public health, public safety or public security should be repealed. Registration certificates cannot be cancelled because of contravening of street vending by-laws since it is not a felony. By-laws shall expressly provide for specific penalties for contravention which are limited to payment of fine only and authorities should not enforce such penalties by means of arrest and prosecution or impounding of goods.

The operation of push-carts should be allowed provided that their dimensions, the dimensions of the cargo they carry and their movements on the roads are regulated under local authority traffic by-laws. Finally, in order to remove the plethora of by-laws which regulate small scale activities, all existing by-laws regulating street vending should be repealed and replaced with one set of by-laws. All in all, these measures imply significant reduction in the red tape with which small entrepreneurs have to contend even in the simplest activities.

Structural Adjustment and the Impact of Social Development Funds

In this section the focus will be on the Socio-economic Development Fund (SDF), established as part of the structural adjustment effort. The aim was to shield disadvantaged groups from decline in welfare arising from restructuring activities or stabilization programmes. This fund has influenced the business environment in Zimbabwe substantially by providing some 2,500 loans for investment in small enterprises.

In addition to the inauguration of the fund in 1991, Social Dimensions of Adjustment (SDA) activities in Zimbabwe included food-for-work programmes, public work programmes (carried out by the Department of Public Service, Labour and Social Welfare) and other programmes for poverty alleviation such as the Grain Loan Scheme and the Child Supplementary Feeding Programme as well as a number of drought relief measures. The SDA formed an integral part of the five-year ESAP launched in 1990 (van Dijk, 1995).

The two main components of the SDF were the Social Safety Nets (SSN) Programme, also called the Social Welfare Programme (SWP), and the Employment and Training Programme (ETP), which provided assistance to those made redundant from both the private and the public sectors as a result of ESAP.[6] This was a Z$100 million soft-loan programme to start small scale enterprises. Originally it was intended to transform retrenched employees into entrepreneurs by providing an introductory one-week training course in how to start up a new business and loans for small enterprise start-ups.

A course is mandatory for ETP beneficiaries, called 'How to start and run your own business'. This course is organized by the Department of Employment and Employment Development (DEED), with offices in all six provinces, which allow them to provide training outside Harare. It includes skill training in fields like welding and carpentry. Sometimes the candidates already have an SDF loan, sometimes they have a project proposal pending and in a number of cases this proposal has already been approved by the Loans and Grants Allocation Committee (LOGAC) of the SDF.

The ETP credit scheme was evaluated by Moorsom *et al.* (1996) and they note that the scheme introduced business training and achieved a certain outreach. It is estimated that one-third of all private and public sector retrenchees completed a course before the suspension of the programme in August 1995. 1,889 loans worth US$16 million were approved in three years and the employment created is estimated at 7,500 people by January 1996. The average loan (US$9,250 in early 1996) was high and outside the scope of micro- or informal enterprises, and thus the programme did not compete with the existing NGO programmes for micro-enterprises.

However, procedures in the co-ordination unit were not adequate, which led to a backlog of nearly 7,000 project proposals by mid-1995. In addition, there was a strong gender bias and a marked urban bias in the implementation of the programme. More generally, there was a lack of professional business and financial expertise at all levels. Officers running the programme did in particular lack experience of micro-lending. Lastly, since the LOGAC approved nearly all the projects it considered, the scheme 'took on the character of an entitlement program' (Moorson *et al.*, 1996).

As a next step, the Poverty Alleviation Action Plan (PAAP) was presented to the Consultative Group meeting for Zimbabwe in Paris in December 1993 and later to the Social Summit in Copenhagen in 1994. The plan was endorsed by the government as national policy in 1994. The plan is intended to transform the traditional poverty alleviation approach by moving from a social welfare approach towards an approach based on self-reliance and self-sustenance, focusing on both temporary and chronic poor. It stresses participatory methods and the involvement of interested civil groups in the alleviation of poverty. The most important changes in all these plans are:

- the transition from a welfare orientation to a more business-oriented approach, stressing the importance of micro-loans instead of providing grants;

- the involvement of micro-credit institutions, instead of handing out loans directly by a ministry, without an adequate supervision system;
- the involvement of the International Labour Organization (ILO) in providing technical assistance (see below);
- a reconfiguration of the SDF, turning it into an on-lending financial institution, which manages and monitors its portfolio.

Generally, developing small enterprises with loans and business training is emphasized, whereas the importance of technology and marketing and of the exploration of export possibilities is largely overlooked.

The ILO provides support to the second phase of the SDF and in particular for the Micro-Enterprise Development Programme (MEDP), which is also called the Poverty Reduction and Employment Creation through Micro-Finance Programme. Its objective is to reduce poverty and create employment by empowering the entrepreneurial poor. The SDF will channel funds through MEDP to Micro-Finance Institutions (MFIs) with the capacity to reach out to micro-entrepreneurs.

After an evaluation of the first phase of the SDF it was found that the repayment rate of the loans was very low. In order to ameliorate this, it was decided to work through intermediaries in the future and for the second period (1996–99) five partners were identified: AFC, SEDCO, Zambuko Trust, ZWFT and ZECLOF. Later other institutions also asked to qualify as an intermediary. Instead of getting directly involved in lending, SDF now lends to organizations which are considered to be in touch with the target groups. ILO issues a newsletter (*ILOSDFINFO*), which keeps the organizations involved informed about the approach chosen and the progress made.

The main emphasis of the ILO support is on developing a well-functioning SDF loan facility. It focuses on financial intermediaries, which should be professionally managed, financially self-sufficient and reach the poor (*ILOSDFINFO* No. 1). For this purpose a co-ordination unit has been created, and the financial intermediaries operate as subcontractors to this unit. The project follows the 'Guiding Principles on Micro and Small Enterprise Finance' which have been developed for donors to help them selecting and supporting financial intermediaries (Gibson, 1997). This approach stresses the importance of simultaneous outreach and sustainability.

Effects of Liberalization for Small Enterprises

According to the IMF (1996), significant progress has been made in deregulating product, labour and foreign exchange markets, as well as foreign investment in the economy, during the first phase of the economic reform programme, which ended in 1995. The key thrust of further deregulation in the framework of ZIMPREST is to eliminate unnecessary restrictions on the informal sector. The Deregulation Committee does again examine issues such as access to and use of water for agricultural purposes, controls on access and use of land for agricultural, commercial and industrial uses; access to mining rights for small-scale operators and legislation covering entry, transparency, competition and systems of redress in the professions. At the same time, the Monopolies Commission is expected to carry out a series of reviews of restrictions on competition in key sectors, including statutory monopolies.

The chapter in ZIMPREST devoted to deregulating the domestic economy is called 'Removing the last shackles'. It stresses that the majority of the recommendations made by the Deregulation Committee have been accepted by the Government. It notes that some changes have taken place which have eased the plight of the informal sector operators regarding licensing requirements and gaining official recognition by both government and local authorities. However, during the period of ZIMPREST the pace of implementing change shall be accelerated, especially at the level of local authorities.

The impact of small enterprise policies, projects and programmes is usually difficult to assess. A large number of other organizations are active in Zimbabwe in the field of small enterprise promotion, focusing on different areas, for example:

- *Training:* Several NGOs and government institutions are active in this field.
- *Credit:* Among those involved are SEDCO, AFC and Barclays Bank. A score of micro-credit initiatives exist in Zimbabwe, but only two of them have been active for more than five years in 1997.
- *Business associations* and promotional organizations such as the Zimbabwe Farmers' Union (ZFU) and the Confederation of Zimbabwe Industries (CZI).
- *Technology development:* Among the organizations working in this field are ENDA-Zimbabwe, Intermediate Technology Development Group (ITDG), Silveira House,[7] the Zimbabwe Women's Bureau (operating an

Agriculture and Nutrition programme) and the Development Technology Centre (DTC) at the University of Zimbabwe.

The development of the co-operative movement has also attracted considerable attention in Zimbabwe. The results of these efforts are not always clear. An editorial in *The Herald* (11 May 1990, p. 7) speaks of many co-operative societies that have flourished, but 'many more have fallen victim to the pitfalls that await the unwary in any business adventure'. Bare (1985) describes Zimbabwe's first experiences with the formation of women's self-help groups, which would become pre-co-operatives and eventually co-operatives. The advantages of such a development is that training will be provided to the participants. The co-operatives will eventually have access to credit and the Co-operatives Act provides limited liability to its members. The Ministry responsible for co-operatives is also expected to assist in the proper utilization and management of funds.[8]

A major disadvantage is the complicated procedure for registering a co-operative society. It must have the promotion of economic and social interests of its members as an objective and must submit a copy of its by-laws to the Registrar. These by-laws should prescribe the minimum number of shares in the society that shall be held by each member and the circumstance and manner in which shares of ex-members will be disposed of.

Although there is some willingness to further liberalize the regulations presently hindering the development of small enterprises, the authorities are very reluctant to compromise on health, sanitation and security regulations. The feeling is very much 'we have to keep up the standards'. In practice, many health and sanitation regulations are outdated and do not really serve a purpose in the present situation, except for allowing some people to seek 'informal rent' from enforcing these regulations.

The government of Zimbabwe is following two strategies in this regard. On the one hand it tries to change laws at the national level, hoping this will create a more positive environment for small enterprises. At the same time lower levels of government are instructed that certain laws and regulations do not apply any more. However, since these laws usually have not been changed yet, this creates an ambiguous situation. Which laws apply and which ones are not implemented any more? In such a situation local officials may pretend that a law is still in force and expect consideration for not enforcing it.

Social services and infrastructure for small enterprises, task 3 in the good governance definition above, hardly exist in Zimbabwe. For example, it is very difficult for a small enterprise to obtain space with water, sanitation and electricity. As mentioned above, obtaining land to build on is often difficult as well. The hawkers' licence system could also be more flexible with respect to the places where they are allowed to sell and the range of products that can be sold and it should be easier to get a licence. These are among the tasks that need to be addressed if credit provision is to achieve its goals. Such problems do in particular affect the situation for otherwise vulnerable people which the government is bound to protect (task 4) who often end up in the informal sector.

As far as protecting the environment (task 5) is concerned, there is not yet a policy on how small enterprises could contribute to the protection of the environment. However, it was recently announced (*The Herald*, 31 October 1997, p. 11) that Zimbabwe has been included in a German Development Agency (GTZ) Programme for Small and Medium Enterprises incorporating environmental aspects into management tools.

Finally, there is no real consultation structure for small enterprises in Zimbabwe. This point is not mentioned explicitly by the World Bank (1997) as a key task of the government, but could be considered as an extension of the definition of good governance. Another important extension would be the need for effective local government. As we saw above, local governments influence the practice of small enterprise support in far from non-trivial ways, which are, however, inadequately understood (cf. Zaaijer, 1997).

Conclusions: a Business Support System is Developing

There is a foundation of law in Zimbabwe, but it is not yet adjusted to the new reality of the urban informal sector. The changes suggested by the Deregulation Project Team will take a long time before they will be implemented through new laws. A legal foundation at the national level may not be the most efficient option in this case, given the time it takes and the possibilities for lower levels of government to deregulate and to create a more favourable environment locally for small enterprises. In Zimbabwe, the emphasis of policy has been to regulate small enterprises rather than facilitate their activities. This is also the case in rural areas.

There have been a number of side-effects of the economic liberalization in general and the functioning of the SDF in particular which are relevant for small enterprise development. It should be noted that similar developments could have taken place in the framework of projects like the World Bank financed Export Revolving Fund. Four such effects of the SDF can be mentioned.

1. To qualify for the support of the SDF many people followed a one week course how to start and run a business. Consequently, a large number of people were trained and acquired some basic skills to run a business.

2. To apply for a loan candidates needed to submit a business plan. Gradually a business support system has developed because a number of private consultants have specialized in writing applications for loans based on some kind of business plan. This was a positive effect of the requirement to submit such a plan in order to gain access to loans under the ETP. The involvement of private consultants is quite unique and their development may be one of the lasting effects of the program.

3. A number of new institutions stepped into the micro-credit business before or after the so-called 'micro-wave', the sudden positive attention for micro-credit after the Conference on this subject in Washington in February 1997 and the support that became available for such programmes under the second phase of SDF. It is not clear yet whether all these efforts are financially sound but in the current situation the prognosis is reasonably positive. However, it will take time before this can be evaluated but the business support system in Zimbabwe has, at the very least, developed further.

4. Finally, new export and import markets have emerged, if only because of the new regime in South Africa and the consequently improved possibilities to travel, transport and communicate. This provides new opportunities for small enterprises in Zimbabwe, many of which make use of them already.

However, the trajectory of the SDF is in some ways problematic. The legal status of the SDF remains an important issue. As it is, it is closely linked to the government. An autonomous SDF would perhaps have a better chance of success, due to more effective and transparent decision making process. Further, the SDF is involved in so many different activities that it is difficult to manage them all simultaneously without some streamlining of its structure. The SDF approach can also be criticized for not distinguishing between retrenched workers in general and potential businesspeople in particular. In general, working with existing entrepreneurs is much easier and has a larger chance of success.

ZIMPREST states that implementation of change shall be accelerated, especially at the level of local authorities. It also indicates the two major problems. One is that a lot of these changes are implemented very slowly at the national level, since after the publication of the Deregulation Committee's report the Cabinet had to look first at the recommendations and now a number of recommendations need to be turned into laws to be discussed in parliament, which will take time again. Power to change things is also vested at the local level. Much depends on the attitude of the authorities. In Bulawayo, the local authorities have adopted various measures to support small enterprise (Zaaijer, 1997), but this seems to be an exception.

Finally the NGOs have an important role to play. They can help to formulate the needs of small entrepreneurs, providing them with the voice they otherwise often lack. However, an important role of NGOs is to implement tasks which are carried out inadequately by the government, and which are beyond its capacities in the short and medium term. In the context of decentralization, local government and civil society (including the NGOs) have in fact emerged as major actors to improve the quality of the political and economic governance in many countries (Africa Recovery, July 1997). This has occurred in Zimbabwe as well, a trend that can only be strengthened in the future.

It can be concluded that the key tasks included by the World Bank (1997) in the definition of good governance are important for small enterprises. However, from that point of view, two tasks should be added to the list. The first is the provision of timely and relevant information to small scale proprietors of matters of concern to them. This could be done through a government consultancy structure and a number of donor funded projects aim at improving the capabilities of government agencies in this regard. The second task is reform of local government practices, adjusting them according to the situation and problems of small enterprises.

Notes

1. See also Bradburd and Levy, 1995 and Mhone, 1995.
2. For detailed studies of circumstances in different sectors and areas, see van Dijk, 1992a; Mutambirwa, 1995; Chavarika, 1996; Mhuriro, 1996; Murphy, 1996 and Sibanda, 1996.
3. In Masvingo ENDA (1990) found that the Council had set aside land to allocate to co-operatives free of charge, usually for agricultural purposes.
4. The activities of SEDCO are described in chapter 7 of van Dijk (1990).
5. The DPT was originally asked to review 28 Acts of Parliament. In the course of their research it became necessary to review a body of additional legislation, including subordinate legislation.
6. The ETP target groups are: retrenched and disabled persons entitled for training, with free training course (till August 1996) or a paid training course

(from September 1996) and with a project proposal, or an outstanding SDF-loan. The proposal needs to be submitted to and approved by LOGAC.

7. They developed a solar dryer a number of years ago and provided training on how to use it.

8. See also Otero (1987).

10
Economic Cultures and Industrial Development in the South

Árni Sverrisson

A considerable and growing body of literature now exists which employs some kind of network or cluster approach to issues of entrepreneurship, industrialization and technical change in the developing countries (e.g. Nadvi and Schmitz, 1994; Pedersen *et al.*, 1994; van Dijk and Rabellotti, 1997). However, the researchers involved come from different disciplines, economics, sociology, geography and political science. They also relate more or less critically to different substantive concerns. Some are interested in the long-term paths development can take, others are more interested in the short-term consequences of, e.g. structural adjustment, yet others are primarily focused on particular groups or forms of organization, such as small scale enterprises, or focus on some aspect of development, such as technological change.

Evolving over the last 10 years or so, these different approaches have generated a rich source of empirical material as well as a number of more general propositions about development processes (see Chapter 11, this volume and for a critique Galhardi, 1995). However, there has not been much public reflection over the theoretical and meta-theoretical implications of this within particular disciplines or for interdisciplinary work in this field. In this chapter I will, with the humility such a task calls for, try to address this question using theories of economic sociology (exemplified by the work of Granovetter, 1973, 1985; Burt, 1992; and Callon 1991, for instance). Unavoidably, such an attempt must remain incomplete and partial. Economic sociology is but one of many sociologies, after all. Further, the contribution of unorthodox economics to the development of network/cluster approaches in this particular context is considerable and would deserve a similarly systematic treatment. It is imperative, however, to start a discussion of the implications of network and cluster approaches for the larger issues in development studies, and it has to start somewhere.

In what follows, the emphasis will be on networks rather than clusters, in so far as the two can be distinguished. Combinations of enterprises or enterprise clusters are often, but not always, presented as the loci of intensive networking, i.e. as social entities held together by a logic of complementarities. Each actor then includes other actors in his ambit depending on whether they have something he lacks and needs or not (the actors of economic sociology are, as yet, mostly male). However, the opposite can be true as well. Actors relate to other actors with whom they have something in common. In consequence, clusters can be presented as groups of enterprises and/or business people held together by characteristics they share: common location, a common language, a common educational background, a common ethnic background, a common source of materials, etc. In practice, the two logics tend to be interlaced, which is why networking and clustering are usually, if not always, observed by the same people. However, in such studies, the two logics are frequently conflated, or one or the other is taken as given, while keeping them apart and studying the relation between them could be useful.

Structural Holes

From a social network perspective industrialization problems can be approached from three angles mainly, one based on Burt's analysis of structural holes, the second developing Granovetter's analysis of the social embeddedness of social relations, and the third utilizing Granovetter's concept of weak ties.

Burt's structural hole theory presents networking in terms of complementarities. Its contribution to the problem at hand can be summarized as follows: entrepreneurship consists primarily in creating connections between previously unrelated economic actors, and thereby increasing the availability of finance, competence, or other relevant resources, and in avoiding connections which do not have this effect. In other words, the entrepreneur fills some kind of vacuum or, in Burt's terminology, a 'structural hole'. The important thing to note about this particular definition is that it does not imply that the new constellation of actors is new in the sense that new types of actors are being connected which have never been connected before, or that the result of making these connections is an organizational or technological novelty or innovation not known earlier. It is new in a very concrete sense, and entrepreneurship of this kind is therefore a part and parcel of everyday economic activities, in which new alliances among companies are continuously being created. This can happen in very ad hoc ways as when African carpenters co-operate on fulfilling large orders (Sverrisson, 1993), or be the beginning of a lasting rearrangement of co-operative relationships, sometimes 'technology driven,' as in the cases described by Sandee (1995), or it can happen through close co-operation developed over a number of years. Historically, such connections have been important in technological development, particularly in enhancing the effectiveness and diffusion of the many mundane technologies which together are the material substratum of modernity (Allen, 1983; Scranton, 1997). The main point is, however, that entrepreneurship of this kind is a normal and necessary prerequisite of a dynamic economy, and in order to emphasize this fact, it may be better to denote this particular subspecies of entrepreneurship with a different term, *brokerage*, focusing on the act (or business) of making connections.[1]

For those of us who are primarily interested in the problems of developing countries, the issue arises of what kinds of entrepreneurship or brokerage, understood in this particular fashion, are important in the context we are analysing. Is connection-making important in the economic dynamics of underdevelopment, and if it is, then how?

Context and Embeddedness

Let me briefly summarize a few major characteristics of the economic systems of developing countries, each of which suggest roads along which a network/cluster approach can develop to the point of illuminating general issues in development theory. First, as I have noted elsewhere (Sverrisson, 1993, and many others before me) developing economic systems tend to be bifurcated. On the one hand, there is a large sector which in terms of technology, organization, and often in terms of scale of operation as well, belongs to a global technological system centred in the wealthy North, but spreading its tentacles into every country. These local outposts of the global system often produce export commodities of one kind or another. On the other hand, there is a multitude of local systems, which are, however, remarkably similar. They are based on local markets, usually produce simple consumption goods, formal training and education matter little, and most of the units involved are fairly small. They are local in the sense that their system characteristics are based on local needs, resources and other local circumstances but not, of course, in the sense that they are somehow unconnected to the rest of the world. In using the term system, however, I am indicating that each local economy should be understood as a self-regulating entity. In the case of the global system this is hardly controversial, in the case of local systems, which are then seen as quite distinct from the global system, this proposition is contentious.

However, and that is the important point here, these local systems embody economic dynamics very different from those of the global economic system, and the most significant part of that is that growth takes a different form in local systems: Companies do grow but only up to a point. They rather become more numerous instead. The reasons for this vary: during hard times, local production of simple consumption goods may become feasible, because imports are impossible or prohibitively expensive and new ventures crop up. During good times, opportunities for starting all kinds of locally oriented enterprises in carpentry or dressmaking, etc. obviously increase. In normal times again, population growth at least creates increased needs for simple consumer products, and during hard times again, unemployment provides incentives for self-employment (cf. Havnevik, 1987; Dawson, 1990).

The relative size (in e.g. persons employed) of each of the two types of economic system varies according to time and place, but during industrialization processes, the simultaneous presence of both is ubiquitous. This is somewhat self-evident: the old local systems do not fade away quickly, and the new, global, system takes long to develop. But the corollaries of this often forgotten circumstance are not all that obvious, however. These particular dynamics which stem from the combination of two different economic logics are a universal characteristic of industrialization processes – and a universal problem in the study of these processes.

The exact characteristics of local systems vary, the general similarities observed above notwithstanding. However, a relative absence of network connections between global and local systems seemingly appears everywhere as a corollary of underdevelopment. In brokerage terms one can say that brokers in each system appear to operate primarily within that system rather than creating connections between them. Even relatively simple commercial transactions tend to materialize within systems rather than between them (Knorringa, 1995). The main connections which can be observed are established through people who sell their labour power in the global/modern system but spend the proceedings on products of the local system, and in the provision of raw materials and inputs which are prepared in the global system and used in the local system.

Why would this be the case? In Burt's terms, the bifurcation of economic life should present itself as a sea of opportunities for making new and profitable connections, but yet, in underdeveloped countries, few seem to see it that way. In South Korea, to be sure, subcontracting systems which continue local and traditional forms of organisation are connected to global corporations (Cho, 1994). But this is an exception, so far, and hardly an example of underdevelopment either.

It is here that the concept of embeddedness proposed by Granovetter (1985) can help us. He writes:

> Even when economists do take social relationships seriously...they invariably abstract away from the history of relations and their position with respect to other relations – what might be called the historical and structural embeddedness of relations. The interpersonal ties described in their arguments are extremely stylized, average, 'typical' – devoid of specific content, history or structural location. Actors' behaviour results from their named positions and role sets; thus we have arguments about how workers and supervisors, husbands and wives, or criminals and law enforcers will interact with one another, but these relations are not assumed to have individualized content beyond that given by their named roles.
>
> p. 58

This should be approached differently, according to Granovetter:

> Actors do not behave or decide as atoms outside a social context, nor do they adhere slavishly to a script written for them by the particular intersection of social categories that they happen to occupy. Their attempts at purposive action are instead embedded in concrete, ongoing systems of social relations.
>
> p. 58

This holds, according to Granovetter, both for 'pre-market' economies, in which the effects of embeddedness tend to be overstated and the range of ordinary economic transactions correspondingly underestimated, and for 'market' economies in which the logic of markets is held (by economists) to dominate to the extent that 'historical and structural' features are ignored altogether or reduced to variants of the logic of the 'market'.[2]

We can now observe that the global economic system and the multitude of local systems do not only differ in terms of economic dynamics as identified above, the transactions within them are embedded in very different (economic) cultures as well, and the mechanisms of this embeddedness itself (i.e. the relation between the transactions and their context) are therefore different. This influences the way people relate to issues of both technology and organisation, and not least, how people relate to each other in the course of a day's business. Being a worker in one of the many local systems around the world implies different things than being a worker within the global system. The possibility of 'starting one's own' is for example ever-present in local systems and frequently realized. Because most owners of production enterprises in local systems have once been workers, they tend to interpret their role differently than those in the global system, who usually have no such background, but owe their position to inherited wealth and education, either or both (Scranton, 1997). Further, elementary economic transactions such as buying/selling, lending and borrowing, and production practices such as the physical transformation of things or the acquisition of particular techniques are conducted in different contexts and interpreted differently as well, and therefore acted on and decided about in different ways. Haggling, as an element of ordinary commercial transactions, is a prime example of this: in most local systems haggling is a matter of course and often conducted routinely, almost ritually, whereas within the global north-centred system it is limited to specific occasions and informal contexts when considerable sums are involved, the practical minimum probably being the price of a used car. The examples could be multiplied, but the main point I want to make here should be clear: because of these cultural differences pertaining to histories, structures and their interpretations, networking co-operatively across the bifurcation line is, if not impossible, then at least very difficult, and most of the time, it hardly even occurs to the people involved.

Technology and Society

It is useful at this point in the discussion to bring in the techno/economic network theory represented by authors such as Callon (1991), Latour (1991) and Akrich (1992). The core proposition of this school which deserves further elaboration in this context is as follows: In order to analyse technologies in their social aspect, they must be seen as social actors or, to use the original term, *actants*. Technological artefacts or non-human actors are considered as essentially equivalent to human actors in socio/technical networks. This idea is related to a central tenet of engineering practice (almost self-evident to many), i.e. the substitution of machinery for human labour, in which the machines take over, as it were, the role of human actors in the production process, as if they were interchangeable. This process, that is mechanization, does in turn lie at the core of social development. According to actor/network theory technological artefacts, and machinery in particular, can be usefully analysed as structuring agents a par with the people involved, and hence, available technologies can powerfully shape social networks and economic organisation (and vice versa).

This immediately raises the problem of subjectivity; the ability to be a subject, the capability to act in a social context. Can artefacts be subjects? The actor/network solution to this problem is to endow artefacts with consciousness via human representatives, engineers, economists and policy-makers, which together create as it were the mental states where the substitution of machinery for labour in particular forms are possible – and are often seen as the only possible road. The common sense view of the relations between people and techniques is turned on its head, as it were: Techniques are not always the tools of people – people can also be and often are the 'tools of techniques', i.e. they are caused to act by technical circumstances, make demands which are created by particular configurations of machinery, promote policies which benefit one production system rather than another, etc. Artefacts acquire, as it were, a vicarious consciousness.

However, this problem can also be solved in another way. Social actors are, after all, not necessarily conscious in the sense implied above or to put it differently, social agency does not necessarily imply continuous, and even less, rational reflection. If it did, economic life would be a good deal more contemplative than what it observably is. Hence, in order to act as structuring agents, machines, tools, buildings and other artefacts do not need to be endowed with even a vicarious consciousness. All that is needed is that their structuring characteristics are taken as granted. The machine is operated on its own terms, that is, used for its intended purpose in its intended context. The same applies to buildings: people take their places in a lecture hall according to well known rules.

In other words, if social relations, including of course the pattern of economic transactions in a particular culture, are embedded in technological relations among artefacts which are taken for granted, there is no logical need to endow them with any kind of consciousness in order to explain their structuring effects. Being the products of human efforts and design, machines embody the social circumstances and assumptions underlying that design, and using them reproduces the social structures which created these design criteria in the first place. Hence the problem of subjectivity does not really disqualify theories based on seeing artefacts as actors in networks.

Flexible Technologies

The problem with the actor/network view of technological artefacts goes much deeper. A quick look at social actors in general shows us why. Most social actors participate in many different networks, and they take on different roles depending on the type of network in which they are involved at a particular moment. Taking on a different role implies drawing on a different set of conventions of action and interaction, of meaning, expectations and interpretation, in short, to adopt different social practices. Reasonably, if we take technological artefacts seriously as social actors we would except them to behave likewise.

Wiebe Bijker has developed a concept which can help us to analyze this problem further. He has suggested that all technologies, particularly in the design/innovation stage, possess what he calls interpretative flexibility (Bijker, 1995). The original idea of a technology, embodied in a prototype of say, the bicycle, is subject to a complex process of negotiation and design development, until it receives its final form in what Bijker calls a (temporary) closure. This event is different from an 'ordinary' discursive closure in that its result is not just consensus around a problem definition which identifies a set of solutions deemed feasible for whatever reason and excludes others. It is rather embodied in an artefact which can be used in particular ways and not others. The process leading from interpretative indeterminacy over interpretative flexibility to interpretative closure is in other words the process of negating most of the multiple potentialities of a novel technological idea, and finding a well defined slot or niche in which it fits squarely and securely.

This notwithstanding, technologies tend to retain a degree of flexibility, now embodied in the artefact itself, rather than in its indeterminate concept. We can call this practical flexibility, which allows us to combine two aspects of technological flexibility, the interpretative flexibility of the design process and the material flexibility of the diffusion process, which makes it possible for technologies to be reinterpreted and used in ways more varied than their designers ever imagined. The example of personal computers, the capabilities of which to run different and new types of programmes regularly outruns the capabilities of software designers to invent such programmes is enough to make the point.

Obviously such practical flexibility varies greatly quantitatively and qualitatively among technologies. The usefulness of this type of flexibility also varies depending on the social practices with which particular technologies are integrated. As Sabel and Zeitlin (1985), among others, have pointed out, people need flexible equipment in social environments where the ability to make many different things is a prerequisite of survival and eventually success, and this is the situation in most local production cultures. In social environments where the ability to make many similar things quickly and cheaply takes precedence, as has been the case in the global production culture, and still is to a large extent today, practical flexibility is of little consequence. Just as many, perhaps most of us, only take on a small number of fairly standardized roles, technologies can be perfectly useful even if their social/practical repertoire is extreme limited. However, some of us become veritable social chameleons by virtue of our participation in many and different social networks. Similarly, there are technologies the main point of which is practical flexibility, that is, the capability to adapt to varied social contexts. Multi-purpose machinery is likely to achieve social success in local economic cultures, varied as they are from one place to the next, and shaped by uncertainty, diverse demand and limited standardization.

Strong and Weak Ties

Above were noted elementary economic transactions which cross the lines between different economic systems as they have always done. However, the connections are by no means limited to that. In order to grasp this better it is useful to draw on another distinction made by Granovetter (1973), namely that between strong ties and weak ties. Granovetter's distinction starts from a recurring sociological theme: the relativity of the social order. Not all social relations are equally intense. Interaction with one person is usually more or less frequent than with another, and, moreover, varies over time. Some people are well connected whereas others relate only to a select few, and we tend to be committed subjectively and therefore in actual fact to those we relate to intimately and often. Granovetter sums this up in the distinction referred to above: strong ties are intense, interaction is frequent, and they tend to connect several people closely. Weak ties on the other hand tend to be more ephemeral and temporary: a major characteristic of the weak tie is just this: actual face to face interaction occurs rarely if at all.

Now Granovetter maintains that in the diffusion of novel information weak ties are much more effective than strong ties for the following reason: people connected via strong ties tend, in virtue of this, to share the same knowledge, attitudes and values, and whatever else constitutes information such as similar terminologies, experiences, etc. New ideas and information about such things which are beyond the immediate horizon of a group connected with strong ties tend therefore to come through connections of a very different order, i.e weak ties.

We can for example think of the relations among furniture-makers who all work in the same street or marketplace who know each other well, co-operate when the occasion arises, work for each other from time to time, borrow tools from each other, allow each other the use of the machines which the more fortunate do possess, and generally trust each other up to a point. Although less close knit than small village communities or extended families, such networks would still qualify as an example of fairly strong ties. As Kenneth King and Charles Aboudha (1991) once observed, such clusters are usually characterized by imitation rather than innovation, one reason being that because of the effective information-sharing mechanisms in place the benefits of the first-comer, which could otherwise offset the costs of experimenting, are low or none. From what I know (Sverrisson, 1993) I can only agree. In contrast, weak ties also exist with people outside the close social ambit of such local production networks. These may be links to local economic cultures elsewhere or with local representatives of the global economic culture. Although interaction with them may be rare, it can be (and is according to my experiences) pregnant with technological and organizational information.

This leads to the preliminary conclusion that strong ties and close relations based on trust are likely to reinforce underdevelopment and weak ties which occur as it were as corollaries of instrumental relations such as elementary economic transactions facilitate the diffusion of novelty, and thereby, development.

Innovation and Information

There is a great difference between the global economic culture and its centres in the North, on the one hand, and the different local economic cultures of the South on the other, when it comes to weak ties. In the North weak ties do not only exist in a multitude of informal ways, created in the interstices of working life in large urban agglomerations, but also in institutionalized forms, from the media and public libraries to the internet. This latter type of connections is comparatively rare in the South because of poverty and the prevalence of dictatorship and censorship, which suppresses most media not controllable by government, however innocent.

But yet, information travels in the South if slowly and erratically. People moving from one location to another bring new ideas with them, and people leaving a company to work for another or start their own do likewise. Those who are successful in setting up their own enterprises and keeping them afloat usually have considerable experience in the line of business concerned, ranging from a couple of years to perhaps 20 years. Superficially one would take this as a function of the increased technical and organizational competence that comes with experience and that undoubtedly plays a role here. However, another asset is quite as important, namely the sort of social or network capital which is manifested in extensive customer contacts. Word of mouth is passed among former and potential customers about good and bad (or cheap and expensive) carpenters, blacksmiths and dressmakers, and these networks also spread information about competent workers who start their own workshops. By 'taking with them' customers from a former place of work, proprietors of newly established workshops get a flying start, and through recommendations of these customers the new workshop can thrive, while another one-started by someone just out of school is not getting anywhere.

Continuing with the parameters of success, network theory suggests yet another factor which I have been able to observe on the ground, namely cooperation among workshops. Of particular interest here is the kind of co-operation which arises in consequence of the unequal distribution of machinery, and the resulting division of labour. As I have discussed this at length elsewhere (Sverrisson, 1994a, 1997 for instance) only an outline will be presented here. What basically happens is that someone in a location, well known by colleagues and customers, acquires a machine, e.g. a wood lathe. Although the orders of this particular person or workshop may not justify this investment, the money earned by letting others use the machine or taking orders from others for turned table legs, etc. does. Hence, if, for example, one carpenter in a location has a lathe and there is demand for turned legs for tables, beds, etc. the entire carpentry network will be oriented towards the lathe owner, and his possession of a lathe will have the same effect on the products available as if everyone had lathes.

Henry Sandee (1995 and Chapter 6, this volume) has told a similar story about roof-tile-making in Indonesia. A single machine accessible to all increases the productivity of all, but the distribution of benefits does not have to be equal. Hence, local machine investment is often more a matter of a few machines to which everyone has access in one way or another, than providing a machine of some kind for everyone. However, for this to work as intended, strong ties are needed. The strength of weak ties, which carry the seed of mechanization, depends on strong ties, which are the soil in which it takes root.

Hence, even if weak ties are needed for the diffusion of novelty, the implementation of novelty seems, at least in local economic cultures in the South, to call for the presence of strong ties.

Conclusion

Returning to our discussion of bifurcation, it is striking how little of this type of co-operation spans the border between the global and the local economic culture. Exceptions can be found: gear-cutters for example, a fairly complex, mechanized special operation, serve all kinds of mechanical workshops both in Ghana and Zimbabwe. However, both in the case of subcontracting and of more informal modes of co-operation, they tend to remain within the confines of either culture, as entrepreneurs/brokers follow well-worn paths established in the past.

This brings us again to the core of the problem. Economic transactions and other economic relations are, to speak with Granovetter, embedded in the bifurcation of economic cultures itself. Because the bifurcation as such is a universal characteristic of industrialization processes, it cannot be done away with. Indeed, it appears rather that the bifurcation, which signifies that some companies have taken the lead, is a necessary prerequisite for industrialization. At the very least, there is no known industrialization process in which this has not happened and the appearance of the bifurcation, in itself, should therefore be seen as a positive sign. On the other hand, it appears that this bifurcation is the main obstacle to industrialization. Where does that leave us?

In lieu of an answer, I can only offer observations based on earlier industrialization experiences, or rather, on a comparison of successful experiences and failures. What does it take to industrialize? Undoubtedly, the development and diffusion of mass-production methods is necessary; this has happened everywhere. However, if we look at what has happened to the local small scale, networked economic cultures of Western Europe, USA and Japan during the process, we can observe that they did not disappear. Rather, they were rejuvenated.[3] The exact forms of this varied, across branches, nations and regions, as did the point in time when eventually mass production took the lead and was transformed from an experiment in production organization into the engine of industrialization.

However, it is reasonable from the viewpoint of Third World development to ask the question: was there something common in all these experiences, that made it possible for local economic systems in the now industrialized countries, first, to sustain experiments in mass production, then to support the development of mass production methods (e.g. by crafting the machines used in the new factories), and all the while, retain a growth dynamic of their own leading to a variety of innovations?

Above we have identified a number of circumstances which can be found in the more vigorous local economic cultures of the South. They are:

- Network mechanization based on easy access and cooperation;
- Utilization of network complementarities superimposed on clusters which are based on shared background characteristics;
- Mobilization of strong ties to facilitate creation of weak ties and vice versa;
- Innovative local interpretation of technologies leading to practical flexibility;
- Circulation of technical and organizational information through migration and the establishment of new enterprises;
- Presence of individuals who through the possession of essential technologies or by organizational means (or both) act as brokers of information and opportunities.

All these phenomena can also be observed in the earlier local economic cultures in the North, and constitute together what we could a bit daringly call the universal characteristics of dynamic local economic cultures. Perhaps the prevalence of craft production and polyvalent or all-round skills of workers should be added to this list.

However, observing this only makes the task of explaining the very different outcomes more intractable. If local cultures have similar dynamics everywhere, why do these dynamics lead to industrialization in some cases and not others? One answer can be the extreme competitiveness of local economic cultures in the South as compared to that of the earlier North. Unrestricted competition leads to small margins, less room for experiments and risk taking, hampers the formation of networks both strong and weak, and consequently hinders growth.

Another explanation can be the openness of southern economies relative to those of the earlier North which certainly facilitates the consumption of novelties but hardly supports their local production. A third explanation can be found in the political form of the bifurcation of the two cultures in the South as compared to the earlier North. In the South, mass-production politics preceded mass-production itself; in the North, the order was the reverse. Lastly, in the South, early mass-production initiatives have mainly been focused on import substitution for comparatively wealthy customers, in the North two other customer categories dominated, namely armies and ordinary people whereas craft products were aimed at upscale markets or special niches. In the South, in contrast, cheap products remain the preserve of local economic cultures and insofar as mass-produced goods are consumed, they tend to be imported.

However, the variability of Southern experiences is no less than that of Northern experiences: a case in point is the Republic of South Korea (Cho, 1994). In many countries local mass-production systems struggle to retain their place in the global economic culture, adjust to political demands and take advantage of export opportunities (cf. Chapter 2). The main obstacle, however, is the limited local demand for such products, a direct result of the impoverishment of local economic cultures, and this in turn makes it difficult for local mass-producers to enter a learning trajectory leading to export successes. Structural adjustment, regrettably, seems to exacerbate this problem rather than solve it.

Notes

1. I have not adopted Burt's term *tertium gaudens*, which he in turn adopts from Simmel, because of its opacity. Brokerage instantly signifies what is the key feature here, whereas *tertium gaudens* calls for a lengthy explanation (Burt, 1992).
2. Granovetter explicitly by-passes the issue of 'pre-market' societies in the article quoted here and he has not returned to it since, to my knowledge.
3. There is a large literature which testifies to this. See, e.g. Yamazaki, 1981; Hounshell, 1991; Takeuchi, 1991; Scranton, 1997 and Sabel and Zeitlin, 1997.

11

Conclusion: Research Issues after Structural Adjustment

Meine Pieter van Dijk and Árni Sverrisson

During a long period, the local economies of the South were shaped by more or less successful attempts by national governments to isolate them from the vagaries of global competition through an array of protective measures. Meanwhile, more powerful global actors promoted free trade, mainly among themselves but also in and with the South. Simultaneously, heated debates have taken place among development researchers over free trade policies vs. protectionism. This impasse has now definitely been resolved in favour of free trade and the result is what we can call permanent structural adjustment.

During the last ten years, research on the role of small enterprises in industrialization and on locally grounded development in the South has also developed considerably. Concepts such as flexible specialization, industrial districts, entrepreneurial development and appropriate technology have gained ground at the expense of conventional microeconomic approaches.

In this concluding chapter we discuss the research issues which permanent structural adjustment and the advances in research on local economies have put on the agenda, under five headings. The first concerns structural adjustment itself; how does it look from the point of view of local entrepreneurs? The second issue is clustering and networking. Does structural adjustment change the feasible forms of clustering and networking and increase or decrease its importance? The third issue is what has been called the new dualism, that is groupings of small enterprises around large enterprises to which they do relate in varied ways or don't. Is the development potential of such constellations enhanced by structural adjustment, or are they locked even more irreversibly into the local mechanisms of underdevelopment? The fourth issue is the innovative potential in local economies. Is it enhanced by structural adjustment? Are inequalities in innovation capability ameliorated or intensified? Lastly we suggest a research agenda for the immediate future and discuss how we can go about finding out what we need in order to decide the issues identified. Are broader comparative studies neccessary or is it depth that we lack at the moment?

Structural Adjustment and Economic Development

Currently, structural adjustment has changed the conditions for small- and medium-sized enterprises, but it has not decreased the importance of adaptive strategies. However, as pointed out by Visser, Meyer-Stamer and Trulsson, among others in this volume, the options available depend on the point of departure and the success of adaptive mechanisms depends in this as well. Therefore, it is important to consider carefully a number of case studies before developing a new generic model for small enterprise development, which can both accommodate recent theoretical advances and the new situation created by structural adjustment.

The first step in this direction is to gather and analyse empirical material about the consequences of structural adjustment on local enterprises in particular instances, and this is the main focus of this volume. Perhaps a bit surprisingly, the overall conclusion is rather optimistic. The effects of structural adjustment can be very positive for some enterprises. Meyer-Stamer argues that the shock brought about by structural adjustment forces managers to adjust their strategies, and even if they are slow, they can indeed do it. Similar conclusions are drawn by Trulsson, Halimana and Sverrisson, and Pedersen from their particular cases. Visser, van Dijk and Revoltella argue for a somewhat more pessimistic view, and Sverrisson's theoretical argument in Chapter 10 suggests that these adaptive strategies, which make it possible for the small- and medium-sized enterprise sector to survive, may not be enough to break through the more fundamental constraints on development, often referred to in earlier development debates but somewhat off the mainstream agenda today (e.g. Amin, 1976; Frank, 1978; Wallerstein, 1983).

However, a number of issues remain, which need to be addressed in further research. First, structural adjustment can alternatively be seen as a shock (or a series of identifiable shocks), or as a phase in an evolutionary process. Thus, the focus can be on short-term or long-term effects. Most of the contributors in this volume adopt the former view.

There is, prima facie, no need to doubt the shock character of structural adjustment, nor the view that structural adjustment is in the main an externally conceived strategy more or less imposed on the economies of the South. To expect quick recovery from the shock is not particularly realistic either, although the increasing fluctuations of the world economy might create such an appearance temporarily. Rather, as some firms or even entire sectors, such as small-scale tailoring, are wiped out by structural adjustment in some countries, they are strengthened in others, and in the hard hit countries, new activities crop up or old are reoriented. In other words, the global division of labour and the position of local economies within it does change, but what happens then?

Another way of putting this question is: what kind of dynamism do we have here? Earlier experiences of crisis in the South have shown that people show considerable ingenuity in creating new enterprises out of whatever opportunities they can find, simply because they have to (Havnevik, 1987; Dawson, 1990). Thus, the mere existence of a large number of new or changing firms cannot be read as a sign of a dynamic that breaks out of the old constraints on development. For that to happen, both the internal structure of local economies needs to change in fundamental ways, and their relations to the global economy as well. One aspect of this is the privatization or closing down of parastatal enterprises and government-owned corporations. Another aspect is the changes in how network and cluster advantages are created, maintained and utilized, which we discuss in the next section.

Clusters and Networks Among Small Enterprises

There is as yet little agreement on what a cluster is, and what can be called a cluster. Ongoing research seems to add to the plethora rather than reduce it to manageable proportions. However, a number of criteria crop up in case studies, both in this volume and elsewhere (see further van Dijk, 1997). The first criterion is spatial proximity. However, the relevant distance varies from one kilometre in the centre of a city to about 50 km in the case of some European industrial districts. A second criterion is high density of economic activities. This criterion tends to equal clusters with industry zones or similar phenomena. Prevalence or at least very strong presence of firms involved in the same, similar or subsidiary activities is a third criterion often mentioned, and as a fourth, the existence of inter-firm linkages between enterprises as a result of subcontracting, as well as other forms of networking and co-operation within a limited area. As a fifth criterion, a joint history, and the common understandings, co-operative efforts and dynamic learning effects that come with it have been mentioned, a point particularly stressed by Visser, Chapter 5 and Meyer-Stamer, Chapter 2 in this book. In addition, the members of a cluster may share a cultural background and sometimes a cluster can be identified through institutional arrangements and associations.

These criteria can be developed into what we can call a three-pronged approach to cluster-oriented analysis. The first prong is then analysis of the production network and the transactions immediately neccessary to maintain it. The most basic task here is to understand what kind of networking takes place among a set of companies defined by the intersection of industrial branch and location, e.g. all firms involved in carpentry in the Timber Market in Accra (Sverrisson, 1997). Another task is to investigate what kind of supporting input, repair and marketing networks are maintained in a particular area, and which lead to actors outside the area. Although cluster analysis is often used as a substitute for network analysis, and the actual interaction either assumed or analysed in general rather than specific terms, the issue usually emerges at some point: who deals with whom, where and how?

The second prong is analysis at the cluster level proper, in which the focus is not so much on production as on commercial transactions within the cluster and other forms of local interaction and their likewise locally determined social embeddedness (Pedersen, 1997). If any kind of network tracing exercise will soon lead us out of a cluster, the whole point of a cluster level analysis is to remain within it and study the local business culture in all its variegated forms, including what sets the cluster apart from its environment, and the emergent properties which result.

The third prong is analysis of the dynamics and history of the cluster. How did it come about? What is keeping it together? Which cleavages can be identified between firms in the cluster, which influence its trajectory? This implies an assumption that network level connections, spatial proximity, observed co-operation or frequent transactions among the members cannot adequately explain the presence and development of a particular cluster. Van Dijk (1997) has, for example, developed a distinction based on such dynamic criteria, and suggests that we can distinguish three different stages in the development of most clusters. The first stage is market-oriented clusters, which form around a particular product. As and if a division of labour and technological development occurs, they are transformed into technological clusters. When the resulting subcontracting relations are complemented by other types of (horizontal) relations among enterprises, a fully fledged industrial district results. As clusters will be at different stages at any given point in time, this concept can also be used to classify clusters.

The New Dualism

The phenomenon known as 'the new dualism' has been touched upon above, but it is now possible to spell out more clearly what it means for small- and medium-sized companies in the post-structural-adjustment-era. By the term new dualism, we mean the existence of informal clusters of small enterprises around the clusters of larger and sometimes more dynamic ones. Superficially, this might seem to imply some kind of subcontracting relationship which, however, is rarely the case in the underdeveloped countries in the South, whereas instances of such relationships have turned up in numerous studies of industrialized countries (e.g. Pyke *et al.*, 1990; Axelsson and Easton, 1992; Grabher, 1993). This type of dualism can be found virtually everywhere in the underdeveloped countries of the South (Nadvi and Schmitz 1994).

One way to approach this problem is to see the more dynamic enterprises as the core of the cluster and the rest as its periphery, reproducing the mechanisms of underdevelopment observable at the global level. A number of relations between the core and the periphery can be observed in such cases: peripheral firms produce cheap wage goods for local markets and make it possible for core companies to pay lower salaries than their counterparts in the industrialized countries. Peripheral firms act as unemployment buffers, easing social tensions and thereby facilitating the operations of the core. Peripheral firms in turn acquire inputs from core firms, ranging from sophisticated textiles for local dress makers, to off-cuts and sub-quality timbers for local carpenters. As the examples suggest, core firms are often located farther upstream in the production chain than peripheral firms, export their output on world markets, and provide them to local small firms as a by-product. However, this is not always the case, and both Meyer-Stamer and Visser provide examples to the contrary in this volume. The difference is rather to be found in the degree of integration into global markets, global technological systems and global financial systems (cf. Sverrisson, Chapter 10 in this volume).

The issue here is whether structural adjustment changes the respective roles of cores and peripheries in local economies in fundamental ways? The integration of core firms into the global economy was earlier mediated by the state in most cases. Many locally established core firms were government-owned, they could borrow on preferential terms from government banks, they operated behind protective barriers erected and maintained by governments, and they had preferential access to state of the art technologies brought in on the basis of development co-operation. As these privileges disappear one after the other, their competitive situation is correspondingly changed.

However, local peripheries also owe their existence to the situation which prevailed before structural adjustment. Protective barriers did not only benefit large scale exporters and import substitution producers. Locally oriented firms were also relieved from competitive pressures and could operate at technology levels significantly below those of the industrialized North, and approach issues such as standardization, quality control and timely delivery rather offhandedly (e.g. Trulsson, Chapter 3; Halimana and Sverrisson, Chapter 7 in this volume). As protective barriers are lifted, cheap mass-products and second-hand imports from elsewhere severely constrain their options, even to the point of making local production unfeasible.

Hence, what we can expect structural adjustment to do in this case is to create a new (but not necessarily any more level) ground for the relations between the local core and its local periphery. The shock of structural adjustment seems in most cases to have increased the divide rather than narrowed it, and the peripheral firms have become even more peripheral or even degenerated into day to day crisis management, although exceptions can be found. The core firms have either adjusted quickly utilizing their own, often considerable, resources, or if they were extremely dependent on or even owned by the state, more or less folded down, leaving the way free for imported substitutes. However, as the after-effects of the shock die down, possibilities emerge for entrepreneurs to take advantage of the situation, as documented in numerous instances in this book. Yet, this area remains underresearched if only because the long-term effects of structural adjustment in combination with other developments in the global economy have not yet manifested themselves fully. This issue therefore remains a major concern for a future research agenda, not least the question whether structural adjustment regimes will, in the medium term, encourage subcontracting and therefore, increased integration of core and periphery, in spite of the opposite trends in the immediate aftermath of the shock, observed by virtually all the contributors to this volume.

Innovation and Small and Medium-sized Enterprises

A long-standing concern within the flexible specialization discussion has been the potential for innovation in small and medium-sized enterprises. These discussions have been woven by two rather distinct strands, one concerned with innovative processes in enterprises, the other with innovation processes in clusters or networks. In both cases, local innovation and adaptation of 'off-the-shelf' technologies is the prevalent form (Stewart, 1978). A large number of empirical studies has shown that the innovation potential is very unevenly distributed among enterprises (e.g. Sverrisson, 1990, 1992, 1993; Aeroe, 1991; Rasmussen, 1992; Knorringa, 1995; Sandee, 1995; and Rabellotti, 1997). Clustering can, however, ensure that the benefits accrue to everyone within the cluster, because of co-operation of some kind or through imitative practices. In other cases cleavages within what appears to be a cluster can also be obstacles to the diffusion of innovations and this is one of the features of the new dualism. Hence, the diffusion of innovations depends less on clustering in the spatial sense than on the relations among firms within the cluster, that is, on their networks.

Do these circumstances change through structural adjustment? It has been argued that firms should have more incentives to innovate when competition increases. On the other hand, a surplus of resources, money, knowledge, time, is often the prerequisite of innovation, and such margins are cut by increased competition. The evidence presented in this volume on this point is not conclusive. Meyer-Stamer (Chapter 2) and Halimana and Sverrisson (Chapter 7), for instance, develop examples in this volume where increased competition has fuelled innovation. Visser's study (Chapter 5) leads to the opposite conclusion for his case, but he notes that others in the vicinity have fared differently.

The solution here is to consider a broader spectrum of possible causes and effects. The innovative potential of firms depends on the character of the cluster in which they are located, or more generally, on the local economic environment. However, it also depends on how a particular firm is located in this environment, and in a variety of value-added chains or production chains, over which small and medium-sized enterprises usually exert little control. The result is a thrust towards vertical integration even within clusters which otherwise would appear to be prime candidates for flexible specialization on a co-operative basis, as documented by Trulsson (Chapter 3) and Meyer-Stamer (Chapter 2) in this volume. If this thrust is also supported by macro-economic policies which favour large-scale integrated enterprises and afford little protection for small-scale enterprises, it will be reinforced even more (Scranton, 1997). A scenario in which the prerequisites of innovation are concentrated even more in relatively developed enterprises as a result of structural adjustment is therefore probable, if not certain. Small enterprises would, in this scenario, survive as sweatshops, with a few dynamic entrepreneurs being able to beat the odds and innovate.

However, as Sandee and Rietveld (Chapter 6, this volume) show, this does not have to be the case, and Pedersen (Chapter 8), Halimana and Sverrisson (Chapter 7), and van Dijk (Chapter 9) also suggest in their contributions that certain branches may actually be strongly favoured by structural adjustment which therefore creates opportunities for innovation even among the very small enterprises.

A Future Research Agenda: Three Levels of Investigation

We can now summarize our reflections about structural adjustment and local economies. First, let us note that the effects depend on which aspect is in focus. In this volume three aspects have been lifted out, namely:

- Strategies of proprietors and managers and action at the enterprise level,
- The interconnections between enterprises in networks and clusters,
- The impact of structural adjustment on aggregate growth and development.

Several of the studies have discussed how the reaction of an individual proprietor or entrepreneur very much depends on her judgement of the situation. The responses range from moving the company to changing the product, the service, or the production process. Going into a new line of business altogether is also a possibility, and in volatile environments entrepreneurs often keep a door open by developing several activities simultaneously. Trulsson's (Chapter 3) examples of vertical integration as a reaction to uncertainty and Revoltella's (Chapter 4) analysis of how internal funding supplants credit as an important source of finance can also be mentioned as entrepreneurial strategies to cope with structural adjustment.

In the contributions which focus on clusters the central question has been: what makes the cluster tick? What is the role of policies and projects, of entrepreneurship and of innovation? In this book, Visser (Chapter 5) points to the disintegration of the cluster mechanism in difficult times, while Sandee and Rietveld (Chapter 6) stress that innovation diffusion in clusters of small enterprises may actually help the cluster survive. As the shock of structural adjustment dies down, the issue will remain with us, however. Earlier research shows beyond reasonable doubt that spatial agglomeration and networking are important in understanding small-enterprise networks and cluster development, and it is time to go beyond that, as preliminarily attempted by all contributors to this volume, in order to identify what distinguishes dynamic clusters from stagnant ones (see also Schmitz, 1995a, 1997).

At the level of the political and economic environment the impact of macro policies and deregulation are clearly assessed in the case of Zimbabwe in the different chapters dealing with this country. One observation is that despite more than a decade of structural adjustment programs, Zimbabwe, like a number of other countries, does not have macro-economic and regulatory frameworks which are adequate for small- and medium-sized enterprises.

Further, as Pedersen (Chapter 8) shows, it is difficult to determine on the basis of available data which explanations hold at the aggregate level. Van Dijk (Chapter 9) suggests that prevalent attitudes among established interests are an obstacle as well. When the small and medium enterprises are cast in the role of illegal or disloyal competitors which should be eliminated, rather than integrated, the economic mechanisms behind the new dualism are further reinforced. This theme is also developed by Sverrisson (Chapter 10) who stresses the social and cultural embeddedness of industrial networks, and suggests that the explanations for the relative underdevelopment of clusters in the South need partly to be sought in such factors rather than the discontinuities of economic networks per se.

All considered, the three pronged strategy developed earlier in this chapter yields the following research questions:

- *What is the impact of structural adjustment on economic networks?*
  Certain inputs will, for example, become available from the outside and take the place of homespun alternatives. Marketing channels will change as public sector purchasing is reorganized to adapt to new policy priorities. Repair services will lose importance as new machinery can be acquired more easily. Intensified competition with imports can make a major reconfiguration imperative.
- *To what extent can the local business culture cope with structural adjustment?*
  Does the shock intensify co-operation, or as suggested by several authors in this volume, drive people apart? Do entrepreneurs strike out along different paths or do they follow their old lines of action, with increased vigour? How are the longer-term prospects conceived and interpreted individually and collectively by cluster members? How do collective responses fare in comparison with individual responses?

- *How does structural adjustment facilitate or hinder dynamic development?*
  One issue here is if structural adjustment facilitates technological
  change and division of labour, or if cluster members are thrown
  back on traditional crisis management, cost-cutting and wage-
  cutting. A second issue, which arises in cases where division of labour
  and technological change is already occurring on a general scale, is
  whether the deepening of these processes is facilitated by structural
  adjustment which implies increased competition but also increased
  availability of imports. In the case of developed clusters, in which
  interrelations among companies are established at all levels, to
  the point where they form a meta-enterprise rather than a mere
  agglomeration of companies, the issue becomes if such relations can
  be maintained in spite of the shock, and then turned to a strong
  advantage afterwards, or if a return to or further development of
  existing vertical integration strategies is a likely result.

Lastly, the question can be posed whether the impact of structural
adjustment depends on the character of the cluster? Are market oriented
clusters more vulnerable than clusters built around particular core technologies with numerous subcontracting links? Can well-integrated clusters withstand shocks better than their less integrated but more flexible
counterparts?

Beyond Flexible Specialization

Concepts like flexible specialization (van Dijk, 1996) and industrial
districts (van Dijk, 1993) have been used to explain the dynamics of
certain regions or cities. Each of these concepts stresses the importance
of clustering, innovation and co-operation among firms. However, the
mechanism assumed to stimulate innovation differs. In the flexible
specialization paradigm, innovation is the result of the combination
of skilled labour, multi-purpose equipment and an innovative mentality. In the industrial district literature, innovation is the result of proximity and relations between firms, and the emergent dynamics which
follow.

Van Dijk (1992) defines flexible specialization as a higher order concept, which points to seven important, and often interrelated, characteristics of the dynamic small enterprise sector:

1. An innovative mentality on the part of local entrepreneurs,
2. Broadly skilled personnel, trained on the job,

3. Inter-firm co-operation, often in the form of subcontracting,
4. Spatial clustering of (mainly small) enterprises,
5. Networking among (mainly small) enterprises,
6. Multi-purpose tools and machines,
7. Specialization and proven flexibility.

It has, however, turned out to be difficult to find cases in the field, where all these characteristics are simultaneously present. However, as a summary of what has been shown to be important mechanisms in the dynamics of existing clusters, it is still valid. In order to disentangle the contributions of each mechanism it is important to develop operational variables and collect detailed data at the firm level, in order to ascertain how different mechanisms work out for different categories of firms and in different types of clusters (cf. Dijkman and van Dijk, 1997). In this it is imperative to try to measure the effects of being in a cluster and separate them from other causes of growth and decline, of innovation and its absence (cf. Chapter 6).

Further, much of the earlier research on flexible specialization, clustering of small enterprises and networks of small entrepreneurs has had a very local focus, and although the contributions in this book transcend this partially through their emphasis on the effects of global economic processes and of nationally constructed economic programmes, much work remains to be done in order to facilitate comparative analysis.

It is therefore imperative to go beyond flexible specialization and industrial districts cum ideal types and focus the attention of researchers squarely on the components or to put it another way, the basic mechanisms of growth, and how they operate in different contexts. One can ask, for example, what is the role of the concentration of economic activities, and focus on that, and ignore for the moment, for example, whether craft production is prevalent or not. Innovations and their dissemination is another possible candidate for comparative study as well as querying the role of different networking strategies.

It is also possible to apply a more historically oriented approach and follow particular clusters and other aggregates over a longer period (cf. Chapters 2, 6 and 8). This strategy works, as it were, in the opposite direction. Rather than specifying mechanisms assumed to be operative in a large number of superficially different situations and investigate whether their presence or absence influences innovation and growth, the cases selected are studied in even more depth. Instead of the one-off field study we get cluster histories, which in turn open new avenues of theorizing about long term processes in clusters and enterprises. As flexible specialization and cluster research in the South comes of age, the opportunities for repeated studies, complementary studies over longer periods and even more or less developed forays into the past of clusters will of course increase (Humphrey, 1995).

Both these paths, while leading us in opposite directions, are based on the shared assumption that the main task is no longer to validate the flexible specialization approach or any other similar approach in the Southern context. That has been accomplished by now. At the same time, the research object, with the advent of structural adjustment, has become distinctly different. In the past we and others with similar agendas have sought to show that local economies in the South have considerable potential for growth and development, even if left on their own in the shadow of protective barriers. Nowadays we have to reconsider this issue and ask if this potential can be developed further in the fierce competition unleashed on the South through structural adjustment.

References

Aage, H. (1997) 'Transition and transplantation of economic systems' in J. Hersh and J. D. Schmidt (eds), *The Aftermath of 'Real Existing Socialism' in Eastern Europe*, Macmillan Press, London.

Adelman, I., J.-M. Bourniaux and J. Waelbroeck (1989) 'Agricultural development-led industrialisation in a global perspective' in J. Williamson and V. Panchamukhi (eds), *The Balance Between Industry and Agriculture in Economic Development*, Macmillan Press, London.

Aeroe, A. (1991) *Rethinking Industrialization – from a National to a Local Perspective: A Case Study of the Industrialization Process in Tanzania with Particular Emphasis on the Construction Industry*, Centre for Development Research, Copenhagen.

Akerlof, G. A. (1970) 'The market for lemons: quality and the market mechanism', *Quarterly Journal of Economics*, Vol. 84: 488–500.

Akrich, M. (1992) 'Beyond social construction of technology: the shaping of people and things in the innovation process' in M. Dierkes and U. Hoffmann (eds.), *New Technology at the Outset: Social Forces in the Shaping of Innovations*, Campus, Frankfurt am Main.

Allen, R. C. (1983) 'Collective invention', *Journal of Economic Behaviour and Organisation*, No. 4: 1–24.

Amin, S. (1976) *Unequal Development: An Essay on the Social Formations of Peripheral Capitalism*, Monthly Review Press, New York.

Arthur, W. B. (1994) *Increasing Returns and Path Dependence in the Economy*, University of Michigan Press, Ann Arbor.

Asmussen, T. (1993) *Employment Implications of Flexible Specialisation in Zimbabwe, mimeo*, International Labour Organisation, Geneva.

Avelino Filho, G. (1994) 'Clientelismo e Política no Brasil: Revisitando Velhos Problemas', *Novos Estudos, CEBRAP*, No. 38: 225–40.

Avritzer, L. (1995) 'Transition to democracy and political culture: an analysis of the conflict between civil and political society in post-authoritarian Brazil', *Constellations*, Vol. 2, No. 2: 242–67.

Axelsson, B. and G. Easton (eds) (1992) *Industrial Networks: A New View of Reality*, Routledge, London.

Baer H. and C. W. Gray (1995) *Debt as a Control Device in Transitional Economies: The Experiences of Hungary and Poland*, Policy Research Working Paper 1480, World Bank, Washington, DC.

Banco Central de Reserva del Perú (1994) *Memoria 1994* (Annual Report 1994), Banco Central de Reserva, Lima.

Banco Central de Reserva del Perú (1995) *Monthly Bulletin*, May and Aug., Banco Central de Reserva, Lima.

Bare, R. (1985) 'Women self-help groups in Zimbabwe', Unpublished paper presented at the Royal Tropical Institute, Amsterdam.

Berglof, E. and G. Roland (1995) 'Bank restructuring and soft budget constraints in financial transition', Working Paper No. 1250, CERP, London.

Berglof, E. and E. L. von Thadden (1994) 'Short-term versus long-term interests: capital structure with multiple investors', *Quarterly Journal of Economics*, Vol. 108: 1055–84.

Berkowitz, S. D. (1988) 'Markets and market areas: some preliminary formulations' in B. Wellman and S. D. Berkowitz (eds), *Social Structures: A Network Approach*, Cambridge University Press, London.

Bijker, W. E. (1995) *Of Bicycles, Bakelites, and Bulbs: Toward a Theory of Sociotechnical Change*, MIT-Press, Cambridge, MA.

Bonin, J. P. and M. E. Schaffer (1995) *Banks, Firms, Bad Debts and Bankruptcy in Hungary 1991–94*, Discussion Paper No. 234, Centre for Economic Performance, London.

Bradburd, R. and B. Levy (1995) *Zimbabwe's New Entrepreneurs: An Emerging Success Story?*, World Bank, Washington, DC.

Brand, V., R. Mupedziswa and P. Gumpo (1995) 'Structural adjustment, women and informal sector trade in Harare' in P. Gibbon (ed.), *Structural Adjustment and the Working Poor in Zimbabwe*, Scandinavian Institute of African Studies, Uppsala.

Bryceson, D. (1996) 'Deagrarianisation and rural employment in Sub-Saharan Africa: A sectoral perspective', *World Development*, Vol. 24, No. 1: 97–111.

Bryceson, D. and V. Jamal (1997) *Farewell to Farms: De-agrarianisation and Employment in Africa*, Aldershot, Ashgate.

Burt, R. S. (1992) *Structural Holes: The Social Structure of Competition*, Harvard University Press, London.

Burt, R. S. and I. Talmud (1993) 'Market niche', *Social Networks*, Vol. 15: 133–49.

Callon, M. (1991) 'Techno-economic networks and irreversibility' in J. Law (ed.), *Sociology of Monsters: Essays on Power, Technology and Domination*, Routledge, London.

Camagni, R. (1991) 'Local milieu, uncertainty, and innovation networks: towards a new dynamic theory of economic space' in R. Camagni (ed.), *Innovation Networks: Spatial Perspectives*, Belhaven Press, London.

Capek, A. (1995) *The Bad Loans and the Commercial Banks Policies in the Czech Republic*, Ceska Narodni Banka, Institut Ekonomie, Working Paper No. 39, Prague.

Central Statistical Office (1992/93) *Census of Industrial Production 1992/93*, Harare.

Central Statistical Office (various issues) *Quarterly Digest of Statistics*, Harare.

Chavarika, J. (1996) *Dairy Sub-sector Study*, Ranch House College, Harare.

Cho, M.-R. (1994) 'Weaving flexibility: large–small firm relations, flexibility and regional clusters in South Korea,' in P. O. Pedersen, A. Sverrisson and M. P. van Dijk (eds), *Flexible Specialization: The Dynamics of Small-Scale Industries in the South*, Intermediate Technology Publications, London.

Coffee, J. (1996) 'Institutional investors in transitional economies, lessons from the Czech experience' in R. Frydman, C. W. Gray and A. Rapanczynski (ed.), *Corporate Governance in Central Europe and Russia*, Central European University Press, London.

Corbett, J. and T. Jenkinson (1994) *The Financing of Industries 1970–89: An International Comparison*, Discussion Paper No. 948, CEPR, London.

Cramer, J. S. (1991) *The Logit Model*, Arnold, London.

Daniels, L. (1994) 'Changes in the small-scale enterprise sector from 1991 to 1993: results of a second nationwide survey in Zimbabwe', Gemini Working Paper No. 71, Development Alternatives, Bethesda, MD.

Daniels, L. and Y. Fisseha (1992) 'Micro- and small-scale enterprises in Botswana: results of a nationwide survey', Gemini Working Paper No. 46, Development Alternatives, Bethesda, MD.

Daniels, L., D. Mead and M. Musinga (1995) 'Employment and income in micro- and small-scale enterprises in Kenya: results of a 1995 survey', Gemini Working Paper No. 92, Development Alternatives, Bethesda, MD.

Dawson, J. (1990) 'The wider context: the importance of the macro-environment for small enterprise development', *Small Enterprise Development*, Vol. 1, No. 3: 39–46.

Denzau, A. T. and D. C. North (1994) 'Shared mental models: ideologies and institutions', *Kyklos*, Vol. 47, No. 1: 3–31.

van Dijk, M. P. (1990) *Women in the Informal Sector in Zimbabwe*, Euricur, Rotterdam.

van Dijk, M. P. (1992a) 'Women in the informal sector of industrializing Zimbabwe' in H. H. Bass, D. Hansohm and Wohlmuth (eds), *Africa Development Perspectives Yearbook, 1991/92*, Lit, Hamburg.

van Dijk, M. P. (1992b) 'How relevant is flexible specialisation in Burkina Faso's informal sector and the formal manufacturing sector?' in J. Rasmussen, H. Schmitz and M. P. van Dijk (eds), *Flexible Specialisation: A New View on Small Industry*, special issue of *IDS Bulletin*, Vol. 23, No. 3.

van Dijk, M. P. (1993) 'Industrial districts and urban economic development', *Third World Planning Review*, Vol. 15, No. 2: 175–87.

van Dijk, M. P. (1995) 'Structural adjustment and the role of different actors in Zimbabwe', *Nord-Sud Aktuell*, Vol. 9, No. 4: 103–10.

van Dijk, M. P. (1997) *Clusters: An Evolutionary Perspective*, Euricur, Rotterdam.

van Dijk, M. P. and R. Rabellotti (eds) (1997) *Enterprise Clusters and Networks in Developing Countries*, Frank Cass, London.

Dijkman, H. and M. P. van Dijk (1997) 'Opportunities for women in Ouagadougou's informal sector: an analysis based on the flexible specialisation concept' in M. P. van Dijk and R. Rabellotti (1997).

Dike, E. (1997) 'Structural adjustment and small-scale industrial entrepreneurs in south-eastern Nigeria', Discussion paper No. 81, United Nations Research Institute for Social Development, Geneva.

Dittus, P. and S. Prowse (1995) 'Corporate control in Central Europe and Russia: should banks own shares?', Policy Research Working Paper No. 1481, World Bank, Washington, DC.

Dornbusch, R. (1997) 'Brazil's incomplete stabilization and reform' in *Brookings Papers on Economic Activity*, No. 1: 367–94.

DPT (undated a) 'Specific issues report to the Deregulation Committee on trading restrictions on hawking and street vending, etc.', Deregulation Project Team, Harare.

DPT (undated b) 'Graduation phase report to the Deregulation Committee', Deregulation Project Team, Harare.

DPT (undated c) 'Formal sector report to the Deregulation Committee', Deregulation Project Team, Harare.

ECE (1996) 'Small and medium-sized enterprises in countries in transition' Research Report IND/AC/3/3, (United Nations) Economic Commission for Europe, Geneva.

ENDA (1990) 'Report on a survey of the informal sector', International Bank for Reconstruction and Development, Washington, DC.

Etzioni, A. (1987) 'Entrepreneurship, adaptation and legitimation: a macro-behavioral perspective', *Journal of Economic Behavior and Organization*, Vol. 8: 175–89.

FIESC (1995) *Santa Catarina em Dados*, FIESC, Florianópolis.

Financial Gazette, Bulawayo.

Fleury, A. (1995) 'Quality and productivity in the competitive strategies of Brazilian industrial enterprises', *World Development*, Vol. 23, No. 1: 73–86.

FMB Group (1993) *Highlights Zimbabwe Economy*, FMB Group, Harare, Dec.

Frank, A. G. (1978) *Dependent Accumulation and Underdevelopment*, Macmillan Press, London.

Frank, A. G. (1996) 'The Thirdworldization of Russia and Eastern Europe' in J. Hersh and J. D. Schmidt (eds), *The Aftermath of 'Real Existing Socialism' in Eastern Europe*, Macmillan Press, Basingstoke.

Frischtak, C. and I. Atiyas (1990) *Industrial Regulatory Policy and Investment Incentives in Brazil*, Report No. 7843-BR, World Bank, Washington, DC.

Galhardi, R. M. A. A. (1995) 'Flexible specialisation, technology and employment: networks in developing countries' in *Economic and Political Weekly*, 26 Aug.

Gazeta Mercantil, São Paulo.

Gibson, A. (1997) 'Business development services, core principles and future challenges', *Small Enterprise Development*, Vol. 8, No. 3, Sept.: 4–15.

Goodman, E. and J. Bamford (1989) *Small Firms and Industrial Districts in Italy*, Routledge, London.

Grabher, G. (ed.) (1993) *The Embedded Firm: On the Socioeconomics of Industrial Networks*, Routledge, London.

Granovetter, M. (1973) 'The strength of weak ties', *American Journal of Sociology*, Vol. 78: 1360–80.

Granovetter, M. (1985) 'Economic action and social structure: the problem of embeddedness', *American Journal of Sociology*, Vol. 91: 481–510.

Gray, C. W. and R. Hanson (1993) 'Corporate governance in central and eastern Europe: lessons from advanced market economies', Policy Research Working Paper No. 1182, World Bank, Washington, DC.

Gray, C. W. and K. Hendley (1995) 'Developing commercial law in transition economies: examples from Hungary and Russia', Policy Research Working Paper No. 1528, World Bank, Washington, DC.

Grierson, J. P. and D. Mead (1995) 'Business linkages in Zimbabwe: concept, practice and strategies', Gemini Working Paper No. 49, Development Alternatives, Bethesda, MD.

Haggblade, S. and P. B. Hazell (1989) 'Farm-nonfarm linkages in Sub-Saharan Africa', *World Development*, Vol. 17, No. 8: 1173–1201.

Halimana, C. M. (1995) *The Role of Small Industrial Enterprises in Zimbabwe's Industrialization Future: Focus on Engineering Firms*, Institute of Development Studies, University of Zimbabwe, Consultancy Reports No. 24, Harare.

Harris, M. and A. Raviv (1990) 'Capital structure and the information role of debt', *Journal of Finance*, Vol. 45, No. 2: 321–49.

Havnevik, K. J. (1987) 'A resource overlooked – crafts and small-scale industries', in J. Boesen, K.J. Havnevik, J. Koponen and R. Odgaard (eds), *Tanzania: Crisis and Struggle for Survival*, Scandinavian Institute of African Studies, Uppsala.

Havnevik, K. J. (1993) *Tanzania: The Limits to Development from Above*, Scandinavian Institute of African Studies, Uppsala.

Hawkins, T. (1993) 'Better chance than most', *Financial Times*, 1 Sept.

Helmsing, A. H. J. (1991) 'Rural industries and growth points: issues in an ongoing debate' in N.D. Mutizwa-Mangiza and A. H. J. Helmsing (eds), *Rural Development and Planning in Zimbabwe*, Avebury, Aldershot.

Henderson, J. (1998) 'On appropriate models for transformation in Eastern Europe', in J. Henderson, K. Balaton and G. Lengyel (eds), *Industrial Transformation in Eastern Europe in the Light of the East Asian Experience*, Macmillan Press, Basingstoke.

The *Herald*, Harare.

Hering, M. L. R. (1987) *Colonização e Indústria no Vale do Itajaí: O Modelo Catarinense de Desenvolvimento*, Editora da FURB, Blumenau.

Hosier, R. H. (1987) 'The informal sector in Kenya: spatial variation and development alternatives', *The Journal of Developing Areas*, Vol. 22: 283–402.

Hounshell, D. A. (1991) *From the American System to Mass Production 1800–1932: The Development of Manufacturing Technology in the United States*, John Hopkins University Press, London.

Humphrey, J. (1995) 'Industrial reorganisation in developing countries: from models to trajectories', *World Development*, Vol. 23, No. 1: 149–62.

Humphrey, J. and H. Schmitz (1996) 'The Triple C Approach to local industrial policy', *World Development*, Vol. 24, No 12: 1859–77.

Hungarian National Bank, *Monthly Bulletin*, various issues.

Hydén, G. (1980) *Beyond Ujamaa in Tanzania: Underdevelopment and an Uncaptured Peasantry*, Heinemann, London.

Hydén, G. (1983) *No Shortcuts to Progress: African Development Management in Perspective*, Heinemann, London.

Hydén, G. (1987) 'Capital accumulation, resource distribution, and governance in Kenya: the role of the economy of affection' in M. G. Schatzberg (ed.), *The Political Economy of Kenya*, Praeger, New York.

Hydén, G. (1995) 'The economy of affection revisited: African development management in perspective', paper presented at research seminar on 'Improved Natural Resource Management: The Role of Formal Organizations and Informal Networks and Institutions', Jyllinge, 23–26 Oct.

ILOSDINFO (International Labour Organisation Social Development Fund Information), ILO, Harare.

IMF Survey, 21 Oct., 1993, Washington, DC.

IMF (1996) *Zimbabwe: Recent Economic Developments*, International Monetary Fund, Washington, DC.

Informe Sectorial, São Paulo.

Jeans, A. N. (1995) *Small-scale Light Engineering Project: Phase 1 Report*, Intermediate Technology Development Group Zimbabwe, Harare.

King, K. and C. Aboudha (1991) 'The building of an industrial society: change and development in Kenya's informal sector 1970–1990', Occasional paper No. 30, Centre of African Studies, Edinburgh University.

Kiondo, A. S. Z. (1989) 'The politics of economic reforms in Tanzania 1977–1988' unpublished PhD Thesis, University of Toronto, Toronto.

Klapwijk, M. (1997) *Rural Industry Clusters in Central Java, Indonesia*, Tinbergen Institute Research Series No. 153, Vrije Universiteit, Amsterdam.

Knight, P. (1996) 'Brazilian textiles and clothing: adapting to liberalisation', *Textile Outlook International*, May: 33–56.

Knorringa, P. (1995) *Economics of Collaboration in Producer–Trader Relations: Trans-action Regimes Between Market and Hierarchy in the Agra Footwear Cluster, India*, Vrije Universiteit, Amsterdam.

Knorringa, P. (1998) 'Cluster trajectories in developing countries: towards a typology', paper presented at EADI workshop on 'the Importance of Innovation for Small Enterprise Development in the Third World', Institute of Social Studies, The Hague, 18–19 Sept.

Lambooy, J. G. (1994) 'Networks and proximity: transactions and knowledge', paper presented at the RSA conference, Groningen.

Latour, B. (1991) 'Materials and power: technology is society made durable' in J. Law (ed.), *Sociology of Monsters: Essays on Power, Technology and Domination*, London.

Lazerson, M. H. (1990) 'Subcontracting in the Modena knitwear industry', in F. Pyke, G. Beccatini and W. Sengenberger (eds), *Industrial Districts and Inter-firm Cooperation in Italy*, International Institute for Labour Studies, Geneva, pp. 108–33.

Lazonick, W. (1993) 'Industry clusters versus global webs: organizational capabilities in the American economy', in *Industrial and Corporate Change*, Vol. 2, No. 1: 1–24.

Liedholm, C. and D. Mead (1991) 'Dynamics of micro enterprises: research issues and approaches', Gemini Working Paper No. 12, Development Alternatives, Bethesda, MD.

Liedholm, C. and D. Mead (1993) Structure and growth of micro enterprises in southern and eastern Africa: evidence from recent surveys', Gemini Working Paper No. 36, Development Alternatives, Bethesda, MD.

Lindberg, S. and Á. Sverrisson (eds) (1997) *Social Movements in Development: The Challenge of Globalization and Democratization*, Macmillan, London.

Made, J. and D. Mfote (1995) *Design of Policies and Programmes for Growth and Employment Promotion in the Non-formal Sector in Zimbabwe*, International Labour Organization and Samat, Harare.

Mainwearing, S. (1992) 'Brazilian party underdevelopment in comparative perspective', *Political Science Quarterly*, Vol. 107, No. 4: 677–707.

Malecki, E. J. (1991) *Technology and Economic Development: The Dynamics of Local, Regional and National Change*, Longman, Harlow.

Marris, P. and A. Somerset (1971) *African Businessmen: A Study of Entrepreneurship and Development in Kenya*, Routledge & Kegan Paul, London.

Marshall, A. (1890) *Principles of Economics*, 8th edition, Macmillan, London.

Mayer, C. P. (1990) 'Financial systems, corporate finance and economic development', in R. G. Hubbard (ed.), *Asymmetric Information, Corporate Finance and Investment*, University of Chicago Press, London.

McCormick, D. and P. O. Pedersen (eds) (1996) *Small Enterprises: Flexibility and Networking in an African Context*, Longhorn Kenya, Nairobi.

MacGaffey, J. (1987) *Entrepreneurs and Parasites: The Struggle for Indigenous Capitalism in Zaire*, Cambridge University Press, Cambridge.

McPherson, M. (1991) *Micro- and Small-scale Enterprises in Zimbabwe: Results of a Country-wide Survey*, Gemini Technical Report No. 25, Development Alternatives, Bethesda MD.

Meagher, K. and M.-B. Yunusa (1996) 'Passing the buck: structural adjustment and the Nigerian urban informal sector', Discussion Paper No. 75, United Nations Research Institute for Social Development, Geneva.

Mellor, J. (1976) *The New Economics of Growth: A Strategy for India and the World*, Cornell University Press, Ithaca.

Meyer-Stamer, J. (1997a) *Technology, Competitiveness and Radical Policy Change: The Case of Brazil*, Frank Cass, London.

Meyer-Stamer, J. (1997b) 'New patterns of governance for industrial change: perspectives for Brazil', *Journal of Development Studies*, Vol. 33, No. 3: 364–91.

Meyer-Stamer, J. (1997c) *Systemische Wettbewerbsfähigkeit und Standort- und Industriepolitik: Ansatzpunkte für die Technische Zusammenarbeit mit Brasilien*, Deutsches Institut für Entwicklungspolitik, Berlin.

Meyer-Stamer, J., C. Rauh, H. Riad, S. Schmitt and T. Welte (1991) *Comprehensive Modernization on the Shop Floor: a Case Study on the Brazilian Machinery Industry*, German Development Institute, Berlin.

Meyer-Stamer, J., B. Adam, S. Bantle, A. Lauer and D. Mohaupt (1996) *Industrielle Netzwerke und Wettbewerbsfähigkeit: Das Beispiel Santa Catarina/Brasilien*, Deutsches Institut für Entwicklungspolitik, Berlin.

Mhone, G. C. Z. (1995) *The Impact of Structural Adjustment on the Urban Informal Sector in Zimbabwe*, International Labour Organisation, Geneva.

Mhuriro, G. (1996) *Catering Traditional Meals in Harare*, Ranch House College, Harare.

Ministério da Fazenda (1997) 'Medidas de Redução do 'Custo Brasil.' Versão atualizada com os dados disponíveis em 23.04.97', Secretaria de Política Econômica, Brasilia, mimeo.

Ministry of Finance (1991) 'Small scale investment policy issues and options for rural industry', Working Paper No. 29, Zero, Harare.

Ministry of Finance (1991) Framework for Economic Reform 1991–1995, Government Printer, Harare.

Mishan, E. J. (1971) 'The postwar literature on externalities: an interpretative essay', *The Journal of Economic Literature*, Vol. 9, No. 1: 1–28.

Mizsei, K. (1994) 'Bankruptcy and banking reform in the transition economies of central and eastern Europe', in Bonin J. P. and I. Szekely (eds), *The Development and Reform of Financial Systems in Central and Eastern Europe*, Edward Elgar, London.

Monitor Company (1995) *Construyendo las Ventajas Competitivas del Perú: El Sector Confecciones*, PROMPERU, Lima.

Moorsom, R. with J. Matange and C. Sachikonye (1996) *Evaluation of the SDF in Zimbabwe: A pilot study*. Christian Michelsen Institute, Bergen.

Moreira, M. (1993) *Industrialisation and Interventions: The Role of Governments in Developing Countries: Brazil*, UFRJ, Instituto de Economia Industrial, Rio de Janeiro.

Morgan, G. (1986) *Images of Organization*, Sage, London.

Murphy, A. (1996) *Fruit and Vegetable Drying in Zimbabwe: Opportunities for Microenterprise Development in the Communal Areas*, Department of Food Economics, University College, Cork.

Mutambirwa, S. (1995) *Report on Food Processing as a Small Business*, IKEA Consultants for Development, Harare.

Müller, J. (1980) *Liquidation or Consolidation of Indigenous Technology: A Study of the Changing Conditions of Production of Village Blacksmiths in Tanzania*, Aalborg University Press, Ålborg.

Müller, J. (1997) 'Consolidation and transformation of indigenous technology: prospects for a comeback of the village blacksmiths in Tanzania', paper presented to an Institute of Development Studies and Center for Development Studies conference on 'African Business Systems: Institutionalising Industrialisation in an Era of Economic Reform', Mombasa, 4–6 June.

Müller-Glodde, R. (1993) *Organisationsentwicklung in brasilianischen Unternehmensverbänden: Fallstudie des Partnerschaftsprojekts zwischen brasilianischen Handels- und Industrieverbänden in Santa Catarina und der Handwerkskammer für München und Oberbayern*, Gesellschaft Technische Zusammenarbeit (Aus der Arbeit der Abteilung 403) No. 16, Eschborn.

Nadvi, K. (1997) 'The cutting edge: collective efficiency and international competitiveness in Pakistan', Discussion Paper No. 360, Institute of Development Studies, University of Sussex, Brighton.

Nadvi, K. and H. Schmitz (1994) 'Industrial clusters in less developed countries: review of experiences and research agenda', Discussion Paper No. 339, Institute of Development Studies, University of Sussex.

Ndlela, D. B. (1986) 'The capital goods sector in Zimbabwe', *Zimbabwe Journal of Economics*, Vol. 1, No. 3: 41–53.

Ndlela, D. B., B. M. Zwizwai, J. W. K. Kaliyati and D. Mutungwazi (1990) *A Study of the Metals and Metal Goods Sector in Zimbabwe*, CIID Manuscript Report No. 242e, IDRC/CRDI, Toronto.

Nicholson, N. (1988) 'The state of the art' in V. Ostrom, D. Feeny and H. Picht (eds), *Rethinking Institutional Analysis and Development*, ICS Press, San Francisco.

Nooteboom, B. (1992) 'Towards a dynamic theory of transactions', *Journal of Evolutionary Economics*, Vol. 2: 281–99.

Nooteboom, B. (1993) 'Firm-size effects on transaction costs', *Small Business Economics*, Vol. 5: 283–95.

Nooteboom, B. (1994) 'Innovation and diffusion in small firms: theory and evidence', *Small Business Economics*, Vol. 6: 13–33.

North, D. C. (1994) 'Economic performance through time', *American Economic Review*, Vol. 84, No. 3: 359–68.

OECD (1992) *Technology and the Economy: The Key Relationships*, OECD, Technology and Economy Programme.

Otero, M. (1987) *Gender Issues in Small Scale Enterprise*, Gender Manual Series, Maastricht School of Management, Maastricht.

Pedersen, P. O. (1994) 'Structural adjustment and the economy of small towns in Zimbabwe', in Pedersen, P. O., Á. Sverrisson and M. P. van Dijk (eds), *Flexible Specialization: The Dynamics of Small-Scale Industries in the South*, Intermediate Technology Publishers, London.

Pedersen, P. O. (1997) *Small African Towns: Between Rural Networks and Urban Hierarchies*, Avebury, Aldershot.

Pedersen, P. O., Á. Sverrisson and M. P. van Dijk (eds) (1994) *Flexible Specialization: The Dynamics of Small-Scale Industries in the South*, Intermediate Technology Publishers, London.

Philips, L. (1988) *The Economics of Imperfect Information*, Cambridge University Press, Cambridge.

Piore, M. J. and C. F. Sabel (1984) *The Second Industrial Divide: Possibilities for Prosperity*, Basic Books, New York.

Pohl G., G. T. Jedrzejczak and R. Anderson (1995) *Creating Capital Markets in Central and Eastern Europe*, Technical Paper No. 295, World Bank, Washington, DC.

Polanyi, K. (1957) *The Great Transformation*, Beacon Press, Boston.

Ponce, C. R. (1994) *Gamarra: Formación, Estructura, y Perspectivas*, Friedrich Ebert Foundation, Lima.

Poon, A. (1990) 'Flexible specialization and small size', *World Development*, Vol. 18, No. 1: 109–23.

Porter, M. E. (1990) *The Competitive Advantage of Nations*, The Free Press, New York.

Prahalad, C. K. and G. Hamel (1991) 'Nur Kernkompetenzen sichern das Überleben', in *Harvard Manager*, Vol. 13, No. 2: 66–78.

Pyke, F. (1992) *Industrial Development Through Small-Firm Co-operation: Theory and Practice*, International Labour Organisation, Geneva.

Pyke, F. and W. Sengenberger (eds) (1992) *Industrial Districts and Local Economic Regeneration*, International Institute for Labour Studies, Geneva.

Pyke, F., G. Beccatini, and W. Sengenberger (eds) (1990) *Industrial Districts and Inter-firm Cooperation in Italy*, International Institute for Labour Studies, Geneva.

Rabellotti, R. (1997) *External Economies and Cooperation in Industrial Districts: A Comparison of Italy and Mexico*, Macmillan Press, Basingstoke.

Rasmussen, J. (1992) *The Local Entrepreneurial Milieu: Enterprise Networks in Small Zimbabwean Towns*, Research Report No. 79, Dept. of Geography, Roskilde University.

Rasmussen, J. and A. Sverrisson (1994) 'Flexible specialization, technology and employment in Zimbabwe: the cases of building and carpentry', Research Working Paper WEP 2–22/WP.241, International Labour Organisation, Geneva.

Rasmussen, J., H. Schmitz and M. P. van Dijk (eds) (1992) *Flexible Specialisation: A New View on Small Industry*, special issue of *IDS Bulletin*, Vol. 23, No. 3.

Rietveld, P. and C. Gorter (1990) 'Innovation in small scale industry', *International Journal of Development Planning Literature*, Vol. 5, No. 1: 1–19.

Romero, L. L., J. O. W. M. Vieira, R. F. Martins and L. A. Rossatto de Medeiros (1995) 'Malharias', *Informe Setorial*, No. 1: 111–26.

Rotter, J. B. (1966) *Generalized expectancies for internal versus external control of reinforcement*, Psychological Monographs 0096–9753, Vol. 80, No. 1: 1–28, Washingon, DC.

Russo, M. (1985) 'Technical change and the industrial district: The role of inter-firm relations in the growth and transformation of ceramic tile production in Italy', *Research Policy*, Vol. 14: 329–43.

Sabel, C. F. and J. Zeitlin (1985) 'Historical alternatives to mass production: politics, markets and technology in nineteenth century industrialization', *Past and Present*, No. 108, Aug.: 133–76.

Sabel, C. F. and J. Zeitlin (eds) (1997) *World of Possibilities: Flexibility and Mass Production in Western Industrialization* (Studies in Modern Capitalism), Cambridge University Press, Cambridge.

Saito, K. and M. P. van Dijk (1990) *The Informal Sector in Zimbabwe: The Role of Women*, International Bank for Reconstruction and Development, Washington, DC.

Sandee, H. (1995) *Innovation Adaption in Rural Industry: Technological Change in Roof Tile Clusters in Central Java, Indonesia*, Vrije Universiteit, Amsterdam.

Sandee, H. (1998) 'Promoting small-scale and cottage industry clusters in Indonesia', *Small Enterprise Development*, Vol. 9, No. 1: 52–7.

Sandee, H., P. Rietveld, H. Supratikno and P. Yuwono (1994) 'Promoting small scale and cottage industries: an impact analysis for Central Java', *Bulletin of Indonesian Economic Studies*, Vol. 30, No. 3: 115–42.

Sanner, L. (1997) *Trust Between Entrepreneurs and External Actors: Sensemaking in Organising New Business Ventures*, Department of Business Studies, Uppsala University, Uppsala.

Schmitz, H. (1989) *Flexible Specialisation: A New Paradigm of Small-Scale Industrialisation?*, Discussion Paper No. 261, Institute of Development Studies, Brighton.

Schmitz, H. (1992) 'On the clustering of firms', in J. Rasmussen, H. Schmitz and M. P. van Dijk (eds), *Flexible Specialisation: A New View on Small Industry*, special issue of *IDS Bulletin*, Vol. 23, No 3: 64–9.

Schmitz, H. (1995a) 'Small shoemakers and fordist giants: tale of a supercluster', *World Development*, Vol. 23, No. 1: 9–28.

Schmitz, H. (1995b) 'Collective efficiency: growth path for small-scale industry', *Journal of Development Studies*, Vol. 31, No. 4: 529–66.

Schmitz, H. (1997) *Collective Efficiency and Increasing Returns*, Working Paper No. 50, Institute of Development Studies, Universtity of Sussex, Brighton.

Schumpeter, J. A. (1942) *Capitalism, Socialism and Democracy*, Harper and Row, New York.

Scitovsky, T. (1954) 'Two concepts of external economies', *Journal of Political Economy*, Vol. 62: 143–51.

Scoones, I. *et al.* (1996) *Hazards and Opportunities: Farming Livelihoods in Dryland Africa, Lessons from Zimbabwe*, Zed Books Ltd. in association with International Institute for Environment and Development, London.

Scranton, P. (1997) *Endless Novelty: Specialty Production and American Industrialization, 1865–1925*, Princeton, Princeton University Press.

Sequeira, J. H. (1990) *World-Class Manufacturing in Brazil: A Study of Competitive Positions*, American Chamber of Commerce, São Paulo.

Shapiro, H. (1994) *Engines of Growth: The State and Transnational Auto Companies in Brazil*, Cambridge University Press, Cambridge.

Shleifer, A. and R. W. Vishny (1996) *A Survey of Corporate Governance*, NBER Working Paper No. 5554, National Bureau of Economic Research, Cambridge, MA.

Sibanda, A. (1996) *Fish Subsector Report*, Troparg Consultants, Harare.

Sibanda, A. (1997) *Baseline Study of Aspiring Entrepreneurs in Nyamutumbu, Murewa*, Ranch House College, Harare.

Singh, A. (1995) *Corporate Financial Patterns in Industrialising Economies: A Comparative International Study*, IFC Technical Paper No. 2, World Bank, Washington, DC.

Small Enterprise News, Gesellschaft Technische Zusammenarbeit (GTZ), Harare.

de Soto, B. F. (1993) *Da indústria do papel ao complexo florestal no Brasil: o caminho do corporatismo tradicional ao neocorporatismo*, IE/Unicamp, Campinas.

Steinherr, A. (1993) *Reform of Financial Markets in Eastern European Countries*, European Institute of Banking, Luxembourg.

Stewart, F. (1978) *Technology and Underdevelopment*, Macmillan, London.

Stewart, F. (ed.) (1987) *Macro Policies for Appropriate Technology in Developing Countries*, Westview Press, London.

Stewart, F., H. Thomas and T. de Wilde (eds) (1990) *The Other Policy: The Influence of Policies on Technology Choice and Small Enterprise Development*, Intermediate Technology Publishers, London.

Stiglitz, J. and A. Weiss (1981) 'Credit rationing in markets with imperfect information', *American Economic Review*, Vol. 71: 393–410.

Stone, A., B. Levy and R. Paredes (1992) *Public Institutions and Private Transactions: The Legal and Regulatory Environment for Business Transactions in Brazil and Chile*, Policy Research Working Paper No. 891, World Bank, Washington, DC.

Sverrisson, Á. (1990) *Entrepreneurship and Industrialisation: A Case Study of Carpenters in Mutare, Zimbabwe*, Research Policy Institute, Lund.

Sverrisson, Á. (1992) *Innovation as a Collective Enterprise: A Case Study of Carpenters in Nakuru, Kenya*, Research Policy Institute, Lund.

Sverrisson, Á. (1993) *Evolutionary Technical Change and Flexible Mechanization: Entrepreneurship and Industrialization in Kenya and Zimbabwe*, Lund University Press, Lund.

Sverrisson, Á. (1994a) 'Gradual diffusion of flexible techniques in small and medium sized enterprise networks', in P. O. Pedersen, Á. Sverrisson and M. P. van Dijk (eds), *Flexible Specialization: The Dynamics of Small-Scale Industries in the South*, IT-publications, London.

Sverrisson, Á. (1994b) 'Making sense of chaos: socio/technical networks, entrepreneurs, careers and enterprise morphologies', *Acta Sociologica*, Vol. 37, No. 4: 401–17.

Sverrisson, Á. (1997) 'Enterprise networks and technological change: aspects of light engineering and metalworking in accra', in M. P. Van Dijk and R. Rabellotti (eds), *Cooperation, Clusters and Diffusion Networks in Emerging Economies*, Frank Cass, London.

Takeuchi, J. (1991) *The Role of Labour-Intensive Sectors in Japanese Industrialization*, United Nations University Press, Tokyo.

Ternes, A. (1986) *História Econômica de Joinville*, Meyer, Joinville.

The *Economist*, London.

Tripp, A. M. (1989) *Defending the Rights to Subsist: The State vs. the Urban Informal Economy in Tanzania*, World Institute for Development Economics Research Working Papers No. 59, Helsinki.

Tripp, A. M. (1997) *Changing the Rules: The Politics of Liberalization and the Urban Informal Economy in Tanzania*, University of California Press, Berkeley.

Trulsson, P. (1997) *Strategies of Entrepreneurship: Understanding Industrial Entrepreneurship and Structural Change in Northern Tanzania*, Linköping Studies in Art and Science No. 161, Department of Technology and Social Change, University of Linköping.

Vega-Centeno, M. (1988) 'Desarrollo Industrial y Exportaciones Industriales', *Economía*, Vol. 11, No. 21.

Visser, E. J. (1996) *Local Sources of Competitiveness: Spatial Clustering and Organisational Dynamics in Small-Scale Clothing in Lima, Peru*, University of Amsterdam, Amsterdam.

Visser, E. J. and J. I. Távarra (1995) *Gamarra al Garete*, Consorcio de Investigaciones Económicas, Lima.

Wahjana, J. (1994) 'Women and technological change in rural industry: tile making in Java', *Economic and Political Weekly*, Vol. 29, 30 Apr.: 19–33.

Wallerstein, I. (1983) *Historical Capitalism*, Verso, London.

Weiss, U. (1997) 'Governo anuncia programa de incentivo ao setor têxtil', *Jornal de Santa Catarina*, 20 May.

Whalley, P. (1986) *The Social Production of Technical Work: The Case of British Engineers*, Macmillan Press, Basingstoke.

World Bank (1990) *Making Adjustment Work for the Poor: A Framework for Policy Reform in Africa*, World Bank, Washington, DC.

World Bank (1997) *The Role of Women in the Informal Sector in Zimbabwe*, World Bank, Washington, DC.

World Bank (1996) *Brazil: The Custo Brasil since 1990–92*, Report No. 15663-BR, World Bank, Washington, DC.

World Economy Research Institute (1996) *Poland: International Economic Report 1995/96*, Warsaw School of Economics, Warsaw.

Yong-Il, Y. and F. Wilkinson (1994) 'Competition and co-operation: towards understanding industrial districts', *Review of Political Economy*, Vol. 6, No. 3: 259–78.

Yamazaki, M. (1981) *Innovations in Japan's Community-Based Industries: A Case Study*, Asian Productivity Organisation, Tokyo.

Yuwono, P. (ed.) (1993) *Subkontrakting: sistem adopsi ataukah sistem ekspoitasi?*, Satya Wacana University Press, Salatiga.

Zaaijer, M. (1997) *Urban Economic Restructuring and Local Economic Response: The Case of Bulawayo*, IHS, Rotterdam.

Zeman, K. (1996) 'Key problems of service sector transformation in the Czech Republic', paper presented at the 12th Seminar on Service Economy of Progress, Geneva, 28–31 August.

Zwizwai, B. M. and J. Powell (1991) *Small Scale Metalworking/Light Engineering Industries in Zimbabwe: A Sub-sector Study*, Intermediate Technology Development Group Zimbabwe, Harare.

Index

Aage, H. 3
Aboudha, C. 176
Adelman, I. 135
Aeroe, A. 187
Africa Recovery 165
Akerlof, G. A. 66
Akhrich, M. 172
Allen, R. C. 169
Amin, S. 182
Anfacer 30
Argentina 35
Arthur, W. B. 42
Asmussen, T. 118
Atiyas, I. 23
Avelino Filho, G. 37
Avritzer, L. 37
Axelsson, B. 185

Baer, H. 73
Bamford, J. 77, 78
bankruptcy 5, 7, 31, 69ff., 88
Berglof, E. 72, 73
Berkowitz, S. D. 124
Bonin, J. P. 73
Botswana 132, 145ff.
Bradburd, R. 165
Brand, V. 133, 141–3
Brazil 4, 19ff.
Bryceson, D. 135
Burt, R. S. 122, 167–9, 171, 180
business associations 4, 13, 30, 35ff.,
    39, 89ff., 161

Callon, M. 167, 172
Camagni, R. 79, 93
Capek, A. 73
capital 3, 7, 32, 35, 60ff., 80, 98–100,
    102, 105, 108–9, 115, 122, 133–4,
    152, 177
Chavarika, J. 165
Cho, M. R. 171, 180
clothing 19, 31 ff., 77ff., 115–16,
    145–6, 148, 152

clusters 3–6, 9ff., 20ff., 39ff., 77ff.,
    95ff., 134, 167–9, 176, 179, 181,
    183–4, 188, 191
Coffee, J. 73
collective efficiency 19, 33, 45, 58,
    77, 80, 83, 86–7, 91–3
Congo 151
co-operation 6, 13–14, 20, 26, 31–3,
    38–9, 41, 77–84, 87, 89ff., 97,
    104, 169, 177–8, 183–4, 187,
    189–91
copper crafts 99ff.
Corbett, J. 60
Cramer, J. S. 104
culture 9, 19, 23, 58, 92, 157, 165ff.,
    184, 189
Czech Republic 5, 61, 63, 66, 69ff.

Daniels, L. 133, 135, 139,
    142, 145
Dawson, J. 170, 183
Denzau, A. T. 78
deregulation 1, 3, 15, 118, 120ff.,
    150ff., 189
Dijk, M. P. van 9, 12, 44, 77, 79, 154,
    165, 167, 183–4, 190–1
Dijkman, H. 191
Dike, E. 134
Dittus, P. 73
Dornbusch, R. 27
DPT 155ff., 165
dualism 11, 169ff., 181, 185ff.

East Asia 33
Eastern Europe 5
Easton, G. 185
Economist, The 88
economy of affection 5, 43, 45
embeddedness 4–5, 9, 43ff., 79,
    100–1, 103, 110–11, 169ff., 189
ENDA 154, 165
engineering 4, 7, 20–1, 24–5, 27,
    33–5, 39ff., 113ff., 155, 173

entrepreneurship   4–5, 20–3, 43ff.,
   79, 118, 157, 160, 167ff.,
   181, 188
Etzioni, A.   44

family   5, 26, 31, 39, 43ff., 86,
   92, 97ff., 104, 120–2, 134
FIESC   30, 35, 41
Financial Gazette   153
Fisseha, Y.   145
Fleury, A.   34
flexible specialization   6, 11, 44,
   124–5, 181, 190ff.
FMB Group   152
food processing   12, 20, 141
foreign investment   22, 150, 161
Frank, A. G.   1, 182
Frischtak, C.   23
furniture   9, 21, 116–17,
   120–1, 176

Galhardi, R.   167
garments   20–1, 39, 84ff.,
Ghana   178
Gibson, A.   160
Goodman, E.   77, 78
Gorter, C.   100, 106
Grabher, G.   185
Granovetter, M.   5, 45–6, 167–8,
   171, 175, 180
Gray, C. W.   72, 73
Grierson, J. P.   134

Haggblade, S.   135
Halimana, C. M.   7, 113–14
Hamel, G.   27
Hanson, R.   72
Harris, M.   62
Havnevik, K.   59, 170, 183
Hawkins   151
Hazell, P. B.   135
Helmsing, A. H. J.   139–40
Henderson, J.   1
Hendley, K.   73
Herald, The   155, 163
Hering, M. L. R.   20
Hosier, R. H.   147
Hounshell, D. A.   180
Humphrey, J.   11, 95, 192

Hungary   61, 66ff.
Hydén, H.   5, 43, 45

ILO   160
IMF   151, 161
Indonesia   6, 95ff.
industrialization   8–10, 19, 23, 89,
   132, 135–6, 144, 167ff., 181, 183,
   190–1
industrial districts   19, 27, 31, 33,
   77–9, 181
informal sector   8, 21, 115, 131ff.,
   152, 154ff., 161ff.
innovation   6–7, 11, 40, 77, 80ff., 93,
   95ff., 126–7, 168, 174ff., 181–2,
   186ff.
interest rates   25, 28–9, 32, 47, 60ff.,
   68, 116–17, 150
Italy   31, 33–4

Jamal, V.   135
Japan   178
Jeans, A. N.   115
Jenkinson, T.   60

Kenya   132, 145ff.
King, K.   176
Kiondo, A. S. Z.   59
Klapwijk, M.   95
Knight, P.   32
Knorringa, P.   3, 45, 95, 97,
   170, 187

Lambooy, J. G.   81
Latour, B.   172
Lazerson, M. H.   42
Lazonick, W.   40
learning   10, 20, 25, 41, 77, 80–2,
   176, 180, 183
Levy, B.   165
Liedholm, C.   134, 144
Lindberg, S.   1
local government   9, 24, 36ff., 101,
   103, 163, 165

MacGaffey, J.   14
Made, J.   152
Mainwearing, S.   37
Malecki, E. J.   82

Marris, P. 53
Marshall, A. 78
Mayer, C. P. 60
McCormick, D. 134
McPherson, M. 140
Mead, D. 134, 144
Meagher, K. 133–4
Mellor, J. 135
Meyer-Stamer, J. 4, 11, 23, 27, 33, 41–2, 83, 119
Mfote, D. 152
Mhone, G. C. Z. 165
Mhuriro, G. 165
Mishan, E. J. 80
Mizsei, K. 72
Moorsom, R. 159
Moreira, M. 23, 41
Müller, J. 136
Müller-Glodde, R. 35–6
Murphy, A. 165
Mutambirwa, S. 165

Nadvi, K. 11, 42, 77, 79, 96, 167, 185
Ndlela, D. B. 114, 127
NGOs 9, 159, 161, 165
Nicholson, N. 44
Nooteboom, B. 81–2, 93
North, D. C. 78, 81

OECD 27
Otero, M. 166

Pedersen, P. O. 2, 44, 118, 134, 137, 143, 167, 184
Peru 6, 77ff.
Philips, L. 81
Piore, M. J. 124
Pohl, G. 72
Poland 61, 66ff.
Polanyi, K. 1
Ponce, C. R. 84–5
Poon, A. 42
Porter, M. E. 33, 40, 42
Powell, J. 115, 127
Prahalad, C. K. 27
privatization 25, 62, 68, 70, 183
Prowse, S. 73
Pyke, F. 77, 78, 185

Rabellotti, R. 44, 77, 79, 167, 187
Rasmussen, J. 127, 187
Raviv, A. 62
Revoltella, D. 5
Rietveld, P. 100, 106
Roland, G. 72
Romero, L. L. 23
Russo, M. 42

Sabel, C. F. 124, 175, 180
Saito, K. 154
Sandee, H. 6, 12, 97, 104, 112, 169, 177, 187
Sanner, L. 59
Santa Catarina 19ff.
Schaffer, M. E. 73
Schmitz, H. 11, 23, 52, 77–80, 83, 96–7, 124, 167, 185, 189
Schumpeter, J. A. 1
Scitowski, T. 80
Scoones, I. 133
Scranton P. 2, 169, 172, 180, 187
self-financing 63–6
Sengenberger, W. 79
Sequeira, J. H. 23
Shapiro, H. 41
Shleifer, A. 72
Sibanda, A. 165
SIDO 47
Simmel, G. 180
Singh, A. 72
SMEs 3, 7, 9, 60ff.
  agriculture and 119, 132
  clusters of 3, 6, 10, 77ff., 95ff.
  commerce and 12, 105, 135–6, 160
  credit and 5, 13, 47ff., 60ff, 160–1
  governance and 9, 12, 14, 150ff.
  histories 6–7, 77ff., 172, 191
  industrialization 136, 167ff., 179
  leasing and 71
  labour supply and 132–4
  networks 3, 6, 9, 83, 94, 98, 101–2, 104–5, 110, 118ff., 168ff., 191
  policy 11ff., 126–7, 152, 162–3, 179
  production 2, 6, 49, 86–7, 180

SMEs – *continued*
  strategies   3, 4–6, 77ff.
  technical change   6–7, 9, 14, 89,
    101ff., 113ff., 136, 160–1, 172ff.,
    179, 190
Somerset, A.   53
Soto, B. F. de   41
South Africa   151, 155
Spain   31
Steinherr, A.   72
Stewart, F.   124, 127, 187
Stiglitz, J.   66
structural adjustment   1, 4, 8, 11,
  15, 43ff., 77ff., 113ff., 131,
  133–4, 137, 141ff., 151ff., 180,
  181ff., 192
Stone, A.   25, 42
subcontracting   6, 21, 24, 26, 32,
  34, 79, 86, 90–1, 99–100, 105,
  107ff., 111, 120, 123, 126,
  152, 160, 171, 178, 183ff.,
  190–1
Sverrisson, Á.   1, 3, 7, 9, 11–12,
  127, 147, 169, 176–7, 184,
  187

Takeuchi, J.   180
Talmud, I.   122
Tanzania   4, 43ff.
Távarra, J. I.   78
Ternes, A.   20
textiles   10, 20ff., 28ff., 39ff., 84ff.,
  145, 151–2, 185
von Thadden, E. L.   73
tile-making   20, 29ff., 39ff., 98ff.
Tripp, A. M.   14, 59

Trulsson, P.   4, 14, 119, 134
trust   4–5, 24, 43ff., 51–2, 58–9, 92,
  134, 176

UDI   113–14, 152
USA   90, 178

Vega-Centeno, M.   85
vertical integration   4, 11, 14, 19ff.,
  46, 49, 79, 91, 135, 144, 187–8, 190
Vishny, R. W.   72
Visser, E.-J.   6, 11, 77ff.

Wahjana, J.   110
Wallerstein, I.   182
Weiss, A.   66
Weiss, U.   33
Western Europe   178
Whalley, P.   50
Wilkinson, F.   81
Williamson, O.   44
women   98, 105, 110, 143ff., 152, 156
World Bank   1, 42, 43, 150–1, 153,
  163, 165

Yamazaki, M.   180
Yong-Il, Y.   81
Yunusa, M.-B.   133–4
Ywono, P.   100, 107

Zaaijer, M.   163, 165
Zeitlin, J.   175, 180
Zeman, K.   73
Zimbabwe   7, 9, 113ff., 132ff., 145ff.,
  150ff., 178
Zwizwai, B. M.   115, 127